BREATHTAKING

*How One Family Cycled Around
the World for Clean Air and Asthma*

PAULA HOLMES-EBER

LORENZ EBER

Guilford, Connecticut

FALCON®

An imprint of Globe Pequot, the trade division of
The Rowman & Littlefield Publishing Group, Inc.
4501 Forbes Blvd., Ste. 200
Lanham, MD 20706
www.rowman.com

Falcon and FalconGuides are registered trademarks of The Rowman & Littlefield Publishing
Group, Inc.

Distributed by NATIONAL BOOK NETWORK

British Library Cataloguing in Publication Information available

Library of Congress Cataloging-in-Publication Data

Names: Holmes-Eber, Paula, author. | Eber, Lorenz, author.
Title: Breathtaking : how one family cycled around the world for clean air and asthma / Paula
    Holmes-Eber, Lorenz Eber.
Description: Guilford, Connecticut : Falcon Guides, 2022. | Summary: "Carrying one stuffed
    elephant, six panniers, and two tents, Paula and Lorenz Eber set off from Athens, Greece,
    on two tandem bicycles with their eleven-year-old daughter, Yvonne, and her thirteen-year-
    old sister, Anya. Pedaling in an unbroken line through Europe and Asia, along Australia
    and the South Pacific and then across North America, the Ebers promoted a carbon-free,
    environmentally friendly way to travel, encouraging others to try new, more sustainable and
    harmonious ways to interact with new places and peoples"—Provided by publisher.
Identifiers: LCCN 2021047731 (print) | LCCN 2021047732 (ebook) | ISBN 9781493064311
    (paperback) | ISBN 9781493064328 (epub)
Subjects: LCSH: Holmes-Eber, Paula—Travel. | Eber, Lorenz—Travel. | Voyages and travels. |
    Bicycle touring. | Cyclists—Biography.
Classification: LCC G465 .H665 2022 (print) | LCC G465 (ebook) | DDC 910.4/1—dc23/
    eng/20211130
LC record available at https://lccn.loc.gov/2021047731
LC ebook record available at https://lccn.loc.gov/2021047732

♾™ The paper used in this publication meets the minimum requirements of American National
Standard for Information Sciences—Permanence of Paper for Printed Library Materials, ANSI/
NISO Z39.48-1992.

For Bill Holmes and Barbara Sullivan,
whose adventurous spirits, passion for travel,
and boundless love and belief in us
were the seeds for our own bold dreams.

To Matt & Rhonda

Thank you for everything
you did to help World Bible
Breath — from legal advice to
setting up a nonprofit, to giving
us an amazing, loving home while
we were gone.

Patrick Lorenz

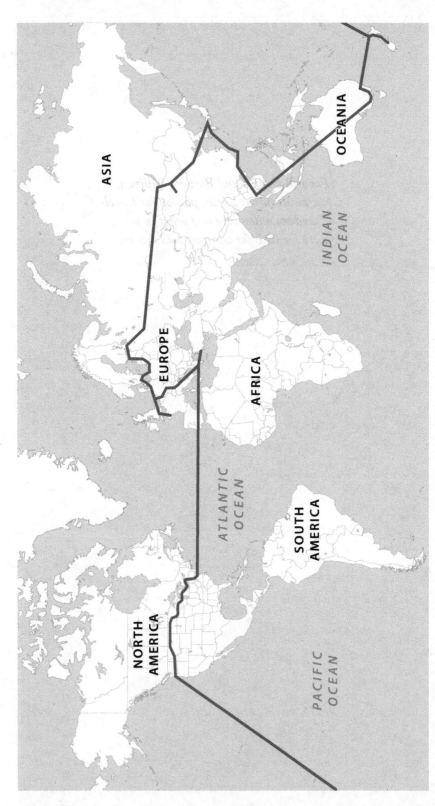

The Eber family's 14,931-km (9332-mile) cycling route around the world, May 2003 to August 2004.

CONTENTS

Contents

Preface

Dear friends, sponsors, and new readers,

It's been a long time since we last wrote. But we did promise we'd tell you the whole story one day. As you would only expect from the Eber family, each one of us wanted to have a say.

Memory is a fickle thing. And since we were all concerned that you got the *true* story, we have included as many actual archival materials about our family's journey for clean air and asthma as possible: *World Bike Bits* newsletters that we sent to you, our sponsors, as we pedaled around the globe; stories posted to the World Bike for Breath website by Yvonne (who was eleven at the time) and Anya (who was thirteen); route updates posted from the road; postcards and letters sent back home, and perhaps best of all, the many emails you wrote encouraging us as we struggled to keep pedaling on our journey.

To write our own personal chapters, we had our many journals and notes to referee any sticky details—along with over three thousand photos and two file drawers filled with receipts, tickets, and maps from our travels; newspaper and magazine articles about our ride; personal financial notebooks recording our bank balances as we traveled; and the minutes and bank statements of World Bike for Breath. In the process of trying to reconstruct the past as accurately as possible, some details may have fallen by the wayside. If there have been any omissions or errors, we will have a family meeting, debate some more, and then, hopefully, apologize.

Lost and Found

Paula

Day 197—Shikoku Island, Japan

"*Shosanji. Shosanji.*" The petite Japanese farm woman gesticulated, pointing her muddy trowel to a steep mountaintop to our west. I fingered the map in my hands awkwardly. Somewhere our family had taken a wrong turn in between the black lines and strange Japanese characters that wiggled up and down the island of Shikoku on the creased map in front of me. Half an hour ago, I had been certain that our two-thousand-foot

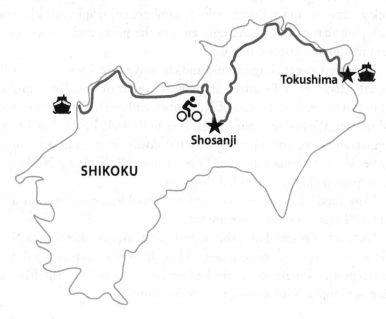

descent from the lush mountain ridge behind us would wind downward to a busy urban river of cars, people, and bicycles wending their way into the city of Kamojima. Instead, I stared, tired and hungry, at a tidy patchwork of vegetable fields and this sunburned woman kneeling in the dirt between rows of daikon radishes.

"*Wa doku desu ka?*" I poked my finger on the map, stumbling over the words that my Japanese phrase book had translated as "Where is?" I had been unable to find a translation for "Where are we?" presumably because the book assumed that the readers (our bicycling family not included in their target audience) had at least a vague idea of where they were and where they were going.

Wiping her muddy hands on the pockets of her gray cotton capris, the woman patiently set down her trowel and stood up. The musky scent of fresh-tilled earth wafted over the map as she traced her finger uncertainly along the lines.

"*Shosanji. Shosanji.*" She pointed again, squinting toward the sun, which hung low and hazy orange above the jagged mountain ridge to our west. I followed her gaze up the lush, remote valley into which we had pedaled, praying for a sign of a village, a house, a car. Anything but the thick green, red, and yellow tangle of bamboo, fall maples, and Japanese black pine that spread unendingly around the peaks and grooves of the silent mountains surrounding us.

I shivered, sweat clinging cold and clammy to my back in the cooling late-afternoon air, and glanced at my watch. Four o'clock. Not a problem in July but we were at the end of November, with each day getting shorter and shorter. We had an hour, at best two, until dark, I fretted as I turned the map and compass to line up with the slowly setting sun. *Shosanji.* Or maybe she was saying Chosangi? Or Koshanshi? Nothing. Nothing on the map even closely resembled this name.

"Any luck?" Lorenz peered over my shoulder, munching on a rice cracker. "Figure out where we are yet?"

"Not yet." I reached into the bottom of the rice cracker bag, famished after seven long hours of pedaling and pushing our tandems up some of the steepest mountain slopes we had cycled so far on this trip. My hand came out empty. "Got any more of these things?"

"Nope, that's it," my permanently hungry husband replied. Since arriving in Japan a week earlier, our family of four had been struggling to eke out enough calories from the local diet of fish, rice, and seaweed to keep cycling. Standing six foot tall and accustomed to a more calorie-heavy German diet of sausage and potatoes, Lorenz suffered the most. He carefully peeled the plastic wrapper from the rice cracker in his hand.

"Here." He offered me the cracker. "You can have the last one."

"Thanks." My stomach was growling, and I was beginning to feel a little light-headed from hunger. "Is there anything else to eat?"

"We have a pile of persimmons."

I nodded, remembering a friendly, wizened man in a conical straw hat hurrying up to our tandems as we wobbled slowly past his home earlier that morning, his hands full of freshly picked persimmons from the trees in his garden. We had laughed and smiled, using hands and feet to express our thanks for his unexpected generosity. Now, peering down at the almost empty food pannier, I had an uneasy feeling that perhaps, as he saw us pedaling farther and farther away from civilization, he knew we were going to need the five pounds of juicy orange fruit in his arms.

"That's it? What about food for dinner?" I began frantically rummaging through the food pannier, pulling out a package of ramen noodles, a crumbled box of fried tofu, a strange bag of unrecognizable powder, and a mound of persimmons.

"I don't know. Weren't we planning on stopping at a store in Kamojima?"

Lorenz, Anya, and Yvonne stared expectantly at me, their designated navigator. I didn't know what to say. I doubted there was a store within fifty kilometers of here.

I plonked myself on the ground, the moist soil still warm from the day, and stared at the map again, willing it to give up the secret of our location. Just then an unexpected sound on the deserted road stirred me from my fruitless map divination efforts. Sputtering loudly, a mud-splashed white van pulled over to the side of the road. A sun-browned hand reached out the window, clasping a brown package tied in string.

"A postman!" Lorenz jumped up quickly, grabbing my map. "Come on! Postmen spend their entire day driving all the local roads. He must know where we are." He sprinted over to join the Japanese farm woman, who was clutching her package and chattering excitedly to the man in the van. She pointed to Lorenz and the map in his hand, her words flowing past us without meaning.

The postman gazed at the map, turning it left then right, scrutinizing the Roman characters on the page. "*Shosanji.*" He jabbed his finger decisively at the map. "*Shosanji,*" he repeated, pointing to a steep mountain peak nearby, the same peak that the farm woman had shown us.

Lorenz and I stared at the spot on the map in disbelief. According to the postman, we had pedaled into an uninhabited mountain region in the middle of the island of Shikoku. On the peak above us stood the Buddhist temple of Shosanji. I swallowed hard as I reread the symbol key on the back of the map: Temple Number 12. How was it possible that I had led us into this sacred, isolated mountain valley, cradling the twelfth temple on the Buddhist pilgrimage route through Shikoku's famed eighty-eight temples?[*] Ever since Beijing, I had been hoping that traveling through Asia would get easier with time. Instead, we kept jumping from one crisis to another.

"Bad news." I swallowed hard as I gazed into the tired faces of Anya and Yvonne. Although they were only in sixth and eighth grade, the two sisters had been pedaling just as hard as Lorenz and me behind us on the tandems. They looked completely exhausted. And it was my fault.

"We're at least eighty kilometers away from Kamojima. On that mountain over there"—I pointed to the steep peak the postman had indicated—"is the temple of Shosanji." I indicated our position on the map resting on my handlebar bag.

I saw a look of despair cross their faces as my daughters registered the seriousness of my mistake as their leader. "Somehow at the top of the last pass, we must have headed south down the mountain ridge into this valley instead of turning north to Kamojima and the coast." I waved my arm hopelessly at the ragged four-thousand-foot mountain range that stood between us and the city. "There's no way we'll get there before nightfall."

---

[*] The island of Shikoku is the birthplace of Kobo-Daishi, one of the most revered Japanese Buddhist monks and teachers. Devout Buddhists follow a thousand-kilometer pilgrimage route around the island to the eighty-eight temples and shrines that claim a connection to Daishi.

"So where are we staying?" Yvonne asked tiredly, pushing the buttons on the cycling computer on my tandem in irritation.

"I don't know." I shook my head, looking at the lush valley without much hope. Even finding a spot to pitch a tent looked difficult.

Suddenly, Yvonne looked up with a start. "Hey! Maybe the temple will take us in. I talked to this man once who said that Buddhist temples take care of travelers in distress. We're travelers in distress!"

I looked at Yvonne intently. At first, when Yvonne had pointed out a signpost or told us she remembered seeing something, we had ignored her. What did an eleven-year-old kid know? But slowly we had come to trust Yvonne's keen observation skills. She listened. And she paid attention to details we ignored.

"So the man said he was lost once and couldn't find a hotel or anywhere to stay." Yvonne's eyes suddenly widened in enthusiasm. "Someone took him to this Buddhist temple, and they gave him a room with gold-plated taps on the sink."

I stared at Yvonne. How did she find out these things? Well, it was worth a try. I doubted the taps were gold plated. But maybe the temple would have a room we could stay in.

◆━━◆

The road to Shosanji wound, silent and cool, beneath a dark forest of black pine trees. Swish, swish, our bicycle tires rolled in a soothing hum over the pavement with no other sound but the occasional call of birds and the soft croak of frogs to interrupt the deep evening peace settling on this hauntingly beautiful mountain valley. After a few kilometers, the road turned upward, slithering back and forth like a long green snake as it crept toward the mythical temple of Shosan-Ji. In the fading light, the shadows of the trees grew longer, stretching across the road and down into the thick tangle of vines and ferns cascading to the valley below us.

Faintly in the distance, an even, hollow sound echoed from above us. *Klock. Klock. Klock.* The wooden beat reverberated through the shadowy trees, growing louder as we pushed forward. *Klock. Klock. Klock.* Suddenly the road narrowed and angled straight up. I ratcheted the gears down quickly, pushing hard on the pedals as Anya and I wobbled into a tight curve. And then, without warning, Shosanji rose in front of us, the ancient temple's curved, gray tile rooftops etched starkly against a thin, milky sliver of daylight receding on the horizon beyond. In front of the temple, an enormous wooden entranceway loomed, perched like a gigantic Greek letter π at the top of the mountain. Gazing through the gateway to the silent complex of sweeping pagodas and stone statues, I wondered if we hadn't just pedaled into an ancient Japanese fairy tale.

Klock, the mysterious rhythm beat out once more. Behind the massive entryway, a set of worn stone steps wove their way to a large water-filled urn. A hollow bamboo reed slowly filled it with water. It paused, tilted, then swung against the black metal edge of the basin. *Klock*, the reed reverberated across the silent evening.

"A Japanese washing basin!" Lorenz exclaimed. He dipped the large wooden ladle hanging next to the urn into the water and poured the cool, refreshing liquid onto his face and hands, splashing away the day's sweat.

"It's so beautiful," Anya, our imaginative thirteen-year-old, sighed wistfully, gazing up at a cascading mountaintop garden of soft moss shaded by majestic cedar trees. Granite statues and little shrines poked up from the landscape, inviting us to meditate in this unexpectedly lovely mountaintop retreat. But not now. I shivered in the suddenly chill night air, the sweat on my skin clammy and cold. We needed to find somewhere to sleep. And soon!

Following the beams of our flashlights, we guided the tandems over a gravel pathway around the temple. Ahead I glimpsed a dimly lit, low building on a hill above us. Yellow squares gleamed in a grid through a rice screen doorway. A hunched silhouette moved across the golden glow carrying what looked like a thick book. Were these the monks' dormitories? Maybe Yvonne was right! A warm room sounded wonderful right now. Would we be put in bunk beds? I'd even sleep on the floor on the traditional rice tatami mats.

As Lorenz and the girls waited below, I walked up the hill to the building. Gathering up my courage, I rapped on the door. Tap. Wait. Tap, tap. Pause. Tap, tap, tap. I waited in the silent darkening night. No answer. I looked upward at the sky, at the tiny white light that had appeared above the horizon: the night's first star. Still no response.

Tap. Tap. Tap, tap, tap. I knocked more urgently this time. To my surprise, a second, even more hunched, shadow hobbled to the door and slid the milky screen cautiously to the side. I stared into an ancient brown face crowned by a smooth shaven head. The monk looked at me expectantly, his dark brown eyes searching for an explanation.

"Do you speak English?"

A shake of the monk's head sent my hopes plummeting. I rummaged in my handlebar bag, my fingers trembling in the cold night air, then pulled out our picture phrase book.* I opened the page to a picture of four beds and pointed hopefully.

"We're on bicycles," I began, mostly to fill the awkward silence between us. The man peered at the picture, then looked up at me quizzically, not understanding. I motioned down the hill to the tandems below, almost indiscernible in the dark as Lorenz, Anya, and Yvonne waved their flashlights excitedly, highlighting a handlebar, an arm, a bag tied to the back rack.

The monk gazed thoughtfully at the tandems, fingering the sleeves of his gray robes. Finally, he nodded in understanding and pointed to our picture book. Flipping through the picture book, he found an image of a tent and pointed to the parking lot below the temple. I looked at him, crestfallen. The Buddhist-temple-as-a-refuge-for-travelers-in-distress plan had turned out to be far from what I had hoped.

A heavy wind blasted me as I tried to assemble the metal poles of the tent in the parking lot below the temple. It was only November, but high up on this lonely mountain it was bitterly cold. When we had planned our world cycling route, I had imagined Japan to be a warm, tropical country where we could escape winter as we pedaled south away from Russia. How wrong I had been! My frozen fingers fumbled as I tried to insert the poles into each other. I missed, then tried again, my numb fingers unable to guide the poles properly as I shivered uncontrollably.

---

* We carried a small book that contained pictures to explain what we wanted in the many countries where we could not speak the language: pictures of different foods, street navigation signs, tents for camping, and beds for hotel rooms.

"I think we should all sleep together in our tent tonight," I said as I finally clicked the tent poles together and hoisted the fading blue fabric. "We'll be warmer if we all snuggle together."

Too tired and frozen to argue, Anya and Yvonne pulled their sleeping bags and pads out of their two-man tent and tossed them into the Taj, our three-man tent. As quickly as we could, the girls and I dove into the Taj to escape the wind, abandoning Lorenz outside to create a miracle meal from the dregs in the panniers. Between the howls of the wind, I could hear the flame on the camp stove sputter on, then out, on again, then out—unable to battle the fierce gusts blowing up from the mountain valley.

"Are you OK?" I peered out the tent door to glimpse Lorenz's frozen hands fumbling with a gooey powder that should have created pancakes, according to the strange pictures captioned in Japanese on the back of the package. He motioned to me to stay in the tent as a heavy blast pushed the tent poles down, slanting the fabric onto Anya's and Yvonne's heads. I scurried back inside and hurriedly moved our heavy panniers to the corners to keep the tent in place.

Finally, half-hypothermic and stiff from cold, Lorenz crawled into the tent and handed out four Sierra cups. The four of us huddled together in a circle around the tent walls, cradling the warm cups in our hands. I forced myself to swallow the sticky, burned, tasteless glop in the bowl, then collapsed into my sleeping bag. For a moment, I gazed up at the blue fabric of the roof, my eyes too heavy to focus. Not exactly a room with gold taps. I sighed in disappointment, pulling the sleeping bag over my head.

At dawn, the soft sound of singing and the tinkling of bells pulled me from a fitful sleep. I crawled to the tent door and stared out in wonder at the steep curved roofs of the temple of Shosanji rising above a valley of pink-tinged clouds. Pulling two thick sweaters and a pair of pants over my long underwear, I stumbled, half hopping, half crawling out of the tent's foyer onto the frost-covered pavement of the parking lot. The sharp, cold air struck my lungs like icicles stabbing inside my chest. Numbly, I fumbled for our water carrier, my hands too cold to bend easily around the handle. I hobbled awkwardly up the uneven steps to the water basin, trying to urge the blood into my stiff legs. Around me the temple gardens sat silent and serene, dusted in delicate crystals of ice.

I heard the music again. In between the hollow, haunting *klock, klock* of the water basin, soft rippling voices and the tinkling of tiny bells wafted up from somewhere down the mountain. I turned toward the singing, picking my way back down the crooked, narrow steps to our tents in the parking lot below.

Three steps from the bottom, I paused, wordless, the dripping Platypus water carrier hanging limply by my side. At the far end of the parking lot, a small group of white-clothed Buddhist pilgrims were weaving their way to the temple, singing and chanting. Tiny silver bells danced cheerfully from the tops of their wooden walking staffs, tap-tapping the rhythm of the slow, even-paced steps of the early-morning pilgrims.

By now, Anya and Yvonne had crawled out of the tent to gaze sleepy-eyed and curious at the approaching figures. The flowing white group paused momentarily in front of our tents, settling briefly like a flock of cooing doves landing on a branch. A bald-headed man stepped out from the group, his brown, wizened skin creasing into a broad smile as he gazed at these two young strangers, with crumpled long underwear and untidy blond hair, camping below the sacred temple. Gently, fluidly, he bowed forward in an age-old gesture of friendship and honor. Then, without speaking, the kindly man stepped forward and placed a mandarin orange into each of the hands of the astonished girls.

"*Arigato!* Thank you!" Anya and Yvonne called out in surprise, bowing in return.

The group of flowing white jackets billowed forward as the bald-headed pilgrim joined them again—peaceful doves heading home to roost on the sacred mountaintop. For a moment, I caught the bright eyes of the generous gift bearer. We smiled in friendship and understanding. Each of us pilgrims on our own sacred journey.

Part I

Biking for Breath

Part I

Biking for Breath

Prunes

Paula

a large white-and-black vinyl banner proclaimed in the Safeway produce aisle. The challenge hung enticingly above a stand of brightly colored packages containing Sunsweet's new lemon- and orange-flavored "dried plums."

A roast chicken? Or spaghetti with salad, I debated, hurrying the shopping cart past the tempting banner to a stack of red plum tomatoes piled high on the stand nearby. It had been a sloshy, muddy bike ride home from Seattle in the rain. I shivered as water dripped off my raincoat and pooled in my soaking-wet shoes. I couldn't wait to put on dry socks and eat dinner by the warm fire crackling in our woodstove.

A small sticky hand tugged on my shirt. "I'm hungry." Yvonne stared up at me, holding up a package of lemon-flavored prunes. "*Please.*"

"We don't need those." I reached for the bag, then paused. Standing patiently next to her younger sister, Anya was clutching a bright orange prune package hopefully. "Well—" They looked so little and tired. It was a long day for them too: eight hours at the elementary school on our little island in Puget Sound and then another three at the Boys and Girls Club after-school program.

3

"OK," I sighed and walked back to the Sunsweet prune stand. "Which flavor shall we get? Lemon or orange?" Clutching her lemon prunes, Yvonne stared at Anya. Anya glared back, unwilling to let go of the orange-flavored package. "Or both?" I glanced down to the edge of the stand and suddenly noticed a stack of three-by-five-inch coupons. "If you could fulfill your dream, what would it be? Tell us and you could win," the coupon challenged provocatively.

On an impulse, I tore off a coupon and stuffed it into my purse.

That night after dinner, as Lorenz and I were loading the dishwasher, I broached my new plan with classic undiplomatic Paula style—you know, break the news immediately and then pick up the pieces. Somehow I have never learned the art of tiptoeing around a subject and playing touchy-feely for hours until finally you just casually mention what you are *really* thinking.

"I found this coupon in the store," I began while rinsing tomato sauce off a plate. "Well, actually, it was a contest. Anyway, I was thinking—"

Lorenz's six-foot frame stiffened slightly. Whenever I started *thinking*, it usually meant I had a *great idea*—the kind that required Lorenz to solve all sorts of impossible practical problems. Early on in our marriage, we naturally drifted into our own career niches. I'm an anthropology professor. I love to research and come up with great theories and plans. Luckily, Lorenz, the engineer, keeps our feet on the ground. Like me, he loves adventure; in fact, he craves it. But when it comes to figuring out how to fit an eight-foot, six-inch tandem bike into a thirty-six-inch shipping box or rewire the kitchen . . . well, he's just so good at it, I see no point in interfering in his domain.

"Yes . . . go on." He had that cautious tone, which suggested I should probably step carefully.

Sensing that I had already started at the wrong end of the stick, I concluded I might as well just rush in and skip the small talk. "Here." I pulled out the Sunsweet prunes competition guidelines from my purse.

Wiping his hands on a dishtowel, Lorenz looked at me suspiciously and reached for the three-by-five coupon.

"Remember at the end of our Alaska bike trip?" I continued, one eye on Anya and Yvonne, who were currently negotiating loudly over whether Samantha or Felicity should wear the black velvet coat I had sewn for their American Girl dolls last Christmas. "We said if we could bike six hundred miles from Fairbanks to Seward—you know, with all the grizzly bears and mountains and remote campsites ... Well"—I struggled to make this all sound so very reasonable—"Yvonne and Anya were only five and seven on that trip. And they had a great time."

Lorenz was studying the contest rules carefully. "Fifty thousand dollars to fulfill your dream? What would that be?"

I took a deep breath and plunged in. "We said if they could bike through Alaska with us"—I swallowed hard—"then why couldn't we bike around the world with them?"

He laughed. "Bike around the world? You're crazy!"

I must have looked crestfallen because he took a second look at the coupon. After a few minutes, he handed the rules back to me and grinned cheekily. I suspected he was about to make one of those impossible-to-refuse deals.

"If you get the money, can I pick where we go?" he asked.

I braced myself, wondering what concessions I'd have to make.

"I want to see the South Pacific. Tahiti. Or Fiji." His eyes lit up as he imagined pedaling along lush tropical beaches, palm trees waving to the sound of crashing waves. "Or both."

"No problem. You have a deal," I jumped in before he had a chance to change his mind.

I'm pretty sure he thought I wouldn't win the contest. But then again, considering that Lorenz was constructing the fuselage of a two-seat, homebuilt experimental airplane in our garage, when it comes to being up for crazy adventures, I'd say we were about even.

———

I struggled to concentrate on the student papers heaped on the desk in front of me. Instead of grading yet another essay on Edward Said's *Orientalism*, I kept turning the three-by-five-inch ad over and over, reading and rereading the details of the contest. "Entries will be judged without bias, and judging will be weighted on the basis of originality of dream wish (50%), reason for desiring dream wish (30%), and creativity of entry presentation (20%)," the entry rules stated. "Submissions must be five hundred words or less."

Several years later, a television reporter in Seattle posed the question that has consumed me ever since that day: "Why?"

As she stood beside me, impeccably dressed in a tasteful suit with a perfect no-stray-wisps hairstyle, she did not add the rest of the question. But gazing at the camera in my cycling jersey dripping with sweat, my hair frizzy from bicycle helmet head, I understood her need to know. Why would a family with perfectly good jobs, wonderful schools for their children, a beautiful home—with soft beds and a hot shower—want to pack it all up and head off on bicycles into the unknown?

I stared at the contest rules in my hand: five hundred words or less. I needed something catchy. Unique. Maybe I could try a poem. It was clear I was not going to finish grading the papers. So I pulled out my computer. I should title it—hmm,

Breathtaking Bicycling
Sunsweet Prunes Contest Entry

Two dusty world-worn tandem bicycles,
sleeping bags snuggled
by a long-loved stuffed bunny and blanket.
Outside the well-traveled tent
the camp stove sputters into life,
aromas of America, Asia, Australia
floating above the laughter
of two sun-browned blond-haired girls
playing tag.

It wasn't always this way.
I remember another blond-haired girl
with protruding rib bones and dangling emaciated arms
wheezing, coughing, choking.
When I was diagnosed with asthma,
a blue-lipped gasping toddler,

the helpless doctors shrugged unsuccessful suggestions—
move to the pollen-free desert;
sleep upside down;
take breathing lessons,
allergy injections,
counseling sessions.

Childhood was a blurred haze
of sleepless nights in emergency rooms,
breathless days in steamy suffocating hospital oxygen tents,
long lonely months wasting away while watching
laughing, skipping, jumping children
from my window.
It has been a long journey
traversed by miracle medicines and faith.
Terbutaline, Theophylline, Proventil, Beclovent.
Each new discovery breathing hope into me.

Somewhere I began sleeping under the stars
instead of in oxygen tents;
taking trips to Africa rather than to the emergency room;
and cycling tens of thousands of miles
with my own laughing, skipping, jumping children
while others watched curiously from their windows.

One day, I dream
I will cycle around the world with my family.
Each mile raising another dollar for research;
Each news story about us raising the hopes of another child;
Each day raising my spirit in thanks
that those lonely impossible childhood dreams at the window—
were but reflections of a tomorrow I could not yet see.

I pack the memories into my panniers
and cycle off to a new day
pedals clicking to the rhythm of my breath.
Come, the road calls. Follow me
to lollipopped cotton-candied summer county fairs;
to silent snow-laden mountain peaks
and windswept ocean coastlines;

to craggy castles and medieval nights;
to onion-domed cathedrals and holy days;
past shouting rickshawed drivers shadowed by the Great Wall
and desolate kangarooed desert byways.

Come, the way whispers. Let us share
new stories
new friends
new challenges;
a new hope.

—Paula Holmes-Eber

Putting Asthma on the Map

Paula

THE AWARD LETTER NEVER CAME. I RAN TO THE MAILBOX EAGERLY FOR weeks after the posted award date of August 15. I received plenty of coupons for Sunsweet's latest line of flavored "dried plums." Even a few samples. I imagined that the prize went to someone a bit more conventional—someone who wanted to study art in Paris, or to fund the down payment on a house for their five homeless children, or even to go to Africa and run an orphanage. Practical dreams.

After Sunsweet had made the obvious mistake of awarding their $50,000 prize to someone more sensible, I stubbornly forged ahead. I may not have won the prize, but the lemon-flavored prune company had given me a much greater gift: a dream. One that gnawed at my mind and fed on my imagination like an insatiable tapeworm. A dream to change the world.

With the confidence that only the truly inexperienced can exude, I marched off to our local library, returning home with a stack of books on how to start and run a nonprofit organization. According to the various experts, one of the first tasks was to convince a few other equally naive and starry-eyed colleagues to sit on my new nonprofit's board of directors.

⮞⬥⮜

Five potential board members sat around our long pine dining room table, staring curiously at a large map of the world stretched across its center. Lorenz was describing our proposed journey. He leaned over the colorful map, pointing to a black line we had drawn across the world in an unbroken, continuous circle.

"Our plan is to travel the entire route by bicycle. No cars, buses, trains, or planes. Except across Siberia. And the oceans, obviously. We'll cycle through twenty-four countries and four continents." Lorenz's fingers followed the black line. "Starting in Washington, DC, we'll fly to Greece—and bike across Europe to Russia. Then we'll head south through Asia"—his fingers moved over Mongolia and China, then down along the islands of Japan and Taiwan—"across the south Pacific." He motioned over Australia and New Zealand. "We'll end by cycling across the US and Canada, coming back full circle to DC, where we started."

My eyes slid across the faces of our prospective board, worried. I had spent months carefully researching a continuous route that would cross through relatively stable and safe countries and follow the seasons, dropping to the warm southern hemisphere from January to March and staying far north of the hot equator from June to August.* But now, show-ing the map to my friends and peers for the first time, I was not so sure.

"How are you going to get across Russia?" Tom, the tall, lanky owner of BI Cycle, pointed to an enormous uninhabited region on the map from Moscow to Beijing as he munched on a chocolate chip cookie I had baked for the event. For the past six years, Tom had repaired our bicycles as they came in and out of his shop from our family's various long-distance bicycle adventures. Replacing bike chains destroyed by sand as we camped and pedaled along the Oregon coast. Overhauling frayed derailleur cables that had done too much shifting while dragging a Trail-a-Bike loaded with camping gear up the steep hills of the Gulf Islands of Canada. And rebuilding a cracked bottom bracket that had crumpled from hauling more than two hundred pounds of kids plus trailer through Alaska.

I nodded, having expected this question. "No roads cross Russia after the Ural Mountains." I pointed to an enormous region of barren, forbidding, roadless steppe and taiga. "So there's no way to bike across

---

* Initially, we planned to cycle in a westerly direction. But to follow the seasons to the best advan-tage, we ultimately switched the route to head eastward. Since the prevailing winds around the world go from west to east, this route traveled with the wind—at least in theory.

Siberia—at least not on paved roads. Across that section, we'll take the Trans-Siberian Railway from Moscow to Ulaanbaatar. And then to Beijing."

Tom looked at me, puzzled. I pointed to a small dot on the map, south of Siberia. "Ulaanbaatar's the capital of Mongolia."

My throat tightened. What were they thinking? For that matter, what was *I* thinking to propose this audacious journey? Who takes their kids through Mongolia? For the past six months, I had been buried deep in maps and books covering our planned route. Absorbed with the lines, contours, and photos, it seemed perhaps I had lost sight of reality. For the first time in months, I stared at the planned route in front of us, seeing it from my prospective board's eyes. Crap. They must think I'm crazy!

Who was I kidding? I wasn't a cycling professional. Or even a weekend racer. Sure, I could bike long distances. But with my asthma, I was anything but fast. I struggled to breathe just pedaling off the ferry to Bainbridge Island. As the hordes of speeding daily bicycle commuters from Seattle whizzed up the hill past me to the traffic light, I huffed and wheezed as I cycled slowly at the back. What was I thinking even suggesting that I could bike around the world?

I could feel my cheeks getting hot. Take a deep breath. Maybe two. I swallowed and pressed ahead, aware I was talking too quickly. "Our goal is to educate people about clean air and asthma. Most people don't see the link between declining air quality around the world and rising rates of the disease." I tried to slow down the rapid torrent of words and relax. Instead, my entire face began to feel like it had caught on fire. Was I even making *any* sense? "That's why we're cycling. To encourage people to consider alternate clean-air forms of travel."

Noticing I was beginning to look more and more like a tomato, Lorenz rushed to my rescue. "On the way, we plan to talk to newspapers and radio and TV stations. The finale will be a fundraising and educational media ride across the US and Canada. The goal is to put asthma on the map. Literally."

I scanned the faces of my guests, unsure of their reaction. Curiosity? Disbelief? Excitement?

"How do you plan to raise the money?" Maureen, a doctor at the Winslow Clinic, asked, her long dark hair brushing the table as she reached for one of the mugs of tea I had set out.

I swallowed hard. My nonprofit fundraising experience was limited to selling Campfire Girls candy in front of Safeway with Anya and Yvonne. But I had watched many of my friends raise money for charity by running marathons or biking in organized events. It seemed easy enough to me. "Through individual and corporate sponsorships. Sponsors will receive special newsletters and updates from our website as we cycle around the world. Our goal is to cycle fifteen thousand kilometers." I penciled the numbers on a piece of paper. "So that would be one hundred and fifty dollars for someone sponsoring us at one cent per kilometer."*

"Well, it's certainly ambitious!" Maureen said. She gazed thoughtfully out the wall of windows lining our dining room. It was an unexpectedly lovely May evening, with no rain and few clouds—a welcome break after the wet, gray Seattle winter. The sky spread crimson over Manzanita Bay below, glimpses of the water poking through a grove of tall red cedars towering over our A-frame house. "But maybe it's just what I need right now. A way to feel like I'm doing something more than just working and raising a family. Being part of something larger than me."

I understood that feeling—a hunger to live a meaningful life, to not drown in the dailyness of kids' carpools, trips to the vet, and cleaning the house on weekends.

"If no one else wants the job, I'll volunteer to be the treasurer."

"Treasurer?" I looked at her in surprise. Maureen just didn't seem the type to like accounting. She was one of the most compassionate and caring doctors on the island. Somehow, I had always assumed that her husband, Brett, an engineer who was currently a stay-at-home dad, managed the family finances as well as running the household and arranging playdates with our daughters.

"You won't believe it, but I was a bookkeeper before I went to medical school," Maureen explained. "After a couple of years sitting alone in

---

* With the exception of Liberia, Myanmar, and the US, the entire world calculates distance in kilometers, a convention we followed on our journey—except in the US, where we switched to miles to match the distances on the road signs.

a room talking to numbers, I admit I was very motivated to become a doctor."

Sitting next to Maureen, Tom broke into a wide smile as he began to visualize the trip. "Wow! What an adventure! Well, if anyone can do it, I guess it's you guys. I'm in. I just wish I could join you."

I felt a sudden lump in my throat and swallowed hard. Tom—a former racing cyclist—thought we could do this? He believed our journey was possible? Maybe it was!

Debbie spoke next. "You can count me in. You've been talking about nothing else for months on our ferry rides to work together." She laughed. "How could I say no?"

"Me too," Linda said. "As a pediatrician, I see children with asthma every day. It's a good cause."

I looked hopefully at our last guest: Matt, a young, sandy-haired business attorney.

"I can't be on the board," Matt said. My heart sank. We needed someone to help with the confusing pile of legal incorporation documents, 501-(c)-3 filings, and other requirements I had printed out from the Internet. There was no way I could handle that myself.

"That would be a conflict of interest if I'm going to provide you with pro bono legal advice."

I gasped, hardly able to believe our good fortune. A new board and a free attorney! I opened my mouth, but before I could speak, Matt continued, getting down to business right away. "We'll need a name for the organization so I can start filing the papers—"

Around the table, the seven of us toasted World Bike for Breath, our new charity, with mugs of tea and cookies, dreaming of adventure, challenge, an exciting purpose. Oh, how little we knew!

Top Ten Ways to Fall Off a Tandem Bicycle

Lorenz

10. Since riding around the world on a tandem bicycle is still just a crazy idea in my wife's head and none of us has actually ever ridden a tandem, I ask our friends Maureen and Brett to lend us their tandem for training. Being an expert on all things bicycle, I kindly refuse Maureen's guidance on how to get on this contraption, and in my infinite wisdom I place Anya, the stoker (or rear rider), onto the tandem without me while the tandem is still standing on its bike stand. Promptly the wimpy bike stand snaps, and Anya sprawls onto the driveway. I explain to Maureen that the bike stand is obviously not strong enough and generously offer to buy her a better, stronger one.

9. After installing the better, stronger bike stand, I roll Maureen's tandem out onto my driveway and raise it onto its new stand. I mount the front seat of the tandem alone. Promptly, the stronger, better bike stand collapses, and I sprawl onto the gravel. Picking myself up, I have to admit that, sadly, the quality of bike stands has been steadily declining in recent years.

8. Tom, our local bike store owner, advises me to get on the tandem first and, while straddling it, let Anya, the stoker, climb on without the stand. In light of the current quality-control crisis in bicycle stand manufacturing, I grudgingly adopt this makeshift method

of mounting a tandem. Surprisingly, the method actually works. Unfortunately, some previous misguided tandem captain has left the shifters on the tandem in the highest gear. When Anya and I step into the pedals, there is nearly infinite resistance. We totter and fall onto the parking lot asphalt. Humiliated by the public scene, Anya threatens never to get on a tandem again. I swear to her that I will keep saboteurs away from our tandems in the future.

7. Instituting a mandatory preride shifter inspection rule to prevent tampering by saboteurs, Anya and I mount using Tom's method. Eureka! We manage to pedal around the block. I am ecstatic and have to admit to myself that I am a natural at tandem bicycling, a born tandem captain. Around the next corner, Grow Avenue rises in a steep hill. Nothing against Maureen and Brett and their cumbersome tandem, but the tandem decides to shift very slowly and the gears jam. Unceremoniously, Anya and I fall into the ditch. Dusting off her dirty clothes, Anya suggests that I ride the tandem with someone else in the future.

6. I convince Paula that it is time to buy a more responsive, better-shifting tandem of our own. A divorcée in Yakima has put up an ad for an almost-new Trek tandem. When we meet the woman, she promises that the tandem has only been ridden *once*. Apparently, she filed for divorce immediately after that. Paula and I bike off happily on a test ride. I muse that this is a wonderful way to spend time together as a couple. Gliding down deserted country roads, this truly is quality time, a rejuvenation of our marriage. At the next lonely stop sign, I decide to push through the abandoned intersection. Misguidedly, Paula decides to obey the law and stops the pedals. The tandem jolts, and I lose control. We skid into the stop sign and fall onto the shoulder. In the heated exchange that follows, divorce is threatened on both sides. Bizarrely, we buy the tandem anyway.

5. The world bike ride is now being planned in earnest. Our friend Eric, the photographer, schedules a photo shoot for the official World Bike for Breath brochure. I convince Anya that our new Trek tandem is

much easier to ride, and we head to Hidden Cove, where Eric has set up his photo gear. We feel very important, this being our first photo shoot. It's like being put on a movie poster. I feel that we must look dashing, experienced, and daring, like real adventurers. On our first pass, approaching the ominous black camera lens, I notice that my raincoat is unzipped and take my hands off the handlebars to close it. At the same time, Anya notices a strand of hair out of place and tucks it in with rather quick jerks. I lose control, and we run off the road and into some blackberry bushes. Note to self: never take both hands off the handlebars of a tandem when feeling vain.

4. The Burley bicycle company has committed to be our prime sponsor for the world ride! They invite us to their factory in Eugene, Oregon, and give us free pick of any bike they make. Naturally, I choose the most expensive, coolest-looking bike they have, called the Softride. Paula, being conservatively unimaginative, picks the traditional steel frame Duet. My Softride is a marvel of modern engineering and sports a flexible cantilever carbon fiber boom for the stoker to sit on, promising unmatched rider comfort. We strap our brand-new bikes onto the roof of our van and proudly take them home. The next weekend we test-ride the bikes on San Juan Island. For some unexplained reason, Anya has convinced Yvonne to ride on the Softride with me, preferring to cycle behind her mom on the boring Duet tandem. Behind me, Yvonne is loving the gentle flexing of the carbon fiber boom and is listening to music on her MP3 player. When the Spice Girls blast "Wannabe" into her headphones, Yvonne starts dancing behind me on the bike. The Softride instantly picks up the vibrations and escalates itself into increasingly uncontrollable harmonics. Like the doomed Tacoma Narrows bridge, the bike begins to buck, and the handlebars are torn from my hands. Picking clods of dirt off my sleeve, I vow to beg Burley to replace the Softride with another Duet.

3. Burley, bless their hearts, replaces the Softride with a beautiful green Duet tandem. We now have a matching pair. At the Seattle Bike Expo, a bike dealer convinces me to buy four pairs of cleated pedals and bike shoes that lock into them. He says that cleats can boost

your cycling power by 30 percent because now your legs can push *and* pull on the pedals. We install the cleated pedals on the tandems. The dealer is right, these cleated pedals are *amazing* . . . until we get to the first traffic light. We stop, but we've forgotten how to twist our feet out of the pedals. Our feet are glued to the pedals! Like two planks, the tandems and Ebers keel over and flop onto the road.

2. Since we will be carrying hundreds of pounds of gear on our Duet tandems, Burley is worried that the standard brakes on the bikes are not strong enough to stop the tandems when we sail down the long mountain passes we'll be crossing. Burley adds an extra drum brake to the rear wheels of our Duets and levers on the handlebars to acti-vate them. When set, the drum brakes create an enormous amount of drag, preventing the bikes from becoming runaway trains on a down-hill. On our final gear check-out ride in California, just four months before our departure date, Yvonne and I sail down a two-mile-long hill into Oxnard. We put on the drum brake and voila! The descent is a piece of cake. No need to squeeze the standard caliper brakes at all. We watch the beautiful scenery going by as we zip down the hill and totally forget that the drum brake is set. At the bottom is an imme-diate uphill. Instead of coasting into the uphill, the bike grinds to a halt and flops over. Scrambling out from under the tandem, Yvonne asks with gritted teeth, "Anyone around here maybe forget to switch off the drum brake?"

And the number one way to fall off a tandem bicycle is:

1. I walk into our garage to grab my commuting bike to ride to work, as I do every day. The bike has a flat. No problem, I say, and decide to take my road bike, which incidentally also turns out to have a flat. I cast around for other options, and my gaze falls on the green tandem. Perfect, why not ride the tandem to work alone? Who needs a stoker anyway? I get on the tandem and set off to work. It's a beautiful day, and I go fast as I enter the trail through the woods that takes me to work. I am daydreaming and forget I'm riding an eight-foot-long tandem instead of my zippy commuting bike. I scream down the

hill to the bottom of the trail, where suddenly there is a sharp turn to the left. I turn to the left and nothing happens. I turn harder. Very little happens except that the cedar tree directly in front of me grows larger. I feel like I am commanding an ocean liner instead of the speedboat I am used to. The cedar tree now fills my entire vision. *Bam!* My vision goes black, then I see tiny yellow, pink, blue, and red stars—very beautiful. I wake up lying on top of my tandem in front of a badly marred cedar tree. I limp home. I think I'll go to work another day.

World Bike for Breath Funds Asthma Clinic in India

World Bike Bits

Bits and stories about World Bike for Breath. A Bulletin for sponsors. Volume 1.

World Bike for Breath funds asthma clinic in India

With the arrival of a computerized spirometer, oximeters, nebulizers and peak flow meters donated by World Bike for Breath, a new pulmonary lung function laboratory is opening this December to treat an estimated 20,000 people with asthma and lung diseases in Calcutta, the city made famous by Mother Teresa.

The new laboratory will be part of an asthma clinic run by International Asthma Services. Services will be provided at minimal to no cost. "We are very excited about funding this clinic," says Paula Holmes-Eber, President of World Bike for Breath, "Since respiratory illnesses are the leading cause of death of children in the developing world, we felt that our sponsors would be proud to be part of such an important international project."

Welcome World Bike for Breath Board!

Paula Holmes-Eber, PhD
Maureen Koval, M.D.
Tom Clune, Owner BI Cycle
Linda Warren, M.D.
Deborah Wheeler, PhD

Did you know?

♦ 1 in 10 Americans has asthma
♦ Asthma rates have doubled since 1980; decreasing air quality, especially in cities is correlated to this change
♦ Each year as many Americans die from asthma related causes as from AIDS
♦ Air pollution kills over 7 million people a year

With appreciation to our volunteer staff

Mike Culver—Web design and maintenance
Eric and Cheryl Fox—Visual media
Eileen Magnuson—Office administration
Gabriel Perez—Graphic design and brochures
Matt Topham—Legal Counsel

Many thanks to our World Sponsors

Arkel Over Designs
Burley Design Cooperative
Cascade Designs
MSR
Old Man Mountain
Patagonia
REI
T-Mobile

19

Fogg

Paula

"Hey, how's my big girl?" My dad peeked his head around the door to my room.

He's home! My heart jumped. It was my favorite moment of the long, long day in bed.

"Doing OK," I answered, fighting to pull myself up in the small single bed—an impossible project since the foot end was elevated ten inches on a pile of bricks, making my body slide into the headboard in miserable contortions.

"Here, let me help." Daddy grabbed two pillows from the floor and stuffed them behind me, trying to find a position in which I could sit comfortably in this upside-down bed. It was the latest stupid doctor idea: lie in a bed with my head lower than my feet. Supposedly by sleeping at this awful angle, the blood and oxygen in my toes would flow downhill to my lungs and help me breathe. But I knew better. They just wanted to suffocate me faster. Or kill me with excruciating headaches. It was obvious the blood just skipped my lungs and rushed straight behind my eyeballs, pulsing endlessly in a head-splitting rhythm.

I straightened out my favorite pink nightgown with the frilly lace collar. "Can you read me another chapter? *Please?*"

"Sure. We have a little bit of time before Mommy finishes dinner."

I reached for the pile of books that had been my best friends for the past two months. The enormous stack from the library sat in a special place on my bedside table, next to two half-full water glasses, an uneaten bowl of soup my mom had made me for lunch, piles of Kleenex filled with sticky sputum, and my "monster inhaler." All I had to do was breathe one puff of the white monster and my pulse raced to two hundred million beats a minute. As much as I hated the upside-down bed, I loved the monster. It had saved my life hundreds of times. No, I mean it. I really would be dead now without it. Every time I would think for sure, absolutely no question, this time I would in fact suffocate in a world of unobtainable air, one squirt from the monster would haul the enormous, lung-squishing elephant off my chest. And suddenly, miraculously, air, wonderful whooshing air, would pour back into my lungs.

"Where were we?" Daddy asked, holding the latest book. On its cover was a picture of a train, a steamship, and an elephant (a nice-looking one, not the lung-squishing kind) carrying two men—one in a black top hat, the other in a pith helmet—and a beautiful woman in a sari. Scrolled across the top of the book was the title *Around the World in Eighty Days*.

"Passepartout and Phileas Fogg just rescued Aouda from the fire. And now they are running away through India!"

"They *did*?" My dad looked at me in shock with that mischievous twinkle in his eye that I so loved.

"Yes, Daddy. Don't you *remember*? The Indians were about to throw Aouda on the funeral pyre." I giggled. It was a little game we played— my dad pretending he couldn't remember or didn't know something. It was a game we would play for the rest of our lives—testing my memory, checking my facts and assumptions. It forced me to think critically, to examine issues carefully, and, ultimately, to love the logic of scholarship and research.

"Burn Aouda? Why would they do *that*?"

"Well, because her husband died. *You know*. It was a custom they used to have. Kind of like the Egyptians. The husband needed his wife in the next world."

"Oh dear! How dreadful! Well, we must see what happens to Aouda then." His lips struggled to hide a pleased smile as he flipped through the book to find the right page.

"Daddy?"

"Yes," he answered absentmindedly, skimming the pages to find the chapter.

"Can you *really* go all the way around the world?"

"Well, sure. Today we have airplanes. You can do it in a couple of days."

"No. Not that. I mean, *really* travel *all* the way around the world. Seeing all the countries. Meeting the people and having adventures. Like Phileas Fogg and Passepartout."

"Hmm. I don't know. I guess it depends on the countries you travel through. I suppose you could, theoretically. Depending on your route."

"Well, I'm going to do that then!"

My dad looked down at me, tousling my hair. "Sure, honey." He looked away to the pages of the book, trying not to let me see his concern.

"But first, let's get better. OK?"

⌁

I stared at the wooden A-frame ceiling above our bed, unable to sleep, trying to block out the lost childhood dreams. Occasionally a flicker from the glowing woodstove below played on the ceiling above our bedroom loft, creating eerie dancing figures above my head. Next to me, Lorenz lay wrapped in the heavy blankets, a solid, silent form. Asleep. How could he possibly just lie there, happily slumbering away, while everything we had worked for was falling apart?

Relax my shoulders. Count to ten. Fifty. One hundred. I tried to avert my gaze from the dancing figures overhead, pointing grotesque fingers at me accusingly. *I'd failed!* One hundred one. One hundred two. I sat up, pushing the crumpled sheets away. This stupid counting was a waste of time! Just like going over and over our finances. We had barely $15,000 in our personal savings account. That would pay for one person to bike around the world. Not *four!*[*] Where were we going to find the other $45,000 in the next three months? There was no way we were getting on a plane to Athens on May 7 and pedaling off into the sunset. Maybe we could leave later? Instead of on World Asthma Day? I shook my head,

---

[*] We had budgeted an average of $15,000 per person for the sixteen-month trip, for a total of $60,000.

thinking of the impossible logistics of changing dates now. Any later and we'd be going through Russia in the dead of winter. No, not an option.

Were those eerie dancing figures on the ceiling actually *laughing at me*? I pulled my knees up and tucked my head, curling into a ball, hiding from the accusing faces. Get a grip! Those faces aren't real. They're just flickering lights from the fire.

I bit my lip, pushing back tears. Two years. Two long hard years. We'd come so far since that first hopeful board meeting. Where had I gone wrong? It had all seemed so easy in the beginning. My stomach lurched as I thought about the many dedicated friends who had helped us start World Bike for Breath. Mike, our favorite Microsoft tech nerd, who'd immediately volunteered to build our website for free. My sister, Tina, and her husband, Gabriel, an art director. What a stunning fundraising brochure they had created with our beautiful purple-and-black logo. Our friends Eric and John, who had taken professional photographs for the website and brochures. So many friends and neighbors had helped hold fundraising events, marched in the Fourth of July parade with us, and sponsored our dream. It had all seemed so possible, sitting with my friend Eileen in my crammed home office, recording donations, while Anya and Yvonne built forts with their friend Electra under the tall cedars outside. They had all believed in us. And I'd blown it!

How naive I'd been to count on the pharmaceutical companies for a large donation to World Bike for Breath. Why on earth had I thought that Merck or Schering-Plough would want to donate money to our tiny organization? Just because I had asthma? So did twenty-five million other Americans! I bet they'd taken one look at the ridiculous proposal that a woman with asthma would think she could bike around the world with two kids, laughed hysterically, and burned the documents.

Stop! I shouted silently to the mocking figures on the ceiling as I slid back down in the bed. We'd come so close to succeeding. *We had!* What about our six great outdoor corporate sponsors and all the other businesses that had sponsored us? Or our three partner asthma organizations?* And World Bike for Breath *had* raised over $20,000. Didn't that

---

* We partnered with International Asthma Services, the Asthma and Allergy Foundation of America, and the American Lung Association—all designated recipients of the funds we raised.

count for anything? I sighed. Yes. But at least half of that money was supposed to go for asthma programs and research. No, it was nowhere near enough. I swallowed hard as I faced the grim reality. *We were not going.*

I struggled to wrest the covers back from Lorenz, who was now wrapped like a mummy in all the sheets. How could he sleep so soundly? We were so compatible in so many ways. And yet so different. I attacked problems, held on to them, and worried them like a dog with a bone. Lorenz? He happily went to sleep, figuring the problems would solve themselves by the morning. I envied him.

I groaned. What were we going to do with all the donations? Did we simply roll in to the Burley factory with our used Duet tandems and say, "I'm sure you can polish off the scratches and put on new tires. Really appreciate the loan."

Should we send our used panniers back to Arkel? What about the tents from REI? And the muddy raingear from Patagonia? What about the sponsorships from all our friends and family who had already donated for the kilometers we would never pedal?

We'd come *so* close. We'd done so much right. Except raise enough cash. I stared at the accusing, flickering figures laughing from the ceiling, tears creeping from the corners of my eyes. We'd never see Ulaanbaatar, let alone make it to Washington, DC. All that hard work—for what? My breath pulled in sharply as I thought of the asthma clinic we had already helped fund in Calcutta.* At least we'd done something good with all this fundraising.

Suddenly, I bolted upright in bed. Cold beads of sweat ran down my back. I stared unflinchingly at the flickering shadows on the ceiling. Determined. Clear. I knew what we had to do.

———— ⌒ ————

My hands trembled as I walked out of the bank holding a check for $30,000. Had we done the right thing remortgaging our house and using up every penny of our savings to go on this journey?

"Are you OK?" Lorenz asked as I stood frozen on the curb by our car.

---

* World Bike for Breath provided medical supplies for International Asthma Services' new clinic in India.

I twisted the check around and around in my fingers, wishing it would miraculously double. Even after refinancing our house, we were still short $10,000.*

I nodded and replied, "I'm fine. Just totally excited! And terrified! All at the same time." I stared down at the check in my hand and frowned. "I'm sure we'll find a way to fund the last part of the journey—across the US to Washington, DC. Right?"

"Listen, let's not worry about the rest of the money until we get back to Seattle." Lorenz put his arm around my shoulders, then grinned cheekily. "Who says we'll even make it across Europe? We'll probably kill each other long before we get to Moscow!"

He was right. Who knew what challenges and great adventures lay ahead of us?

"Well, there's only one way to find out." I tossed my head in determination and waved the check in the air. "OK, world—here we come!" I wrapped my arms around Lorenz as he swung me in an excited dance. "Next stop, Athens!"

---

* World Bike for Breath paid $5,000 to cover the costs of our health insurance and flights to Athens. Combined with $15,000 from our savings and $30,000 from refinancing our home, we had a total of $50,000.

Part II

Tandem Trials

An Ill-Fated Odyssey

Lorenz

Day 2—Athens, Greece

Our odyssey began as we stared bleary-eyed at a stopped luggage belt in the Athens International Airport. At our feet lay six bicycle panniers, two bicycle wheel bags, and *one* large gray suitcase. The luggage belt had absolved itself from any further motion with disheartening finality, and it dawned on me that the other gray suitcase, containing our second brand-new custom-designed tandem bicycle, was never going to come. I had feared this scenario might happen in Mongolia, halfway around the world, but it had never occurred to me that we might lose a bicycle before we even started pedaling.

When we inquired about the missing bike, the luggage handler made us understand with a lot of hand waving that there was only *one* gray suitcase on the plane.

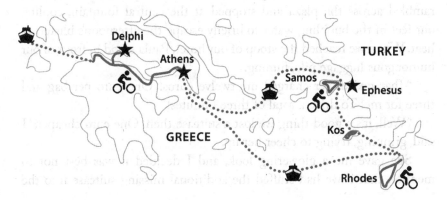

"Always I unload *aeroplano* myself. Only one *valitsa*," he said with conviction.

As I closed my eyes in frustration, I could just see the grinning luggage handler and his hazel-eyed girlfriend pedaling past ancient marble ruins and into the Greek sunset. They were riding a glinting, brand-spanking-new, irreplaceable tandem bicycle—ours. There was nothing else to do but to fill out the lost luggage form and hope the baggage handler's girlfriend preferred sailing to tandem bicycling.

"Don't worry. Always I find," said the luggage handler when I handed him the form.

Sure, you'll find it—right in your own garage, I thought as I walked away, clutching my lost-baggage receipt.

Outside the airport, we caught a city bus that brought us to our hotel. Almost. The bus dropped us off at the edge of the largest city plaza I have ever seen. The plaza, Syntagma Square, was easily a quarter mile across. At the far end, small but clearly visible, stood our hotel. Squinting and shielding my eyes with my palm, I contemplated lugging our nine overloaded bags across the daunting distance of hot, glimmering paving stones.

"Hey, there's a taxi," Paula cried out, waving her arms excitedly to get noticed. "The taxi can drive me and the bags to the hotel, and you guys can stroll on over."

The taxi stopped, and we managed to just shove Paula into the diminutive Fiat after we compressed the last bag into the back seat.

"Ciao. See you over there." She grinned, pointing across the plaza, obviously pleased with having hatched this clever plan. The kids and I rambled across the plaza and stopped at the central fountain, cooling our feet in the bubbling water to briefly escape the afternoon's blistering heat. When we reached the stoop of our hotel, Paula stood in front of our humongous luggage pile, fuming.

"That taxi driver charged me twelve euros! One euro per bag and three for me! To drive a total of three minutes!"

"Well, it's a good thing we lost a suitcase then. One euro cheaper," I said, grinning, trying to cheer her up.

She gave me a glowering look, and I decided it was best not to mention that if we had stuffed the additional missing suitcase into the taxi, Paula would have had to ride tied to the roof of the tiny car. Over the years I have learned there are times when my entertaining mental pictures are best kept to myself.

Paula stared in the direction of the departed taxi. "What a crook. That trip should have cost three euros max! I want my money back!"

"Why did you pay him?" I asked gingerly, knowing very well that in situations like these my wife was best handled delicately.

"I tried not to, but he started to drive off. Threatened to leave with our luggage." Paula threw herself onto the surviving gray suitcase, looking hot and defeated. "That thief. If I ever see him again . . ."

I entertained myself with mental images of Paula setting the tiny taxi on fire and pushing it, grinning, into the sparkling Aegean Sea. Maybe, for good measure, she'd pull our tandem from the baggage handler's hands and throw him and his dark-haired girlfriend into the sea right behind the flaming Fiat.

"Well, the hotel looks nice," I said, moving away from fantasies of revenge and toward sleep. "Let's just go to bed, and I'll bet tomorrow will look much better."

After a good night's sleep, the next morning did indeed appear much improved. The luggage handler's girlfriend had apparently put her foot down and refused to be seen on an odd-looking double bike, which had miraculously led to a midnight delivery of our lost tandem. Overjoyed, we went to a scrumptious breakfast in the quaint hotel lobby, its walls painted with frescoes of ancient temples and statues. Our celebration lasted just long enough to finish our coffee, at which point the front desk clerk informed us that additional nights in this lovely hotel would cost us 140 euros. The rates had just changed to high season. With our Athens budget being only sixty euros per day, we found ourselves back in the hot, dusty street by the clearly posted noon checkout. This time with not nine but ten humongous pieces of luggage.

A fierce negotiation with the next taxi driver *before* we got into the cab landed us for a much more reasonable five euros in front of the Pella Hotel, painted entirely in peeling midseventies orange.

"You're kidding, right?" said Yvonne, staring in horror at the dilapidated building.

"Let's just give it a look. Often these places are charming inside," I said, trying to convince myself more than anyone.

The place was not charming inside. In fact, the place was a dump. When we stumbled into the hot, dark, abandoned lobby, I vaguely noticed a red light near the floor. Thinking nothing of it, I dragged my load of suitcases through the light beam. Instantly a deafening siren pierced our ears. A disheveled woman in a dirty dress raised herself, bleary-eyed, from a cot that stood behind the rickety reception desk. Pointing at the laser beam with some pride, she said something unintelligible over the din that I interpreted as "No sneaking around in my place!"

The alarm was still screeching at unimaginable decibel levels as the woman handed me a pen. Confused by the bizarre scene and noise, I started, almost mesmerized, to fill out the booking form.

"You're not actually checking us in here?" yelled Paula over the racket, but I only heard a snippet.

"What? Check us in here—OK," I yelled back.

"Eighty euros," said the landlady.

Stupefied by the sensual overload, I handed her the money.

"Dad, no!" protested Yvonne, but it was too late. The colorful bank notes had already disappeared in the landlady's lockbox.

The landlady pushed some buttons on a greasy remote control, and the piercing alarm abruptly stopped.

We headed up the paint-chipped stairs to the fourth floor in complete silence. As I opened the door to our room, I knew I was in trouble.

"Look, there are ants in the room!" said Anya in disgust, pointing to a column of ants transporting bits of stale bread from the dirty floor out through the shuttered windows.

"The room smells moldy," said Yvonne. "I think something has died in here."

"We asked you not to check us in here. This place is awful," said Paula as she fiddled with the latch on the window shutters.

"Sorry. I couldn't hear you over the alarm, and the description of the hotel sounded nice . . . in the guidebook," I mumbled.

"Not a great deal for eighty euros, honey."

I was just going to shoot back that Paula had spent twelve euros on a three-minute taxi ride when she finally managed to snap open the wooden shutters. Suddenly, my breath was taken away. Filling the entire window, a magnificent series of white marble temples dotted a hill in front of us: the Acropolis. In the center, almost close enough to touch, the Parthenon (the famous Greek temple to Athena) lay under a sapphire-blue sky.

"Wow," we said in unison and stood in silent awe for a minute. Immediately our moods brightened as the sunlight reflected off the ancient temples and flooded into our room. Paula quickly found an old broom and swept up the floor while I tiptoed into the empty neighboring room, co-opting some nicer bedspreads. Anya and Yvonne lovingly redirected the ant caravan to the geranium flower boxes outside the windows by strategically placing stale cookie crumbs from the bottom of my handlebar bag onto the windowsill. In half an hour, our tattered room seemed almost homey. Feeling much more cheerful, we collapsed onto the lumpy beds for a much-needed afternoon siesta.

Botulism

Lorenz

Day 3—Athens, Greece

The next morning our landlady served us a skimpy breakfast of stale toast and gritty coffee in a dingy room with red velvet curtains, which she called the Red Salon. To our pleasant surprise, we discovered the landlady actually spoke some English. To our unpleasant surprise, she mostly used her English to scold us when we violated one of the seemingly infinite rules surrounding her dubious establishment: "No shoes in Red Salon"; "No banging down stairs"; "No food taking to room, ants will come"—no kidding!

Crunching on a piece of burned toast, I pondered the question of how and where to assemble our eight-foot-long tandem bicycles. Our tiny hotel room was certainly not up to the task, and I did not feel

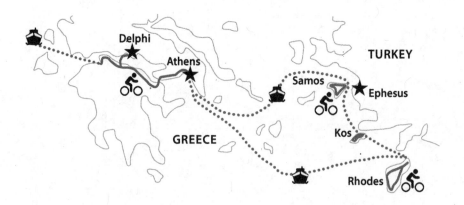

inclined to spread out hundreds of bike parts in the dusty street in front of the hotel. The Greek children who played there seemed all too curious about us, and I could just see some of our precious bike parts disappearing, tied with rusty wire as "hood ornaments" onto their beat-up street bikes. I briefly considered asking the lady of the house for an appropriate work space, but it was all too obvious by the way she plonked down the coffeepot that she was not much of a morning person. I decided this was one of those times when asking for forgiveness was better than asking for permission and began to scour the hotel for a makeshift workshop.

Starting in the basement, I stepped into room after room filled with moldy furniture, junk, and rotting cardboard boxes, stacked high from floor to ceiling. Tiny shoulder-width passageways led through this labyrinth of decay, with hardly a place to turn around. Growing more and more discouraged, I worked my way upward, floor by floor, until I came to a heavy metal door one floor above ours. I heaved the creaking door open and stepped out onto a large flat roof into the sunshine of a glorious Greek morning. I could see for miles through the clear air and was astonished that Athens was dotted with many other ancient temples in addition to those on the Acropolis. One of these temples was only a stone's throw from the roof, and I decided to set up shop right in front of it to make my bike assembly a truly memorable experience. Little did I know.

The roof was off-limits to hotel guests, and only the hotel maid used it to hang bedsheets to dry. She had crisscrossed the entire roof with clotheslines, some of which I moved to make enough room for my "bike shop with a view."

Assembling the bikes was a laborious, four-hour task. Baking in the morning sun, I worked as swiftly as I could, hoping to escape detection by our surly landlady or her maid. I believed the maid did not come to the roof until early afternoon and was hurrying to finish before she saw me. Since we had transported the huge bike frames in just two thirty-by-thirty-inch suitcases, the bikes were literally in a hundred pieces. Each bike frame had been carefully cut into three sections by the Burley factory, and I now connected those frame pieces back together with stainless steel S&S aircraft couplings. All the other parts, like shifters, gears, saddles, and handlebars, lay in a huge, sad pile that seemed to disappear rather slowly as I worked, sweating under the Mediterranean sun. At one point I thought I saw a face peeking around one of the bedsheets, but by that time I felt so delirious from the heat and lack of drink that I could not be sure of anything. At two o'clock I had the bikes back together and hastily hid them behind one of the crumbling chimneys.

Nearly passing out from dehydration, I returned to our room and guzzled down an entire bottle of mineral water. After I flopped, face-down, onto the lumpy bed, Paula broke the bad news. While I had been melting into the tar paper on the hotel roof, she had lugged the heavy bike suitcases (now containing all our emergency spare parts for Russia—tires, wrenches, inner tubes, and even mosquito repellant and maps) to the post office. She had planned to mail the cases to my brother's friends in Saint Petersburg, where we would resupply after traversing eastern Europe. The bike suitcases were then intended to hold our bikes again for the crossing of the roadless expanse of Siberia on the Trans-Siberian Railroad. It had been a well-laid plan, except that it had failed miserably.

"The grumpy clerk at the post office refused to mail the suitcases. Told me they were a few centimeters too large," said Paula, now sitting on the suitcases, grumbling with frustration. "I found a couple of cardboard boxes and moved all the Russia supplies to them. But now what do we do with the cases?"

"We'll have to throw them out. Nothing else we can do. We can't carry them with us."

"Such a waste. They are worth hundreds of dollars," lamented Paula.

But we had no other solution. So I dragged the empty bike cases into the hallway and started down the stairs. Then suddenly I remembered that I had left my irreplaceable bike tools on the roof. I quickly ran up to retrieve them, but when I pulled on the heavy roof door, I was shocked to find it was locked with a chain and a heavy padlock.

That sly old bird, I thought and mumbled, "Here comes the forgive-ness part" as I dragged the suitcases down to the Red Salon. The landlady was sitting on her tattered cot, waiting.

"My maid find funny things on roof," she said.

So it *was* the maid spying from behind the bedsheet, I thought.

I replied, "Yes, our tandem bikes. Will you let me get them from the roof in the morning, before we leave?"

"Why should I? You never ask. First you made bedsheets on the roof dirty. Now you want to put scratches on the walls in stairway. I think not. I think, maybe my grandchildren like bicycles, no?"

My throbbing brain was trying to grapple with this sharp turn of events. Could it be true that the landlady was actually taking our bicycles hostage?

"Look, I'm sorry I didn't ask you. I didn't want to assemble the bikes in our room."

"Hmm ..."

"I figured I would make less of a mess on the roof than in the room."

"You figured ..."

"Yes."

"I figure, I could sell bicycles for a lot of money. Or maybe my ex-husband and I could take a romantic bicycle trip—like old times, no?"

"I think that's a nice idea, but I really need the bikes in the morning."

"You think you need bicycles. Hmm. Anyway, what have you packed in those big suitcases—vacuum cleansers?"

"These? Nothing. They're empty. The bicycles used to be in there."

"That impossible. No bicycle fit in that."

"No, it's true. I was hoping to mail the suitcases to my friends. But the post office said they are too big. Now I have to throw them in the garbage."

"Into the garbage! That crazy business!" she said, tapping her index finger on her forehead.

"Nothing I can do. They won't mail them."

"Why not give the suitcases to me instead of garbage?"

At once I saw the opening and said, "Why would you want them?"

"I collect things."

"I can see that in your basement—" I said without thinking.

"So you have been sneaking about all over!" she said, jumping up from her cot.

"No! I mean yes ... just a little to find space for building the bikes," I replied, sensing the advantage I had gained begin to evaporate.

"Hmm, sneaking just a little . . ."

"Tell you what. If you give me my bikes in the morning, I will let you have the suitcases."

"I don't know. I like bicycles. I could rent them to other guests, or maybe you and I could take romantic bicycle trip together. Much fun, you know," she said, giving me a toothless grin. Then, chuckling, she sputtered, "OK, we have deal." She grabbed my hand, shook it, and immediately lugged the suitcases down to her claustrophobic basement.

Hostages traded, I went back to the room and helped Paula and the girls lug the two cardboard boxes with the Russian supplies to the post office, where they charged us an exorbitant seventy-five euros to mail them. Feeling too poor to eat dinner out in a restaurant, we dejectedly began the retreat back to our hotel, resigned to eating a cold dinner in our stuffy room.

On the way back to the Pella Hotel, Yvonne noticed a small street market in a side alley, where open-air vendors in colorful clapboard stands sold local groceries. Paula flicked open her phrase book and began shopping. She collected a loaf of bread, a wrinkled sausage, a plastic bag full of marinated olives, a dusty jar of pickled vegetables, and even a bottle of cheap red wine; all for less than six euros! Turning back into the Pella Hotel, we almost ran over our landlady, who stood smoking on the rickety entrance stairs.

"Roof open now. You can get bicycles," she rasped.

I suddenly had an idea that could make the end of this mangled day and our last night in Athens a bit more memorable. I said, "We don't need the bikes until the morning. But would you let us eat our dinner up on the roof?"

She took a long draft from her filterless cigarette, blew a column of smoke straight up into the air, and said, "OK, but no more crazy business."

"No more funny business, I promise."

We all clambered up the stairs and onto the roof. The night was mild, and the lights on the Acropolis had just been turned on. We set up our dinner on a plastic table the hotel maid used for her breaks, and we all began to relax. Anya and Yvonne brought paper napkins from the room and decorated the table with a potted geranium from our window box. We sat down, gazing at the lit-up Acropolis while I poured the wine.

I had just taken the first bite of bread, soaked in the oil of the olives, when Paula handed me the jar of pickled vegetables saying, "I can't open that. Could you please give it a try, honey?"

"Sure, no problem," I said, twisting the frozen lid.

With a gigantic pop, the lid shot out of my hand and three feet into the air, supported by a jet of foaming cauliflower and carrots that ejected from the jar, propelled by years of pent-up vile fermentation. A second later, we were all showered in a cascade of putrid, foaming juice. The stench was mind-boggling.

"Agh! Disgusting," cried Yvonne.

"What in the world was that?" gasped Paula.

"Botulism!" screamed Anya.

"What?" I asked.

"Botulism. We're all going to die," howled Anya as she jumped up and scraped foam and vegetable bits from her arms. "It's a deadly toxin that grows in badly canned food. I learned about it in home ec."

"Well, good thing we didn't eat it then," I said as I picked bits of carrots from between the straps of my sandals.

"No, Dad, it can get into your pores or wounds and you die a horrible death," screamed Anya.

Yvonne, her eyes suddenly filled with terror, threw over her chair and sprinted downstairs toward the communal showers.

"Now let's be reasonable. I have never heard of this. Carrots can't kill you."

"Dad, they've threatened to use botulism in biological warfare. It's one of the most dangerous toxins known to man. It paralyzes you while you are completely conscious. You know you are dying, but you can't move." With that, she too shot toward the roof door and was gone. Paula and I stared at each other for a split second, both wondering if our teenage daughter could possibly be right. Then, as if shot from a cannon, we both bolted for the door. Within seconds we were all furiously scrubbing ourselves in the shared showers on the third floor. I was in the men's shower, and the three girls had ripped off their clothes in the hall and crammed themselves into the single women's shower available. I could hear them fighting over the anemic jet of water.

"Anya, move," screamed Yvonne.

"Yvonne, I have a cut on this arm. If I don't wash it, I'm gonna die right here in the shower," pleaded Anya.

"Girls, let me at the water. I'm your mother, and if I die, you'll be orphans," Paula yelled.

Suddenly a fourth voice chimed in. "What is going on? Look at mess. You doing crazy business again?" said our landlady out in the hall.

"Just a little accident," I yelled from the shower, cringing with embarrassment.

"You have big accident if you not clean up this," she said, already descending the stairs and probably shaking her head.

When we emerged from the showers, the girls voted me most qualified to clean up the botulism battlefield on the rooftop. They said they needed to go back to our room and wash our soiled clothes in the sink. Apparently I was the most dispensable, and they could risk exposing me to some more deadly toxin.

Back on the roof, staring at the botulism disaster zone, my stomach growled angrily. There would be no dinner tonight after all. I slumped against the roof railing, feeling burned out. How could this be so hard? Home was thousands of miles on the other side of the world, and we had not even begun pedaling toward it yet. I stared at the illuminated Acropolis framed in the jet-black sky. How many other ancient travelers had gazed at this same sight, wondering if they too would ever make it home?

Next to my leg, laying on the roof, I found a piece of bread still wrapped in a plastic bag and carefully extracted it. Slumped against the roof railing, I started nibbling at the slice. If I died of botulism tonight, staring paralyzed at the lit-up Acropolis, it really wouldn't be such a bad way to go.

110 Degrees and Climbing

Paula

Day 32—Treviso, Italy

"Fane un giro del mondo!" They're biking around the world! the beaming, round-faced café owner exclaimed. In an attempt to hide from the sweltering glare of the Italian summer sun, we had stopped to drink ice-cold sodas on the shady veranda of Carlo's quiet, rustic café by the side of the road. Since we had stepped off the boat in Venice a week ago, we had had only one goal: cool down.

Italy was hot. Unbearable. Scorching. Stifling. By nine o'clock in the morning, the temperature had already reached a miserable ninety-five degrees. By noon, the country gripped in one of the worst heat waves in a hundred years, the louvered doors and white shutters of northern Veneto

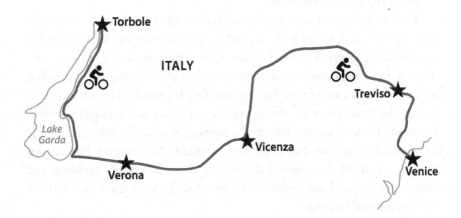

were locked tight against the sun's intense glare. Desperate, we sprayed tepid water from our bicycle bottles down our backs and into our cycling helmets. We jumped into every stream or river we could find along the way. And we stopped at every café to guzzle down ice-cold drinks.

"*Guarda! Guarda!*" *Look! Look!* Carlo stabbed his stubby fingers on our World Bike for Breath brochure, now worn from the many hands that had already thumbed through the pictures and the explanations of our family's unlikely journey for asthma. Shaking the map in front of his smiling, plump wife, our bald-headed café host pointed proudly to a spot east of Venice on the brochure's map.

"*Il telephono. Dove il telephono? Voglio telephonare i giornali!*"

"What'd he say?" Lorenz whispered to me as our excited host disappeared behind the dark wooden bar inside.

"I think he's going to call the newspapers."

"No!" Anya exclaimed, horrified. "Are they going to take photographs? No way. I'm totally a mess."

I shrugged, embarrassed.

"Mom, you *can't*! I'm all sweaty and dirty. And my hair . . ." Anya trailed off miserably as the owner's cheerful wife suddenly reappeared with a mouthwatering tray filled with spicy salami, strong musty slices of cheese, and thick hunks of Italian bread.

"*Mangia!*" She beckoned to the food with her hands.

"Umm. I think we just got invited to a free lunch." I smiled awkwardly at my fuming daughter.

Half an hour later, a pert, cropped-haired reporter chatted vivaciously to the owners as Lorenz and I sipped cappuccinos on the rough wooden benches on the café's veranda. The cappuccinos were the most recent offering in a generous, endless stream of various antipasti, sparkling sodas, and Italian ice cream that our bustling hostess had set on our table during the time between the telephone call and the reporter's arrival. Anya and Yvonne, meanwhile, had disappeared into the cramped simple bathroom behind the café's bar the moment the reporter had shown up with a camera. I imagined the two of them frantically braiding and unbraiding Anya's long, disheveled hair while Yvonne tried to scrub the chain grease off her legs.

"*Perque fate un giro del mondo?*" The reporter smiled, pen poised above her notepad. I gulped on the foam of my coffee, struggling to retrieve the remnants of my college Italian.

"Why are we pedaling around the world?" I repeated her question to Lorenz, who was cheerfully cramming a thick wedge of buttered bread and provolone cheese into his mouth. He waved encouragingly at me as he reached for a handful of stuffed olives to wash it down. Unable to speak Italian, it was clear that Lorenz had happily resigned himself instead to the job of finishing up the generous spread on the rough-hewn wooden table.

"*Io o l'asthme*" *I have asthma.* I stammered awkwardly, digging deep into that ancient forgotten vocabulary, searching to explain.

"*Oggi, con molti molti automobili, la pulizia del'aria e una granda problema. Questo e perque andiamo con bicicletta.*" While my Italian sounded impressive to Lorenz, Anya, and Yvonne, I had a sneaking suspicion that I had just said, "Today with lots lots cars, polluting air is super problem. This is why we go on bicycle."

"*Voglio montrare que l'asthme non prevenire qualcuono di—di—*" *I want to show asthma is not stopping someone from—from—*Ouch! Was it at all possible that as a student in Florence years ago, I had once been fluent in this language? The journalist's pen stopped scribbling furiously, and she looked up, waiting politely.

I hesitated, struggling to shape words from ancient wounds. How could I possibly explain seventh-grade America in my rusty Italian?

A picture of the dreaded gym class tugged at my memory. I could see myself standing awkwardly in line along the wooden wall of the school gym. My blue gym clothes hang shapelessly from my gaunt figure, kneecaps poking out prominently from stringy stick-like legs.

"I'll take Anne," a tall blond-haired girl proclaims, her glossy bouncing ponytail swishing over her lithe, curvy figure. Grinning, Anne leaves the line to join the bouncing ponytail on the springy green floor.

"Mary for my team," calls out a square-faced, muscular girl determinedly.

Not again. Please not again. For once pick me, I pray.

The line dwindles: Alice, Carol, Marcia, Denise, Jane, Elizabeth, Julie, Susan, Adrienne.

Alone against the wooden gym wall, I long to disappear. I stare out at the row of happy, healthy, athletic girls as if facing a firing squad.

"Do I *have* to take Paula?" The blond ponytail bounces angrily, gazing pleadingly at the gym teacher. "She can't even *run!*"

The reporter's pen stood frozen in midair along with her patient smile. Embarrassed, I suddenly let go of the lock of hair I had been twirling nervously and tried again. Those memories, I knew, could never be translated into any language.

Asthma shouldn't prevent someone—"*di essere sportive!*" *from being an athlete!* I blurted out, relieved to have completed a full sentence, regardless of the grammatical flaws.

The journalist smiled and stood up, straightening her skirt over her trim figure. "*Grazie.*" She extended her hand to me as I grinned, thrilled to have survived my first newspaper interview in Italian.

In the photo on the center page of *Il Gazettino di Treviso* the next day, Anya and Yvonne—hair combed and grease stains temporarily removed—smiled cheerfully at the photographer. Leaning against the tandems, Lorenz and I stood next to Carlo, the beaming café owner, dressed for the occasion in his traditional local costume: a top hat, red cape, and silver staff. It was a great photo. If only the picture could have included the scent of olives and provolone cheese, the cool shade and warm chatter of the café, and the kindness of this simple, generous Italian couple who believed in our impossible journey.

❦

"I think we should take *this* road!" I jabbed my finger at the map laying on my handlebar bag. "It will get us off these busy roads."

Lorenz peered at the Michelin map, trying to follow the road crossing the worn and faded crease that should have been the ancient Italian town of Marostica. At a scale of 1:400,000, our Michelin map showed only the busy main roads, filled with smoke, belching trucks, and roaring Lamborghinis speeding maniacally around narrow curves. After a week of cycling in heavy traffic, I was beginning to wonder if Italy had any quiet country lanes at all.

"That road adds at least ten kilometers! I say take the direct route," Lorenz argued.

"I've had enough of being nearly sideswiped by crazy Italian drivers." I wiped the sweat off my forehead, frustrated. "I'd rather cycle an extra ten kilometers in peace."

I leaned against the cool pink stone walls of Marostica's ancient Gothic castle, too hot and miserable to care anymore. Trying to escape from the sun's burning heat, the four of us had retreated to this shady corner on the town's famed checkerboard plaza. Looking out at the silent piazza bordered with quaint cafés and colorful shops, I tried to picture Marostica's famous human chess game being played out on the pink-and-white checkerboard squares inlaid in the plaza's stone pavement. According to the very chatty docent who had just led our family through the castle, in 1454, the winner of the town's very first human chess game won the hand of the beautiful Lionora, daughter of the castle's lord, Doge Parisio.

I gazed across the piazza to a set of romantic tables for two set along the edge of the checkerboard squares. On square A5, I imagined an imposing knight in black velvet standing ready for battle on his live horse. A white queen dressed in a flowing purple cape lined with ermine moves to square B2 next to the floury bread smells rising from the *panneteria*.

"Checkmate!" the doge of Marostica calls from his canopied stage to the right of the piazza, where he has been watching the human pawns in what will, one day, become a famous annual event. I wondered if Lionora was pleased with the outcome.

"If we take my road, we should be in Vicenza by three o'clock," Lorenz pressed on with our debate.

"Hello!" a friendly voice suddenly called out in lilting English. Intent on my imaginary chess game, I had not noticed the tall, dark-haired young man walking up to us. "My name is Giacomo." The friendly stranger thrust a strong, warm hand into Lorenz's sweaty cycling glove. "I am a cyclist—like you." Giacomo beamed, peering down at our Michelin map. "Where are you going?"

"To Vicenza—" I started.

"Vicenza. *Perfetto.*" Giacomo grinned from ear to ear in delight. "I live in Vicenza. You will be there tonight?" Lorenz and I nodded awkwardly. "*E meraviglioso.* Tonight you will join me for some *vino. Non?* I will tell all my friends."

"Ah, *scusi*—" I opened my mouth to protest. Today was our eighteenth wedding anniversary, and I had been hoping for a romantic Italian dinner alone with my husband.

But Giacomo had already grabbed Lorenz by the arm. "The map. This is no good. No good. *Vieni. Vieni!*" *Come!* he exclaimed and marched off to retrieve an armful of maps from the back of his car.

"*Non, non.* Do not cycle on this busy road," Giacomo instructed animatedly as he began penciling lines furiously on the pile of maps he had given us. "No, you must turn"—he paused, puzzling over the route for a moment—"here on this leetle quiet road. There is no name. It is a leetle road. But easy to find. *Si. Si.* You will see a stone house on the corner. And then here—turn right. *Non, non.* I mean left. You will find it. *No problemo.* There is a well under a cypress tree."

"Well, that settles it then." I slid Giacomo's penciled routes firmly under the plastic map holder on my Arkel handlebar bag and pushed the tandem off in what I hoped was the right direction. "This way!"

The sun had already set by the time our hot and dusty family pedaled up to the youth hostel in Vicenza. I never found the cypress tree by the well—although we did manage to pass the same scorched haystack sheltering several somnambulant pigs in a rutted dry field at least three times.

"I've had enough of going around in circles!" Lorenz had glared angrily as we stood sweating and sunburned in front of the pigs for the third time.

"Fine!" I thrust the map at him, almost in tears. "You figure out where we are. Every one of these stone houses looks exactly the same. If I ever run into that Giacomo again—," I muttered under my breath as we dragged our panniers, bumping and banging, up the stone stairs of the hostel. *No problemo,* indeed!

Disheveled, hot, and irritable, Anya and Yvonne were too tired to care that we were sleeping in a two-hundred-year-old neo-Renaissance building in the city of the great architect Palladio. As Lorenz opened the door to a stuffy hostel room outfitted with four single metal bunk beds and an airless window, I almost burst into tears with frustration and disappointment. So much for a romantic wedding anniversary in Italy, I thought and sighed.

—•—

"*Ciao!* How was the bike ride? You came here very late, *non?*"

I looked around in surprise to see Giacomo standing in the doorway, bubbling with enthusiasm. He must have been waiting in the hostel for hours, I thought, wondering how we had missed him on the way up the stairs.

"You must come to my favorite *trattoria* with me. You must be hungry, *non?*" I glanced at Lorenz, trying to shake my head no behind Giacomo's back. "You are tired? Of course. *No problemo.* A little *vino* will fix that!" He smiled eagerly, clasping Lorenz by the arm and cheerfully guiding him out the door.

Unable to refuse Giacomo's laughing eyes and constant chatter, I limped along wearily behind them. After several turns along lovely cobblestoned streets, we arrived at a small outdoor table next to a sparkling fountain.

"*Ciao.* I would like to introduce you to my friends." Giacomo pointed to a group of animated cyclists waiting eagerly at the table. "Would you like a glass of wine?" He reached for the half-filled bottle on the table. "Sit down. Sit down. You are our guests."

I grinned, taken aback by this unexpected little party. It was not the romantic anniversary I had imagined, but sitting under the stars, sharing a glass of wine with a group of passionate, laughing Italian cyclists, I couldn't think of a more memorable way to celebrate.

—•—

The following day, on a terrifying road filled with black belching smoke from the nonstop trucks, Lorenz decided to take over the route navigation.

"Give me the map." He reached over to my handlebar bag. "I'm sure there has to be a better route."

47

He stared at the map for a minute and then smiled triumphantly. "Look!" He pointed to a thin dotted line that paralleled the busy road we were pedaling. "We could cut over to this road and then drop back in on the SR-11 five miles later."

I looked dubiously at the line, which looked more like a crease on the map than a road. "I don't see a route number," I pointed out, worried.

"Oh, stop worrying. It'll be fine." He grinned. "It's just after this road—where the"—he peered closely at the squiggly lines—"E70 crosses our highway."

"Fine!" I shoved the map into the clear plastic reader on the top of his handlebar bag, rather irritated. As far back as I could remember, I had always been the navigator on our bike trips. It was one of those unspoken marital divisions of labor we had worked out on our very first bike trip together around Lake Michigan. Lorenz fixed bikes and cooked meals. I set up the tent—and *navigated*.

"This way." Lorenz pointed confidently a few minutes later as we set off on a very unpromising dirt track following a row of cypress trees.

"Are you sure?" Anya asked as she stared unconfidently at the long, untraveled track of dusty potholes.

"Of course. Trust me. I got it."

Twenty minutes later we stood at the end of the dirt track, staring at a curious farmer on a tractor harvesting his wheat field. I gazed triumphantly at my sheepish husband. "Better job, eh?" I grinned, trying to suppress a laugh.

━━◆◆━━

The next day in Verona, Lorenz bought a compass. I picked up train schedules.

"This heat wave is never going to end," Lorenz began matter-of-factly, reading the weather forecast from our handheld T-Mobile Blackberry as we sat on a brick wall, dangling our legs over the banks of the River Adige by the ancient Roman Ponte Pietra (Stone Bridge). Wrapped in dripping-wet towels, the four of us were munching languidly on a lunch of bread, cheese, and prosciutto. Judging from the hordes of Italian kids and families screaming and shouting in the water in front of us, we weren't the only ones trying to cool off by swimming in the river.

"Highs of forty degrees centigrade—that's about a hundred and five degrees Fahrenheit," Lorenz calculated quickly. "Predicted for at least the next two weeks."

"We can't keep going like this," I sighed, forcing down a disgustingly tepid gulp of water from my water bottle. "Someone is going to get heat stroke. And look—" I lifted my red-brown arm, covered in peeling white patches from extreme sunburn. "I'm so itchy and sore." I started scratching off the layers of dead skin.

"We can't quit now!" Anya and Yvonne cried out in unison.

"All my friends are following us on the Internet."

"I'd rather die than go back to school and face everybody!"

"Well"—I paused, unsure what to say—"I'm not suggesting we quit. Just maybe take a train." I waved my train schedules hopefully. "To the coast of Italy. Or France. Skip Milan and head straight for the Mediterranean. At least we could cool off in the ocean every now and then."

"Forget it!" Anya and Yvonne glared at us over their bread and cheese, suddenly allies.

"We said we were biking," Yvonne cried accusingly. "Everyone's donating for the miles we *bike*. A train is *cheating!*"

I turned to Lorenz, taken aback at this unexpected turn of events. It had never occurred to me that our daughters would be the ones pushing us to continue. Although Anya and Yvonne had both said they wanted to bike around the world before we left, deep down I had worried that sooner or later, when the going got tough, they would want to quit or take a shortcut. I couldn't believe *I* was the one wimping out.

"So you really want to keep biking in this heat?" I made one last feeble bid for the train, my dreams of cool days on the Ligurian beaches evaporating quickly.

"No ... but I'm still not taking a train!" Yvonne reiterated, arms folded stubbornly in front of her. "The rules are the rules."

"The rules?"

"Yeah, no trains." Anya put her arm protectively around her little sister in support.

"And no buses or cars either," Yvonne added.

I raised my eyebrows at Lorenz, looking for some reinforcement. "Well, they do have a point—" he began unhelpfully.

"What about boats? Or planes?" I asked, trying to find a loophole in this rather ironclad logic.

"That's OK." Anya looked at Yvonne for approval.

"Yeah, but only if there is an ocean or something."

"Well, we could rent paddleboats and pedal across the Pacific." Lorenz grinned and made hilarious pedaling motions while holding an imaginary handlebar.

"Dad! We're being serious."

The next day, on the shores of Lake Garda, we finally came to a compromise.

"Innsbruck is only eighty-five degrees," Lorenz announced cheerily as the two of us lazed on lounge chairs by the swimming pool of a five-star campground, complete with aromatherapy baths, bocce courts, and its own private restaurant, bar, and evening disco. Anya and Yvonne were currently cooling off by diving for our keys in the deep end of the swimming pool.

"That's nice," I mumbled as I slurped some more of the raspberry cream from my Italian ice.

"It's a lot cooler than one hundred and ten degrees." Splash! Lorenz threw his keys back into the pool as Anya and Yvonne sprang into the water.

"Innsbruck's in Austria." I set my ice-cold drink down on the nearby table and turned lazily toward Lorenz, who was busily checking temperatures around Europe on the Blackberry. "That's in the Alps. We're not going to Austria. We're headed to the Italian and French Riviera."

"Well, why not?" He stared at me intently.

"You want to bike over the Alps?" I stared at him in disbelief. "Some of those mountains are over ten thousand feet high!"

"With snow on the top." Lorenz grinned teasingly.

Snow! I stirred the last melting pieces of ice in my cup longingly. Curious, I pulled my handlebar bag from underneath the lounge chair and started rummaging through our maps. Impossible, I thought as I looked at the tight squiggly lines of road winding up through the Dolomites to Austria. But then—eighty-five degrees in Innsbruck! A whole twenty-five degrees cooler than Italy. Imagine: pedaling along a refreshing mountain valley under the shadows of snow-capped mountains. Stopping to eat lunch at the banks of a sparkling glacier-fed mountain stream—

"Can you throw the keys again, Daddy?" Yvonne stood dripping water over us, waiting eagerly.

I reached for my cup and gazed down in disappointment. The ice at the bottom had melted into a sickening warm pink froth.

Letters to World Bike for Breath

Lake Garda, June 13

Hi, Brett—

It's great to have you on board as the new executive director of WBB. Thanks for all your hard work.* I know it's a huge job to manage all the records for the ride. Here is a new pile of receipts. We have collected mostly receipts from supermarkets and campgrounds. In the last two weeks, we've only stayed in two hotels—prices in Italy are unbelievable and so are restaurants.

I'm also sending the front page and copy of an article in the *Treviso Gazette* (near Venice) about World Bike for Breath for your files. It might be fun to scan the article and have Mike post it on the web.

Hope all is well in Seattle. It has been 90° to 100° for the past week, and cycling in this heat has been excruciating. We're delighted to be at Lake Garda and cool off in its waters.

—Paula

---

* During the journey, we mailed letters, postcards, and packages back to World Bike for Breath. We have tried to keep the content of Paula's letters as close to the originals as possible, while removing unnecessary material and occasionally adding a few words or a sentence to integrate the letters into the story.

Con Bici and Bambini

Paula

Day 41—Torbole, Italy

The early-morning sun was already warm as we pedaled out of our camp-site on the beach at Torbole, on the northern banks of Lake Garda. Along the village's sleepy, narrow cobblestone streets, shopkeepers were busy setting out their tables of flowers, beach balls, and sundresses. At a corner café, a few early risers sipped cappuccinos while reading their newspapers. They looked up curiously as our bicycles for two cycled on by. Above us a plump woman hummed to herself as she lifted up a freshly washed white shirt and pegged it to the line hanging over her balcony. She waved cheerfully at Anya and Yvonne pedaling behind us on our tandems below.

Abruptly, the village ended. In front of us the precipitous barefaced rocks of the Dolomites loomed chal-lengingly, towering above the deep, narrow chasm chiseled by Lake Garda. My heart sank as I realized, for the first time, the absolute enormity of the mountains rising higher and higher in the distance: the snow-covered Alps.

"That's the road." Lorenz pointed to a steep, narrow black line, which twisted and turned like a writhing snake up the face of the precipitous cliffs surrounding Lake Garda.

"You want us to bike up *that*?" Anya stared at the sheer wall in front of us in disbelief.

"No way," Yvonne chimed in. "That's crazy."

I had to admit they had a point.

"Come on. You can do it," Lorenz urged. "You're tough."

I raised my eyebrows, not exactly convinced.

"Hey, you wanted to get out of this heat—"

I glanced up at the sun, which was already bright yellow and glaring heat despite the early time of day. He was right. I really could not bear another 110-degree day of bicycling. "Sure, we can do this." I rushed to his aid. "This steep stuff should only last a few kilometers." I waved to what I hoped was the top of the cliffs.

"Once we get above the lake, it won't be so bad," I added, not really sure this was true.

Within five minutes of creeping upward along the twisting road, however, I seriously doubted that we could even manage a few kilometers. Glancing down at the odometer on the handlebars, I noted we were pedaling (or rather wobbling) barely four kilometers an hour. Never in my life had I pedaled such a torturously steep road. Narrow and without a shoulder, the pavement barely hung from the face of the rock, clinging desperately, like lichen on a barren mountaintop, searching for a permanent hold along the wall. With only an occasional scrawny tree to shield us from the sun, the cliff radiated the growing heat of the morning, burning our arms and faces.

Each turn of the pedal was misery. Hot air rushed into my lungs, suffocating me as I gasped for breath. My legs shook violently as I pushed down on the pedals. And my forearms and hands ached with the strain of trying to control a wobbling tandem, overloaded with almost three hundred pounds of clothes, food, camping gear, and two people. I stared at the slowly receding ice-cold waters of the lake, lamenting that I was not swimming down there instead of climbing this hill from hell.

For the next two hours, we pedaled in agonized silence, barely able to breathe let alone speak—pushing, heaving, panting, crawling up the zig-zagging route chiseled into the side of the cliff. Inch by inch our tandems crept up the narrow road. Minutes seemed to last hours. Up down, up down. I focused all my energy on the pedals glued to my feet like heavy lead weights, staring mindlessly, numbly at the few inches in front of my wheel, not thinking, not caring, no longer able to do anything but turn and push. Turn and push. Feet turning round and round and round and round, willing the pain to end.

Suddenly, bizarrely, a voice shouted above my haze, seemingly coming from the desolate rock walls. "Bravo! Bravo!"

Lifting my head, I stared in astonishment at a lively group of cyclists dressed in blue-and-white cycling jerseys. Holding temptingly sparkling glasses of cold sodas, they were relaxing at two long wooden tables on the veranda of a café that seemed to have appeared out of nowhere. As I gazed in confusion at their bicycles stacked in shiny rows next to the tables, I realized we had reached the end of the climb. A beautiful Alpine valley spread ahead of us. And below us lay a breathtaking sight: the sparkling deep blue waters of Lake Garda reflecting the steep cliffs of the mountains surrounding it. Dotted along the lake's coast, a string of tiny red-roofed villages lay tucked in protectively under the gray-and-white cliffs of the Dolomites. Far away I could see Torbole at the top of the lake, its slender church bell tower poking up above the flower-filled piazza in the center.

"*Una famiglia con bici. E bambini!*" *A family on bicycles. With children!* the strange voice called in excitement, breaking my reverie. "*Guarda.* Look at these beautiful girls." The wiry cyclist pointed a glass at Anya and Yvonne, who immediately blushed from ear to ear. "You bicycled up this mountain? *Incredibile!*" He grinned broadly.

"*Vieni!* Come! Join us. You must be thirsty." Another man, with curly dark hair, held up a chilled bottle of sparkling water and beckoned to a seat next to him. "Here, sit down. I am Paolo. We are a cycling group from Abruzzi. Near Roma." Paolo pointed to his blue-and-white shirt—obviously a team shirt—and grinned proudly. "We are cycling from Roma to Budapest."

"Are you hungry?" Paolo leaned toward the girls. "Eh, Giacomo," Paolo called over to a tall, thin man. "They must join us for lunch. *Non?* Such a beautiful strong family." He opened his arms wide as if to enfold all of us within them.

"You will come to lunch with us, *non?*" the man called Giacomo insisted earnestly to Anya and Yvonne, who seemed rather overwhelmed with the noisy, excitable group.

"*Si, si.* You must join us. Our wagon is waiting—ahead five kilometers. We will have spaghetti for lunch. It is the best pasta. From Roma, of course! Our cook, he is *fantastico.*" Giacomo put his thumb and forefinger to his lips and kissed them, raising his arm in ecstatic thought of the delicious meal ahead.

"It is an easy ride now." Paolo pointed to the winding valley ahead, lined with shady apple trees. "*Andiamo!* Let's go!" he called enthusiastically as the blue-and-white group jumped onto their racing bicycles and sped off down the flat valley road to their sag wagon waiting ahead.

A bubble of cheerful chatter and laughter rose from the crowd around the white van, parked in a wide picnic area under a cluster of shady larch trees.

"*Prego, prego!*" Paolo smiled as he held out a paper plate heaped with steaming pasta. "Please, this is for you. Pasta from Roma. The best!" He smiled at the friendly, rotund chef who was ladling enormous spoonfuls of spaghetti onto the plates of the hungry cyclists clustered around his huge metal pot. "*E molto buono, Antonio!*" Very, very good! Paolo waved a forkful of the spaghetti in the direction of the chef. He rubbed his stomach, laughing. "We're lucky to have such a good cook follow us on our bicycle trip. We Italians cannot cycle without good food."

Giacomo wandered over, two bags of sugar-coated almonds and a plate of cream-stuffed pastries in his hands. "A gift for your daughters," he said, pressing the almond bags into Anya's and Yvonne's hands. He stood back for a moment, speechless, searching for words. "*Mervegliosso!*

So young. Two girls bicycling over the Alps." Giacomo shook his head, smiling proudly. "I have never heard of such a thing!"

I reached out for the gooey pastry. What an immense contrast from this morning! Just an hour ago, we had been groaning in misery, straining to keep the tandems upright as we struggled to climb the steep cliffs of the Dolomites. And now, suddenly, we were relaxing in a beautiful valley under the snow-covered Alps, the guests of honor of a jovial Italian cycling team.

As I licked the cream from my fingers, I could not remember eating anything more delicious. Strange how much more intensely I felt about everything—a simple dessert; a dry, soft bed; a hot shower. Even the simplest of pleasures had taken on an almost surreal quality since we had begun this journey. Living outdoors, in a world of extreme opposites, every inch of my body tingled alternately with pain, pleasure, exhaustion, strength, misery, ecstasy. For perhaps the first time in my life, I felt completely and powerfully alive.

❧

We discovered the bike path just outside of Trent the next day. Winding along the babbling Adige River, the paved trail was a welcome change from the past month of narrow roads filled with roaring Lamborghinis and smoke-filled trucks. At a thousand feet above sea level, the mountain air was already far less humid. And the sun, filtering through groves of leafy larch and birch trees shading the path, no longer scorched our sunburned and peeling skin. As our pedals clicked softly along the quiet path, shadowed by the towering dolomite cliffs on both sides of the Val d'Adige, a warm sense of contentment and even a bit of pride filled my chest. We had climbed a thousand feet from hell, and we were still going. Maybe, just maybe, we *could* bike over the Alps.

"What a beautiful day!" I exclaimed, unable to contain my happiness. "Don't you love this path? It's awesome. No traffic. No people. It's perfect," I oozed, practically jumping up and down in my saddle. "Don't you just *love* biking?"

Anya and Yvonne shared a knowing smile across tandems and giggled. "Yes, Mom. It's beautiful."

At a grassy spot by the river, Lorenz laid out lunch: a baguette, slices of prosciutto, a slab of Asiago cheese, and a bulb of licorice-flavored fennel, a new favorite vegetable that tasted amazing filled with ricotta. Anya and Yvonne waded in the river, laughing and splashing each other. Lorenz and I lazed below an oak tree, full and content. Gazing lazily up at the puffs of clouds drifting slowly over the oak leaves, I wanted to grab this moment and hold on to it forever.

For the next few hours, following the easy grade of the Adige, we pedaled quickly along the quiet, flat path. Behind me on the tandem, Anya hummed to a song playing on the MuVo—a cool new pocket-sized gadget that stored songs electronically. One of the few luxury items we had purchased for the trip, the MuVo was a coveted possession—all the more treasured since it had been selected over the purchase of a GPS (which we figured would be pretty useless once we entered eastern Europe and Asia), a video recorder (too big and heavy), and a laptop computer (way too big and heavy). Besides, Lorenz, our team photographer, had insisted on bringing along a two-pound Olympus I-S5 Deluxe film camera, which took up an entire handlebar bag. In comparison, the MuVo was a tiny electronic marvel. If only it could store a few more songs. It seemed like we were always stopping at Internet cafés to download a new set.

"Anya," Yvonne called over to her sister. "What are you listening to?"

"Huh?" Anya pulled out her earphones.

"Who are you listening to?"

"Here. Listen!" Anya reached an earphone across the trail. With no one on the bike path, we were pedaling the tandems side by side, making it possible for Anya and Yvonne to chat easily in the stoker seats.

Yvonne grinned as she heard the music on the MuVo. "Oh, it's another redneck girl song!" Lorenz, who shared a love of country music with Anya, had once nicknamed our daughter his "redneck girl" in a moment of fatherly approval. It had stuck.

Bouncing to the music as she pedaled, Yvonne began singing, "My name is Private Andrew Malone—"

"And if you're reading this, I didn't make it home," Lorenz chimed in. "But for every dream that's shattered, another one comes true—"

By now all four of us had taken up the refrain to David Ball's ballad and were singing along gleefully in a noisy, out-of-tune chorus:

This car was once a dream of mine, now it belongs to you,
And though you may take her and make her your own
You'll always be riiiiiiiding with Private Malone

The sun had started to slip toward the horizon, and I began to get worried. During the past forty kilometers, the trail had crossed almost no roads, passed few houses, and skirted only one tiny red-roofed village.

"I haven't seen a person since Trent. Can we stop and check out the maps?"

That morning we had inherited a stack of cycling maps from a hardy-looking older couple, who had just pedaled over the Alps from Germany. Whizzing south past us on the downhill route to Lake Garda, they had braked suddenly, surprised and curious to meet a family pedaling north over the mountains.

"You're sure you don't need these maps?" I greedily clutched the stack they had given me. Other women have addictions to shoes or jewelry or purses. But me? The way I saw it, a pile of maps covered in symbols for campgrounds, bike trails, and bicycle shops was worth at least a couple of diamond earrings or Gucci bags.

"*Nein, kein problem.*" *No, it's not a problem.* The wiry gray-haired man shook his head.

"We don't need them anymore," his lean, muscular wife explained. "Our trip is just about over."

I stared at this almost sixty-year-old German couple with a mixture of admiration, hope, and intimidation. If they could pedal over the Alps, then surely we could too. But then again, they looked like they lifted weights daily and had lived on a diet of muesli and yogurt their whole lives. So maybe not.

"*Na, vielen vielen Dank!*" *Thanks so much!* Lorenz replied cheerfully.

What luck that Lorenz is German, I thought as I stuffed the precious cache into my handlebar bag. I had fallen for Lorenz because of his foreign accent. In the first week of my chemistry class at Columbia University, a cute sandy-haired guy was sitting in front of me chatting in German to a friend. Eager to practice my own German language skills (and in desperate need of notes from the previous class I had missed), I had asked him where he was from.

Now I was cycling over the Alps to Austria with a bag full of maps in German, a husband who had a penchant for any food ending in *wurst*, and two bilingual daughters. I'm not sure a foreign accent is the best basis for selecting a spouse. But it has its advantages.

I pulled out the treasured maps.

"We should be about here." Lorenz pointed to an empty section of the bike trail on the map.

"That can't be! There's not a village or town for another twenty kilometers," I protested in dismay.

"Well, you do the math. It's sixty kilometers to Bolzano from Trent. And we've cycled forty-two since we left Trent."

"The map shows a campground in Bolzano. But nothing until then. We'd have to ride in the dark."

"I don't want to bike in the dark." Yvonne jumped into the conversation. "It's scary."

I had to agree with her. Generally, we never cycled after dark. It was too dangerous.

"I think it would be OK on a bike trail. There are no cars to hit us," Lorenz mused.

"But what about cows or sheep?" Yvonne mumbled miserably. "Or owls. Or bears. Do they have bears in the Alps?"

"I think biking in the dark would be fun!" Anya's eyes glistened with excitement. "C'mon, Boo. It would be an adventure! I'll protect you." She raised her arm, holding an imaginary sword.

That girl has been reading far too many fantasy books, I thought as Anya pranced around, fighting imaginary forest dwellers in her pretend knight's tunic and tights.

"We'd have to put up the tents and cook in the dark," I observed unenthusiastically. Pitching our tents after nightfall was something I hated with a passion. Weary of arguments over who had lost the tent stakes and whether we were holding the rainfly upside down or not, Lorenz and I had long ago agreed on an informal rule that we always made camp before sunset. I wasn't happy about changing the rule now.

"Well, I don't see many other options," Lorenz pointed out practically. "Unless you want to stay in a hotel."

"I want a bed!" Yvonne exclaimed hopefully.

"Me too! And a shower." Anya stopped jabbing at imaginary enemies for a moment.

"That's too expensive. We don't have the budget for it right now." I was feeling rather frustrated. Democracy was a wonderful principle. Sharing every decision and discussing every plan among the four of us had seemed like a fair way to travel together, but it was not working. Everyone spent hours arguing about where to stay, what to eat, which road to take, and even if we should camp or not. It was a luxury we couldn't afford right now, I thought, glancing anxiously at the fading sunlight.

"We could just camp along the trail," I suggested. "There really is no one here. I'm sure we'd be fine."

"Well, that's an idea," Lorenz conceded. "We can get water from the river. And we have iodine to treat it. Why don't we bike on, and if we find a good spot, we'll put up the tents?"

Yvonne didn't look too happy with the plan.

"Honey, it's just like backpacking," I tried to mollify her. "We do it all the time at home."

"But this isn't home!" she mumbled miserably.

Emails to bikeforbreath@hotmail.com

GREAT TO SEE YOUR PROGRESS
Dear Ebers,
You have certainly covered a lot of ground since we
last met back in Rhodes, Greece. I trust that it is
all going well and that the fun and adventures are
still plentiful.

I have emailed my father your website for a bit of
inspiration as I am determined to get him to realize
one of his childhood dreams, which is to ride from
Cairns (north Queensland) to Sydney. Dad has even gone
out and made a few tentative enquiries about buying a
tandem. It will happen all in good time, I am sure.

Keep pedaling and ride safe.
                    —Mary (Australian cyclist from Rhodes)*

GREETINGS FROM MAROSTICA
Thanks to the inspiration you provided us, Adriana
and I have both seriously stepped up our own bicycling efforts. It is such a wonderful way to exercise
and to see and experience the beautiful countryside

---

* These are original emails from the many kind and generous people we met along the way. To
protect their identity, names have been changed.

of Veneto. Even more important, the example of your family—close-knit, happy, and committed to making a difference in the world—remains a model for us to aspire to.

—Jacopo and Adriana, Italy

The Hunt for Harry

Paula

Day 43—Bike Path Near Bolzano, Italy

We pitched our tents on a small grassy spot next to the bike path as the last moments of dusk disappeared with the sun. Anya and I quickly unfurled the two tents, hoping the spots we had selected in the beams of our headlamps did not turn out to be sloping downhill or set on a hidden ant heap. Nearby, shadowy figures darted back and forth in front of the flame of our Whisperlite stove. Amid the pots clanging, I could hear hurried instructions to "hand over the pot grip" and "turn the flame down. *Now*," as Lorenz and Yvonne coaxed a dinner of macaroni from the backcountry stove in the dark.

After six weeks of camping and touring, we had fallen into an efficient family division of labor. Lorenz and Yvonne had gravitated to any activity that involved eating immediately (i.e., cooking). Anya and I preferred to make sure that our makeshift homes for the night were clean, dry, organized, and, most important, comfortable, searching for spots without rocks, sticks, tree roots, and anything else that would jab into our backs or shoulders in the night, leaving us bruised and cranky in the morning. By now, both of us could practically set up our tents with our eyes closed, which is pretty much what we were doing on this black, moonless night. Muttering curses under my breath, I fumbled around on my hands and knees in the pitch-dark, feeling around for the tent stakes. Nearby, I could hear water babbling. I hoped that we were not sitting next to a muddy, mosquito-ridden stream. Or near a rutted, dung-filled cow trail down to the river. Though neither seemed likely given the soft grass and dry patches of dirt under my hands. I disliked having no clue what our little "backcountry" site looked like. And I was rapidly regretting my suggestion that we try out this idea of "camping wild."

I gasped in amazement when I poked my head out of the door of our Taj tent the next morning. I had not expected this! Our tents lay a few yards from the river, tucked under an orchard of fragrant apple trees. In every direction, rocky green-and-gray mountain ridges surrounded us, the quiet chirping of birds the only sound to disturb the silence. On the far bank, a vineyard, small purple grapes hanging from the vines, wound upward along the craggy, steep mountain walls. And there, perched precariously on a precipitous, bare, rocky outcrop above us, stood the ruins of a crenellated Italian castle—looming majestically as if it had just jumped out of one of Anya's fairy tales. We could not have picked a more beautiful spot!

Outside by the river, Lorenz crouched over the tiny single-flame burner. Years ago, after a few unsuccessful attempts at lighting the grass on fire, sending three-foot shooting flames into the sky, and burning simple meals like canned beans, I had gladly yielded the outdoor cooking to my engineering husband, who actually liked tinkering with obstinate mechanical objects.

Rather intimidated by the temperamental stove, I generally gave it a wide berth. With one exception. Occasionally, on quiet early mornings when the sun crept pink along the horizon and my family slumbered happily, I would sneak out of the tent and, in secret, attempt to boil a cup of coffee on the dreaded three-pronged stand long before the others awoke. Those were cherished moments. Alone watching the sunrise, fingers laced around the warmth of the metal cup as I sat on a viewpoint overlooking a river, a mountain, or the ocean. If Lorenz noticed that I had actually succeeded in lighting the stove without assistance, he never commented on it. And I never dared set foot in his backcountry kitchen during the day.

I wished we could stay in this lovely camp spot a little longer, but we needed to be off before the first early-morning walkers strolled down the trail to find two unexpected ochre-colored tents on their path. Plus, I was getting very hungry. The sorry collection of leftover food in our panniers—some powdered coffee, a few packets of hot chocolate, a squished banana, and several crumbling dry biscuits—was not going to keep us full for long. We had to find a supermarket and restock as soon as possible. Fantasizing about Italian pastries in the next town, I began stuffing our sleeping bags and pads into the panniers.

As we cycled off from our impromptu campsite, I stared, surprised at the time on the clock on my bike counter: 7:18 a.m. A record! After more than a month of getting on the road at ten and eleven in the morning, we had managed to break camp before 8:00 a.m. A miracle!

This is great, I thought as the trees whizzed by in the cool morning air. Wouldn't it be awesome if we could always set out this early? The cool mountain air was fresh and clear, the bike path empty, and only an occasional rustle of a bird or squirrel in the bushes interrupted the whirring of our pedals. I felt as if the four of us were the only people in the world and this spectacular mountain valley belonged just to us.

I wished that Lorenz and the girls would share my passion for these precious early-morning moments alone in the world. They agreed—in theory—with my many practical arguments for getting out early. But still, my family preferred to sleep in, as the sun streamed into our tents, waiting until the noisy buzz of people around us dragged them out of their sleeping bags. Why anyone in their right mind would *like* to get up at dawn was unfathomable to them. But maybe there was hope. I began to like this idea of "camping wild" more and more.

———

"Molly emailed. She said someone important is supposed to die in the next Harry Potter book," I overheard Yvonne saying to Anya as they paddled lazily back and forth in the pool of Camping Gamp the next day. "Maybe it's Ron."

"No way. Ron's my favorite. And he's Harry's best friend."

After three days of climbing up the steep Alpine roads, we had voted to spend our weekly layover day in this spectacular campground, nestled below not one but two Italian castles guarding the road to the mountain pass ahead. The bike path—and the flat, easy ride through the Val d'Adige—had ended abruptly after Bolzano, some fifty or so kilometers earlier. Although the climb had not been as excruciatingly steep as the twisting route out of Lake Garda, our calloused palms, throbbing shoulders, and sore legs were screaming for a day off. Writing emails via Blackberry on the stone terrace of Camping Gamp's café, and lying under an umbrella by the pool in a bikini (the only clean clothing left) as our stinky clothes churned away in the washing machines, sounded like a fabulous idea to everyone.

"I hope it's not Sirius Black," Anya fretted. "He can't die. When I grow up, I'm going to marry him." She leaned up against the wall of the pool in the deep end, the snow-covered Alps looming tall behind her. Anya had read every single one of the Harry Potter books at least twice and some as many as five times. I was never quite sure if Anya really lived on this planet. It seemed to me that most days she was practicing new spells learned at Hogwarts or taking knights' lessons in the land of Tortall.

"Maybe it's Snape. That would be great!" Yvonne was not far behind Anya in Harry Potter obsession. She shivered, adding, "Snape's so *creepy*."

Jumping up, she pinched her nose, plunged down under the water, and reemerged down at the other end of the pool. Anya lived in imaginary worlds, Yvonne underwater. The moment we approached any body of water, Yvonne would tear off her clothes and dive in—bathing suit or not. She would wiggle, glide, and flip so gracefully that at the right angle I could swear I was watching the shining, sleek, undulating body of a . . . girl-fish.

Shaking her head left and right, droplets flying around her, Yvonne continued, clearly worried, "Regina and Franz have already preordered their books. They each have a copy waiting for them when they get back home to Germany!"

The girls had spent the entire afternoon swimming, diving, and racing in the pool with two newfound German friends, Regina and her brother, Franz. A few minutes earlier, their friends had been called back to their camper van to cook dinner with their dad—leaving Anya and Yvonne behind in the pool to worry about their current serious predicament.

According to Regina and Franz, an awful lot of important world news had occurred while Anya and Yvonne had been pedaling for a month and a half without TV or radio and only sporadic Internet at cafés. Britney Spears had kissed Madonna. Jennifer Lopez had almost caused an international incident by showing off her legs on German TV. Germany now had its own version of *American Idol, Deutschland Sucht den Superstar*. And, worst of all, everyone in the world was planning to celebrate the latest Harry Potter book's arrival on the summer solstice. Everyone, that was, except Anya and Yvonne.

"Hallie wrote and said there's going to be a Harry Potter party at midnight when the book comes out."

"I know. Lila already has tickets for the party at the bookstore on Bainbridge."

"Yeah. And we're stuck here on bikes!" Yvonne complained loudly, glancing toward me. I was lying on a chaise lounge by the pool, tallying up our expenses for the past two days in our little logbook. We had saved a good fifty to sixty euros by camping wild the previous night, and, at that moment, I was feeling rather pleased with the numbers.

"Mom?" Anya leaned her elbows on the edge of the pool. "How are we going to get a copy of *The Order of the Phoenix*? It's coming out in *two days!*"

"Umm." I looked up, not sure what to say. Like the other small red-tile-roofed hamlets we had passed through on our climb up the Alps, there were no bookstores in the town where we were camping—called Chiusa. Or Klausen, depending on which side of the Italian-Austrian language border you preferred.* Every town had two names here in southern Tyrol, the Italian version and the German one. But neither language was going to help me in this situation. I had no idea how we were going to find an English copy of Harry Potter in the middle of the Alps on bicycles.

"I can't believe they don't have a single store that sells books!" I sighed in frustration as we stood in the Piazza del Duomo admiring the lovely cream-colored Baroque church of Bressanone—the Italian name. Or Brixen—the German name. For the previous half hour, we had pedaled down Bressanone/Brixen's cobblestoned streets, past rows of charming three-story green, pink, and lemon stuccoed buildings that seemed to belong more to Austria than Italy, hunting for Harry Potter. We had found a bank, a post office, a bakery, and several attractive clothing stores and tourist shops. But no bookstore. In the bakery, we had ordered *Apfelstrudel* and cream-filled Berliner from the smiling Italian baker—surprised and pleased to find German pastries in an Italian town. Realizing that the baker also spoke fluent German, Lorenz had asked the man in the flour-covered apron if he knew of anyone who sold books in the entire area.

"*Ne, nichts.*" The kindly baker had shaken his head and then thrown an extra pastry in the bag for Anya and Yvonne. The girls will need it to bike up the steep roads ahead, he explained with an odd look that suggested he was not sure whether to be impressed or worried about an eleven- and thirteen-year-old cycling over the Alps.

June 21 came and went with no *Harry Potter and the Order of the Phoenix*—in English, Italian, German, or any other language—to be found in the quaint, steep mountainside towns of the Italian Alps. We

---

* Tyrol, on the border of Austria in northern Italy, is bilingual and bicultural, speaking both Italian and German.

camped wild again that night, pitching our tents on the edge of a lush green Alpine meadow surrounded by snow-capped mountains. As we sat cross-legged on the grass, scooping spaghetti from our Sierra cups,* Anya and Yvonne were unusually silent. Perhaps they were imagining their friends drinking butterbeer and eating golden snitch cakes at the midnight party. Or lying happily on their beds, opening the crisp new pages of *Harry Potter and the Order of the Phoenix*. Without them.

We reached the top of 4,495-foot Brenner Pass the next morning. I was sweaty, exhausted, and somewhat dazed. For the past three hours, I had wheezed, gasped, and puffed, fighting with every breath to pedal the heavy tandem higher and higher up the increasingly steep mountainside. While my asthma inhalers usually helped open up my lungs, they didn't seem to have much effect at this altitude. I suspected it was the thinning air. No medicine was going to put more oxygen in my lungs if there wasn't any to begin with. As I crawled off the tandem, I didn't know whether to be angry that my crappy lungs had to work so much harder than everyone else's at such a modest elevation or to be proud that I had made it despite my asthma.

I didn't have much time for reflection, however. The hunt for Harry was immediately on in earnest. For the next half hour, my legs stiff and cramping, we walked (or, more truthfully, hobbled) into every single tourist shop along the small main street of Brenner, inquiring after the book. We found shelves of green felt hiker's hats, tinkling crystal bells with "Brenner Pass" etched into the glass, gold and silver Brenner hiking pins, and tempting glossy photo books of Tyrol. But no *Harry Potter*.

Reluctantly accepting defeat, we pedaled out of town, once again *sans* Harry. In front of the sign at the border of Austria, we stopped to take family photographs. By now I had shaken off my dazed fog, and it was slowly dawning on me that the climbing was over. No kidding! We had cycled over the Alps with two children! How awesome was that? I grinned at Lorenz, who was beaming ear to ear. Did I look that happy

---

* To save weight and space, each family member was restricted to one fork, one spoon, and one Sierra cup—a metal cup that could be heated and served as bowl, cup, and plate. We carried two knives for food preparation and one large plate that served as a cutting board, serving platter, and all-around food preparation surface.

and proud? Then I glanced over to Anya and Yvonne. The grin quickly fell off my face.

"This is a big deal, you know." I tried to garner some excitement from our two disappointed daughters. "You girls are amazing. You know what you've done?"

They both shuffled distractedly.

"Mom, stop," Yvonne grumbled, kicking a stone on the ground in embarrassment.

"Mom's right. I don't know how many other girls in the world have biked over the Alps. Maybe none!" Lorenz added, trying to inspire some enthusiasm from our melancholy team.

"You *said* there would be a *Harry Potter* book in one of the stores." Anya glared at me, completely uninterested in discussions of grown-up achievements such as biking over stupid mountains. "We *have* to have a copy." She struggled to hold back tears. "You don't understand at all! I can't read any of my emails from my friends. I can't look at anything on the Internet. I can't call home. I'm afraid someone will tell me what happens in the book and ruin it!"

"Look, we'll be in Innsbruck tomorrow," I tried to appease her. "They'll have tons of bookstores. I'm sure we can find the book there."

Anya frowned, doubt written all over her face. "You promise?"

"Of course they'll have it," I answered, sounding more confident than I felt. A huge city like Innsbruck must have plenty of bookstores. Certainly one of them would sell books in English.

<hr>

"Bad news," Lorenz began bluntly as we stood at our fourth bookstore in Innsbruck. "They *did* have a *Harry Potter* in English. But it's sold out already."

"What about a German one?" Anya asked hopefully. "You could read it to us in German. We could understand it." Yvonne, standing next to her, looked doubtful. But at this point, we were all desperate. I would have even tried to translate an Italian version for them if I had to.

"Nope, all gone." Lorenz looked at me, anticipating my question. "Italian too."

We had spent the entire morning fruitlessly roaming from bookstore to bookstore. The story was the same everywhere. Sold out! After our interview with the *Tyroler Tageszeitung* that morning, the Austrian newspaper reporter had sent us to this store, hopeful that it would still have some copies of *Harry Potter and the Order of the Phoenix* left. It was a mega-bookstore. A super Barnes & Noble on steroids. Two floors of books containing everything from ancient history to Austrian cooking to fiction, translated into at least twelve different languages. Everything but *Harry Potter*.

Anya and Yvonne stared down disconsolately at the empty display table in front of us. Above it hung a huge sign with an enormous golden bird and the title *Harry Potter und der Orden des Phoenix*. I shifted my weight uncomfortably. My arms were clutching a heavy collection of books and maps of bike routes through Europe that I had discovered upstairs in the travel section. I knew I would only buy one or two books and then immediately destroy them, cutting out the relevant chapters and tossing out the unnecessary pages to save weight. But for one luscious moment, I could hold them, pretending I was planning to buy them all.

Anya stared at me resentfully. "How come you get to buy all those books?"

"Yeah," Yvonne chimed in. "And we don't even get *Harry Potter*."

I opened my mouth and then closed it. Some arguments you just knew you were not going to win. Even if you *were* the parent.

⸺❧⸺

That evening, twenty kilometers out of Innsbruck, we found a picnic table nestled on the banks of the babbling Inn River and set up another "wild camp." We were overjoyed with our good fortune. Imagine that—a picnic table! Something we had not seen in a single private campground in Europe, where tents and caravans were stacked in narrow, tight rows on large, overused meadows.

After a luxurious dinner seated on a bench instead of on the ground, we all piled into the Taj. I don't know if REI had actually named the tent after the Taj Mahal, but in our minds, it was a gigantic palace. Technically a three-man tent, the four of us would often sit cross-legged inside, spread in a circle around its blue nylon walls, sharing a meal in the middle. The Taj was our family's living room, rain-day dining room, study, and master bedroom.

Tonight, as we lazed on top of the sleeping bags, I pulled out our very worn and tattered copy of *The Odyssey* and opened it to the final chapters. Traveling over 1,500 kilometers with us since Athens, Homer's epic poem had long surpassed its role as simply Anya and Yvonne's homeschool literature assignment. Each night, as Lorenz and I read a new chapter aloud, the adventures and struggles of Odysseus seemed to spring off the page, becoming intertwined with our own intrepid journey. Snuggled in our tent under the stars on the island of Samos, it seemed that perhaps Odysseus had been trapped on that very same enchanting island under Calypso's spell. As we camped below the eerie, steaming cave where the Oracle of Delphi sat foretelling prophecies, we could almost hear Odysseus battling with the cyclops down below.

Now, here, on the banks of the Inn River, we were coming to the end of the odyssey. As I sat cross-legged against the tent wall, I glanced around our tiny living room. Anya and Yvonne lay side by side on their stomachs. Yvonne was doodling a new picture in her sketchbook, Anya writing in her journal. Lorenz sat against the opposite wall, checking the patch on the inner tube he had just repaired. I loved these family nights together—a soft calm spreading over us as we all relaxed, happy to be resting after a hard day of cycling.

I opened the creased and torn book to chapter 23, describing Odysseus's tearstained return to his wife, Penelope. Only two chapters left. And then? I had been sure that by now we would have found a copy of the new Harry Potter to read out loud next. I quietly sighed in frustration.

———

We spent the next few days pedaling and camping along stunning, quiet bike paths meandering along the picturesque Inn River valley. Surrounded by snow-capped peaks dotted with wooden-balconied houses cascading with geraniums, the trail wound through pristine Alpine forests. Despairing that we would never find an English copy of the coveted

Harry Potter, I left flowers and lit candles at the many picturesque tiny pink-and-white roadside chapels that dotted our route through staunchly Catholic Austria. I doubted that the Virgin Mary would look kindly on requests for a book about witches and warlocks, but then again, she was a mother. Perhaps she would understand my desire to give our daughters a little bit of a normal childhood.

Finally, one week after all their friends had already cried their hearts out over the disastrous ending of Sirius Black, Anya and Yvonne discovered a thirty-five-euro, 870-page, three-and-a-half-pound hardcover English-language version of *Harry Potter and the Order of the Phoenix* in a bookstore in Reutte, on the border of Germany.

"Oh no you don't." I stared warningly at Yvonne, who was squeezing the enormous book into my rear bicycle pannier in front of the bookstore. "I'm not carrying *Harry Potter*. Find space in your own panniers."

"There's no room. Look!" She stood hopelessly in front of her tiny twelve-by-eighteen-inch backpack already overflowing with dirty socks and colored pencils and a wet bathing suit drying in the mesh pocket outside. "Anya, you take it!"

Anya frowned at Yvonne. "I don't have any more space than you do. Where am I supposed to put it?"

She had a point. *Harry Potter* was almost a third of the size of either girl's tiny pannier. And so, reasoning that it would only be a few days before Anya and Yvonne had read about Professor Umbridge's evil inspections, gasped about the battle with the Death Eaters, and cried over Sirius's mysterious end, I tucked the enormous book under a bungie cord next to the tent on the top of my bike rack. Little did I know that Harry and his friends in the Order of the Phoenix would travel 960 kilometers up the Rhine into France and England with us.

"Forty-eight divided by six is—"

"Seven?" Yvonne looked up hopefully at Lorenz, who was sitting cross-legged on a soft patch of grass in front of our tent pitched in a farmer's field near Fussen. In front of them, CliffNotes' *Basic Math and Pre-Algebra* lay open to the chapter on long division.

74

"No, eight." Lorenz stretched out his left leg tiredly. He massaged the muscles on his calf, aching after a day of pedaling up and down the green hills of southern Germany's Romantic Road. "Start again. Forty-eight divided by six. Six goes into forty-eight eight times." He pulled his left knee to his chest and began kneading his ankle.

"Oh, right." Lying on her stomach, Yvonne lazily wiggled her legs in the air. It was a beautiful soft summer evening. White puffs of clouds drifted indolently above in an azure sky. A herd of brown-and-white cows stood chewing leisurely on fresh summer grass in the meadow nearby. And a traditional German song wafted from the farmhouse that had kindly offered us this little patch of grass and heaven in the field behind their house.

"How much longer do I have to do this?" Yvonne gazed longingly at a wild patch of yellow-and-white daisies a few feet away, visions of daisy chains and crowns weaving their way through the tiresome mathematical calculations in front of her.

"Two more problems. And then you can read *Harry Potter*."

Half an hour later, I looked up to see Yvonne and Anya, decorated in crowns of daisy chains, leaning contentedly under a large oak tree. *Harry Potter and the Order of the Phoenix* lay carefully between them. Anya, already on page 709, was rapidly reading about the upcoming O.W.L.S. exams, while Yvonne, the younger reader, sat engrossed with Harry's hopeless lessons with occlumency on page 516. Lorenz was whistling as he fried up some farm-fresh eggs given to us by the kindly farm woman in the house behind us—along with four pieces of warm, crumbling homemade cherry torte she had offered us for dessert.

I smiled as I scrubbed eight pairs of dirty underwear under the faucet next to the barn, the chill water splashing refreshingly on my arms and face. It was not on your average touring cyclist's packing list, but I was happy to be carrying all three and a half pounds of *Harry Potter* along on this journey.

World Bike Bits

Bits and stories about World Bike for Breath. A Bulletin for sponsors. Volume 2

European (K)nights

"IT HAS BEEN A LONG TIME SINCE ANYONE HAS CAMPED IN OUR FIELDS!"
The kindly, plump gray-haired Bavarian woman smiled wistfully as
my husband, Lorenz; our eleven-year-old daughter, Yvonne; Anya, our
thirteen-year-old; and I sat chatting and drinking *Apfelscholle* in her cozy
farmhouse kitchen.

"Twenty, thirty years ago," her thin, wiry eighty-year-old husband
added, "we had many bicyclists stop by—from Holland, Germany,
Austria. But no longer."

"Perhaps it's more comfortable to stay in campgrounds or hotels
now," his wife, Irma, added.

That evening, like many others we have shared in farmers' fields
during the two months we have been pedaling through Greece, Italy,
Austria, and now Germany, a constant stream of little gifts arrived at
our tent: farm-fresh eggs for breakfast, candies for the girls, and slices of
homemade chocolate cake. The next morning as we pedaled off down the
Romantische Strasse after Irma's tearful hugs and waves of goodbye, it
was clear the elderly German farm couple had enjoyed our interruption

of their quiet and perhaps sometimes lonely routine as much as we had appreciated their hospitality. As we cycled over a sparkling river to a picture-book German marketplace surrounded by *Fachwerk* (wooden-framed) houses, it occurred to me that it was neither the spectacular mountaintop Greek ruins of Delphi nor the gondola-filled canals of Venice that have been the most memorable features of the almost 2,500 kilometers our family has pedaled through Europe to date. No indeed, our most treasured stories and adventures have come from the people we have met and the places we have stayed along the way.

On the island of Samos, Greece, after arriving at 2:00 a.m. by boat to a sleeping red-, blue-, and green-painted town, an overbooked hotel keeper let us roll out our sleeping bags on the flat whitewashed rooftop from which we watched a spectacular rosy sunrise a few hours later. In northern Italy we were treated to Italian pastries and coffee with grappa on the stuccoed veranda of an Italian grape cultivator, overlooking our tents tucked between their horse stables and surrounded by hillside rows of neatly cultivated vineyards. And in a little *Zimmer Frei* (room to rent) along Germany's famed Romantic Road, the owner and her husband invited us to a huge dinner of grilled *Bratwurst*, *Schnitzel*, and *Kartoffelsalat*. That night she washed our limited collection of grungy cycling clothes, delivering them the next morning to our room, soft, folded, and smelling sweetly of homemade German warmth and hospitality.

Initially our decision to seek out unconventional sleeping spots in Europe was driven by financial and practical factors. Cycling and camping with a family of four in Europe, we discovered, is significantly more expensive than in the US. Campgrounds charge per person and per tent. And while European campgrounds are often a luxury experience—with swimming pools, private beaches, rows of sparkling clean and hot showers to fill any cyclist's fancy, washing rooms for dishes and clothes, and even stores, restaurants, bars, and nightly entertainment—the price tag, averaging between thirty and fifty dollars per night, quickly began to eat into our budget. Likewise, the modest pensions that had seemed so reasonable when Lorenz and I had pedaled through northern Europe on our honeymoon now cost $120 or $130 per night for two and double that for four.

Yet, truthfully, after a few weeks, a more important motivation for our predilection for sleeping off the beaten track began to grow: the freedom to travel and stop when and where we wanted and the opportunity to glimpse into a world most tourists never see. Our European cultural experience does not end as we lock up our tandems against a tree, unloading our gear after a day of pedaling along the lazy former barge towpath along the Rhine River, gazing up at crenulated castle after castle perched on the cliffs. To the contrary, the nights are when the stories and friendships begin.

Indeed, my most poignant memory of Europe is not of castles and knights but of a simple tired Italian woman in a long skirt and scarf, clipping the grape vines near her house in the countryside south of Vicenza. As we set up our tents under her apple and olive orchards, she offered us bottles of cold iced tea and insisted on washing our clearly sweat-filled clothes in her small machine. Seeing our dinner of macaroni and tomato sauce cooked by Lorenz on our small Whisperlite stove, she insisted that we join her, her elderly mother, and her twenty-year-old son in their simple, untidy, yet warm kitchen for a second meal of fried zucchini, roast potatoes, boiled eggs, fresh-picked green apples, and white wine. But we were sworn to promise to tell her son, Salvatore, that we were only cycling one week through Italy, not one and a half years around the world. For she feared Salvatore, who was an avid cyclist, would want to follow after us.

We left early the next morning, waving goodbye to Salvatore's pumping arm and beaming face, our secret still untold. Yet perhaps, I dream, one day Salvatore may just pedal unknowingly in our tracks over the Alps and ask to put up his tent in Irma's German hayfield, closing the circle of friendship and hospitality that has nurtured us so warmly on our journey through the homes and hearts of southern Europe.

World Bike For Breath

Route Update—Greece to England

Hi, dear friends and sponsors,

We would like to thank all of you for your many encouraging and supportive emails over the past three months. Your faith in our ride for clean air and asthma has kept us going despite cycling in intense heat in Italy and Greece, over mountain passes in the Alps, through clouds of bugs that splattered our bodies from head to toe with their carcasses as we pedaled through southern Germany, and through the noise, air pollution, and traffic of one hundred miles of Germany's Ruhrgebeit—the German equivalent of twenty Pittsburghs and Detroits strung together along the Rhine. (Instead of being splattered with bugs, we were covered with black soot from factory smokestacks.) After intense headwinds in Holland and rain in England, we have come to accept that living outdoors on a bike and in a tent, we will always be facing a natural challenge wherever we are. Knowing that you care and are behind us all the way has made all the difference.

Here's our route so far:

- Kilometers for asthma and clean air: 2,949
- Miles for asthma and clean air: 1,798

- Countries cycled for asthma: Greece, Turkey,* Italy, Austria, Germany, Netherlands, England

Since we skipped France when we rerouted over the Alps, we're headed to the ferry to St. Malo in Brittany for a brief round-trip visit. Then it's another ferry from England back to northern Germany and on to eastern Europe.

Have a wonderful summer.

—The Ebers

---

* We visited Turkey briefly from Greece but did not cycle there.

Bribes

Paula

Day 102—Near Hamburg, Germany

"Bribes. *Schmiergeld!*" Lorenz's brother, Mori, leaned forward on the red-and-green-striped antique Biedermeier couch at their parents' house near Hamburg, Germany. After our short cycling detour to England and France, we were back in northern Germany, outfitting at the Ebers' house for the next stage of our journey—through eastern Europe to Russia.

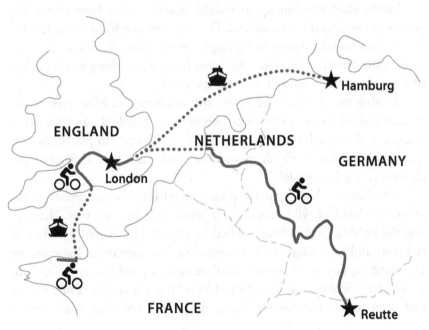

"You'll need to carry cash for bribes." Tall, stocky, with a beaming round face, Mori was usually the cheerful, easygoing member of the Eber family. But now, elbows on his knees and hands tightly clenched together, Mori looked positively worried. "And strong locks. Everything gets stolen there. Cars, bicycles, motorcycles. Anything that's not tied down."

I shifted uncomfortably in my high-backed Empire armchair in Lorenz's parents' living room, not liking the direction of this conversation. I'd assumed that after fifteen years of independence from the Soviet Union, eastern Europe would be completely rebuilt—a new, expanded version of western Europe. Completely safe to cycle through with children. Bribes and strong locks had not been part of the plan.

"They'll even take the hubcaps off your car in broad daylight while you're running in to the grocery store to pick up milk! Why do you think Kassia, and Julian, and I live here, in Germany—not in Poland?"

At that moment, I fervently wished Kassia had been able to join us while we visited Lorenz's family in their tiny farm town. But Kassia was off collecting algae for her research somewhere in the Baltic. So Mori and Julian had driven over to the grandparents' house without her.

Surely after growing up in Poland, Kassia would have something positive to say about her homeland. Didn't Julian love his trips back to his Polish grandparents' home in Danzig? Gentle, sweet Kassia would have calmed the conversation down. Said that Mori was making too big a deal of things. At least I wanted to think she would.

Sensing that Lorenz and I were still unconvinced, Mori pressed on. "Kassia always figures in an extra two or three hundred euros for every shipment of research equipment she sends to Russia—to pay the border guards and customs officials. Sometimes they even have to pay off the director of the biology lab!"

"*Die Russen!*" Vati, Lorenz's dad, jumped into the conversation. He shook his head of wild, thick, curly white hair in contempt. "Kassia's not the only one who's been robbed by them!" He swirled his glass of red wine and took another sip, absorbed in dark memories. I guessed he was thinking about the former family estate in Parei, eastern Germany. Invaded by the Russians after World War II, the beautiful family manor had been turned successively into a hospital, a boarding house, and a barracks under Communist rule. Now crumbling and uninhabitable, the house sat abandoned in the woods, too derelict to be worth claiming under the property restitution law enacted when East and West Germany reunited.

"Mori's right!" My father-in-law set his wineglass down hard on the inlaid walnut coffee table in front of us. Vati had a passion for rescuing antiques, otherwise destined to oblivion under stacks of hay or forgotten behind tractors in the local northern German farmers' barns and stables. The Ebers' living room was furnished with two- to three-hundred-year-old finds, lovingly restored in my father-in-law's workshop. Their centuries-old timber-framed *Fachwerk* farmhouse near Hamburg could have easily been a museum in the US.

"Russia's a horrible country. The mafia runs everything. You can't trust anyone."

"Maybe you could skip Russia, and Poland, and the other eastern countries?" Mutti interjected, her low, even-toned voice unusually high-pitched. "Couldn't you take a train from Berlin instead?"

Lorenz swallowed, trying to maintain his composure. But I could see the red creeping up the back of his neck.

"Mutti." Lorenz reached over to his mother, touching her arm. "Don't worry. We'll be fine. We're already taking the Trans-Siberian Railway from Moscow to Beijing. That's the dangerous part. It'll be OK."

I struggled to ignore the tight knot in my stomach. I was beginning to think that everything *wouldn't* be OK at all. I did appreciate Lorenz's German stoic calm, but there was a fine line between being coolheaded and sticking your head in the sand.

"Are you bringing along any weapons?" Mori stared earnestly at Lorenz.

"*Waffen?* Weapons?" Lorenz was taken aback. "No, nothing. It's illegal to carry weapons into a lot of countries. And the last thing we want is some border guard hassling us because we're carrying Mace. Don't even think about a gun."

"What about a dagger? Or a switchblade?"

The knot in my stomach did flip-flops. Weapons? Daggers? What on earth were we doing? We weren't some invincible, crazy, testosterone-filled boys on bikes, thrilled to prove our masculinity. We were a *family*. With *children*. Maybe we *should* take a train from Berlin straight to Moscow after all.

The next morning, Lorenz, Vati, and Moritz disappeared into the workshop across the cobblestoned courtyard. I hid myself away in Mutti's sewing room. Anya, Yvonne, and Julian ran next door to their aunt Susanne's house to see if their cousins, Lukas and Jonas, wanted to feed the horses with them.

Just before lunch, the male Eber trio emerged from the workshop looking very pleased with themselves.

"Our new weapons!" Lorenz held up our bicycle flags. Waving high above our tandems as we cycled, the red flags usually warned drivers that something bizarre was moving along the road ahead.

"How are we going to protect ourselves with those?" I had no idea how a wobbly, thin flagpole could be dangerous.

"Look! Daggers!" Mori held up the bottom end of the white poles. A deadly sharp three-inch steel point was attached to each of the poles.

Lorenz brandished the pole, parrying and lunging at an imaginary enemy. "*En garde!*" He flourished the makeshift foil, thrusting toward my chest.

I jumped back. "Hey! Be careful!" Then, suddenly, I laughed, impressed. "Pretty clever. Fencing foils! I assume you and Anya will do the fighting?" I had thought that Anya's obsession with being a knight had gone a little far when she first asked for fencing lessons, but perhaps there was a value to all those afternoons listening to Lorenz and Anya shouting, "*Allez*" and "*Arret*" as they twisted and jumped in their fencing jackets and masks, trying to stab each other on our driveway.

"And here's the best part—" Looking very pleased with his latest invention, Lorenz tucked the flagpole into one of the U-shaped holders attached to the bike racks. The metal tips slid behind the holder, completely out of view. "The border guards aren't going to stop us for these!" I had to admit, it *was* rather ingenious.

"I have something too!" I pulled out the rain covers I had been modifying on the sewing machine. "See, we can cinch the cover tight here," I explained, tightening it over a pannier and fastening my newly fashioned clips around the back. "When the panniers are locked to the bikes, it will be impossible for nosy fingers to pull off the covers and get into the zippers and pouches."

"Good job." Lorenz fingered the pannier cover approvingly. "And if any thieves start pulling hard on the panniers, the alarms will go off." He shook the tandem and a shrill beeping noise emanated from the motion sensor bike alarm under the bike seat.

Vati and Mori grinned curiously, poking at the little black box under the seat as Lorenz showed them how to activate the alarm. "*Nicht schlecht.*" *Not bad.* Vati patted his son affectionately on the back, an odd mix of pride and worry playing over his face.

"We're ready for the Eastern Bloc now!" Lorenz grinned.

I tried to join in his confident smile. Instead my lips twisted oddly as I choked down the bitter taste of bile at the back of my throat.

PART III

STAYING WARM AFTER
THE COLD WAR

Leader of the Day

Paula

Day 105—Nusse, Germany

We had barely pedaled twenty kilometers from Lorenz's parents' house when the skies burst open in a torrential downpour. For almost an hour, we huddled under the shallow eaves of the redbrick church in Nusse, shivering as we tried to hide from the whipping cold wind and rain. Although it was still the middle of August, I could already feel autumn approaching early this far north.

"Do you need a hat?" I looked over to Lorenz as he sneezed, worried about him. "You look terrible."

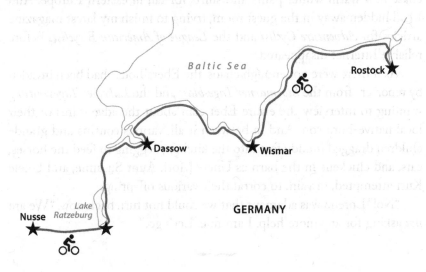

Alternately shaking violently and sweating profusely, Lorenz pulled the hood of his rain jacket tightly under his chin. Mori and Julian had arrived at Lorenz's parents' house with nasty colds, and for the past two days Lorenz had been fighting off a sore throat and runny nose.

"I'm OK," Lorenz insisted, coughing loudly.

Yvonne snuggled up to her dad, wrapping her arms around him. "I'll warm you up, Daddy," she said.

He gave her a hard squeeze. "Thank you, Vonnie. See, I feel better already!"

He didn't *look* any better. Perhaps we should just call Lorenz's parents and ask for a ride back to their house, I thought. Or not. I suspected our visit had felt more like the invasion of the Mongols than a family holiday with the grandchildren. During our five-day stay, we had overhauled most of our equipment; spent hours on calls, emails, and post office trips for World Bike for Breath; and somehow squeezed in time for *Kaffee und Kuchen* (the daily afternoon German "coffee and cake" ritual) with Lorenz's extended family. Vati had dragged the tandems back and forth in a rickety trailer over winding, narrow farm roads to be overhauled in the bicycle shop in Bad Oldesloe. Mutti had bustled Anya and Yvonne off to the huge glass-and-steel Penny superstore in Ahrensburg to purchase new warm winter pants and shirts for fall in eastern Europe. And I had hidden away in the guest room, trying to finish my latest magazine articles for *Adventure Cyclist* and the *League of American Bicyclists* before reliable Internet disappeared.

As if there were not enough chaos, the Ebers' house had been invaded by reporters from the *Stormarner Tagesblatt* and the *Lubecker Tageszeitung* wanting to interview the entire Eber clan about the adventures of their local native-born son. And in between it all, various cousins and grandchildren dragged muddy feet into the kitchen, begging to feed the horses, cats, and chickens in the barn as Uncle Mori, Aunt Susanne, and Uncle Kurt attempted, in vain, to corral their various offspring.

"No!" Lorenz was adamant that we could not turn back now. "We are *not* asking for any more help. I am fine. Let's go."

— ·~ —

We arrived at the bright, modern youth hostel in Ratzeburg that evening, dripping wet and chilled to the bone. In the morning, Lorenz's coughing and sneezing was slightly better. I woke up sweating and achy with a fever.

Despite the coughs and sniffles, Lorenz was eager to press on, thrilled to finally visit the side of his country walled off from him as a child. Lake Ratzeburg lay on the border between the former East and West Germany, barely half an hour's drive from his parents' home. As a young boy, Lorenz would go on picnics to the lake with his family. Munching on buttered *Brotchen* (rolls) with Tilsiter cheese and Black Forest ham, he would gaze across the blue water, thinking of the hundreds of kilometers of barbed-wire wall and guards pointing machine guns from their watchtowers, caging in the Communist half of his country on the other side. Visiting East Germany was like finding a whole new room in your house you had never seen, he explained in excitement as we pedaled off from the hostel.

As soon as we swung around the bottom of Lake Ratzeburg and headed up its east coast, it was obvious we had left western Europe, even though Germany had been unified for almost fifteen years. The paved roads suddenly became narrow paths of bumpy cobblestones, rattling the tandems in an exhausting bouncing motion. The whitewashed houses were no longer clean and cheerful. Instead, their walls were covered in black soot, their dark, depressing facades broken occasionally by brown patches where the stucco had peeled off. Several houses still belched burnt coal from their chimneys. And a thick, acrid smell hung in the air.

The day was damp from the heavy rain the night before, and streams poured into the ditches along the muddy, flat fields bordering the road. Every few kilometers, the crumbling ruins of a tall, narrow East German watchtower would loom above us, the narrow, metal-cased observation windows creaking in the wind high above us. Bizarrely, our T-Mobile Blackberry and cell phones abruptly lost their signals. It was as if the horrendous wall of barbed wire and concrete towers were still there, blocking out all communication with the Western world.

Although the sun peeked out occasionally from the gray clouds, I could not get warm. By the time we got to Dassow, I was alternately sweating and shivering, focused solely on finding a dry bed and hot shower. Dassow's drab, stuccoed houses, stretching along the marshy coast of an inlet off the Baltic Sea, did little to lift my mood. If this was a sign of the eastern European towns to come, I could see why Mori and Kassia preferred to live in Germany—the western side, that is.

Lorenz located a *Zimmer Frei* (room for rent) just as we entered the town.

"Thirty-nine euros," the friendly owner answered as his teenaged daughter peeked curiously from behind him at the front door. Five minutes later, Lorenz practically danced back up the stairs after checking out the two-bedroom apartment below the owner's house.

"It's gorgeous! And the best part is"—his eyes twinkled—"they offered to reduce the price to twenty euros because we're biking for asthma!"

I sniffled an incredibly grateful smile, then hurried down the stairs and crawled straight into bed.

The following day I slept. And sweated and ached. And slept. I had learned a long time ago to take colds and flus seriously. If they settled into my asthmatic lungs, I'd end up with bronchitis or even pneumonia— something I couldn't afford while living on a bike for a year and a half.

The rest of my family spent the day on the beach with Pippi, the owner's teenaged daughter, and her grandfather. As I tossed and turned in bed, I had to laugh at the absurdity of it all. The only time I had fallen sick on this journey was after spending a week in a dry, warm house with a cozy bed and hot showers! So much for all the paranoia about unhealthy dirt and germs in nature. I was certain there was something innately healthy about living outdoors—feeling the wind, rain, and sun on our skin, sleeping when the sun set, waking when it rose. Something that we had lost in our world of artificial light, glowing computers, and hermetically sealed, heated, and air-conditioned rooms.

The next morning, Anya and Yvonne drove off to school with Pippi to talk to her English class for an hour about their cycling adventures. And then we were off again, speeding along the flat, easy Baltic coastal road. We reached Wismar in the early afternoon. Designated a UNE-SCO cultural heritage site, Wismar's medieval townhouses and churches were in the process of a major restoration. With a chill drizzle falling on steel construction frames that obscured the buildings, the city felt gloomy and forbidding. No one was in the mood to go sightseeing. Lorenz wanted to press on, but by then I was feeling like a truck had run over me and just wanted a bed.

"Can we please check out the youth hostel?" I begged.

Twenty minutes later we were standing in front of a featureless, U-shaped brick building that looked like it had been a barracks under the East German government.

"It looks like a Communist interrogation facility," Lorenz protested as we dragged our panniers down the long, narrow, white hall.

Anya wrinkled her nose. "It smells like a hospital."

I mumbled an apology. Then, too tired to argue anymore, I crawled into my sleeping bag, took two puffs of my inhaler and a handful of cold pills, then fell straight to sleep.

❧

"I calculate two hundred and fifty kilometers to the border of Poland." I set my index finger on the map laid out on the hostel's long, narrow cafeteria table the next morning. Moving my finger along the line of the Baltic coast between Wismar and Swinoujskie, I tried to measure out the distance. "Each finger length is about fifty kilometers. So times five—that's two hundred and fifty kilometers to Swin-ooo—er, Swin-oj-sdrk-ee." My mouth mangled the impossible string of consonants. Hopefully people in Poland spoke English. Or maybe German. Because there was no way I was going to be able to say *anything* in a language that didn't believe in vowels.

"And then how far to Lithuania after Poland?" Lorenz asked, buttering another roll from the hostel's breakfast buffet.

I slugged down a gulp of coffee and began the finger-wiggling measurement process again. "About a thousand kilometers to Kaunas."

I wiped the back of my hand on my forehead. It was cold and damp. My head was pounding. I had a sore throat, and my nose was running. I still felt crummy, and the last thing I wanted to do right now was plan another thousand kilometers of biking. Especially through boring, flat, sooty, depressing East Germany and scary Poland, where they'd probably steal the panniers off our tandems the minute we hit the border.

"A thousand kilometers?" Lorenz reached for the map. "Let *me* calculate."

"Why don't you ever believe me?" I grabbed the map possessively. "It's a thousand kilometers! I calculated it twice." My voice began to rise. *Every day* since this ride began our entire family had bickered about some stupid decision—the navigation, where to camp, what hotel to stay in. We even argued about what time to get up! Why couldn't he just leave me alone?

"Hey. I just wanted to check—"

"Do you have to challenge *everything* I do?" My face felt red and sweaty. "Why can't you trust a single decision I make?"

Some of the other hostelers were now turning their heads toward us.

"Listen. Chill!" Lorenz's neck was reddening. His mouth started to set in that angry line that said I'd better back off. He hated public scenes. Anya and Yvonne began wiggling on the bench toward the end of the table, mortified to be seen with this noisy, embarrassing family.

"No, I will not!" I was past backing off now. It was just all too much. The past three days of sleepless nights, coughing, sneezing, and waking up with terrifying dreams of Russian border guards marching us off to some horrible cell in the middle of Siberia. The dismal, cold, gray post-Communist towns. Biking with dagger-tipped flags.

I clutched the map tightly in my hands. "Why do we have to discuss every decision—*every decision*—endlessly? We practically have to have a family vote just to go to the bathroom!"

Grabbing the room key, Anya and Yvonne bolted for the door.

"How are we *ever* going to make it through Russia alive?" I wailed, feeling more and more panicked. "Are we going to have a two-hour family debate about how much to bribe the border guards while they're pointing guns at us?"

"*You're* the one who wants to analyze everything, discuss everything." Now Lorenz was practically shouting. He shoved the bench away from the table and stood up. "I'm going up to the room to pack. We're leaving in half an hour."

I put my head in my hands. What was I thinking—biking to Russia? Sure, we'd cycled through western Europe with our kids. Anyone could do that. Give the girls a swimming pool, some books, and a couple of castles and chocolate croissants every now and then, and they would pedal happily for hours. Well almost. *Harry Potter*, fairy-tale castles, and chocolate croissants *did* encourage pedaling. Most of the time.

So far we had been on home territory. Lorenz and I had variously lived in Germany, England, Italy, and France for months, even years. But ahead? Poland, Russia, Mongolia, China. Countries with cities whose names I could not pronounce. Or read. Crap—they even had different alphabets. If we already argued about directions now, what would we do when the road signs were in Cyrillic or Chinese? I could just see the four of us debating at every intersection: "Look, that squiggle on the sign looks like the one on the map here." "No way. See the two weird prongs coming off the squiggle? That's definitely this town over there."

I pressed the useless buttons on the Blackberry stashed in our valuables pouch. Would we ever get a signal again, or was this it? Biking into the unknown alone—through countries supposedly filled with corrupt, scary, dangerous people. Was Lorenz's family right? Were we dragging our family into mortal danger?

———

"I'm quitting!" I burst into the hostel dorm room ten minutes later, red-faced and flustered. Anya and Yvonne stared in confusion as I slammed the door behind me.

"This is too dangerous. I'm getting a plane ticket and flying home. Anyone who wants to can join me." I strode over to my pannier and started throwing clothes into it.

"That's ridiculous! You can't just quit. This was your idea in the first place!" Lorenz looked over at Anya and Yvonne, shaking his head. "Don't listen to your mom. She's just upset."

"I've made up my mind." I grabbed two pairs of dirty underwear and shoved them in a Ziploc bag. Ugh. Even with a serious cold, I could smell them. "For once I'm making my own decisions. *Without* a family vote!"

"Mom, no!" Yvonne cried. "Don't leave us."

She looked ready to cry. Then stopped. I had a sneaking suspicion that behind my back Lorenz was playing the clown again. Under normal circumstances I would have at least smiled. Instead I spun around, determined. "Listen, we're not some macho expedition of Everest-climbing heroes. We're a *family*! With one guy. And three girls." I pointed at Anya and Yvonne. "And you two aren't even adults!" I wrenched the zipper up on my pannier and looked around for my passport, wiping another wave of feverish sweat from my brow. "So—who's coming with me?"

"No one's going anywhere!" Lorenz sprang to the door with the key in his hand and locked it from the inside. I stared at the door, uncomprehending. A door that could be locked with a key from the inside? How strange.

"So, this is the deal!" Lorenz marched over to the window, threw open the shutters, and dangled the key in the air. "If people don't calm down, I'll drop the key outside!"

Anya burst out laughing. "Ha ha ha ha. You're going to lock us in here together?" She bent over, holding her hands on her belly, struck with the ludicrous situation. "I'm going to be locked in a hostel in eastern Germany with two crazy parents! Ha ha ha ha." Tears began forming at the corners of her eyes.

I dropped my pannier, embarrassed. Lorenz pulled his arm in from the window and shoved the key in his pocket self-consciously. For the next hour, the four of us sat on the bunks in the hostel room, debating. No one wanted to quit, but clearly we couldn't continue on like this.

It seemed we were getting nowhere when suddenly Anya spoke up. "The problem is everyone tries to run the decisions. Right? We don't have a leader."

"That's for sure," I grumbled. "It's dangerous. What happens when we have a *real* crisis? We can't have everyone debating what to do if we have a bike crash or get robbed. Someone has to be in charge."

"Well, what if we had a 'leader of the day'?"

"What do you mean?"

"Well, one day Dad can run the day, and everyone has to do what he says. And the next day Mom can be the leader, and she makes all the decisions. If we don't like the leader, we'll have a new one the next day."

Of course. Simple. Elegant. Obvious. It was brilliant. I felt humbled. Anya was a natural diplomat. It certainly did not come from me! Or Lorenz, for that matter. I gazed at my thirteen-year-old daughter with new eyes. When we had left on this journey, I had just assumed our daughters would be, well, a burden. Children that we'd have to care for and drag along and worry about. But maybe they also had something to contribute. Perhaps the adults weren't the only ones who brought strengths to our little team.

"Why don't you be the first leader? You can start tomorrow," I offered Lorenz. "On one condition."

"What's that?"

I wasn't ready for eastern Europe yet. I wasn't sure I ever would be. "Personally, I'm done with East Germany. It's depressing. And a bit creepy. Why don't we get some practice with this 'leader of the day' thing somewhere easier first—make sure it works before trying it out in Poland or Lithuania."

"Like—"

I dug around in my pannier and pulled out a Ziploc bag filled with maps and torn pages from bike books and travel brochures. "There's an overnight boat from Rostock to Sweden." I moved my finger along the map, calculating the distance quickly while glaring defiantly at Lorenz. "Rostock's about ninety kilometers from here." Wisely, Lorenz decided not to challenge me this time. "The route should be totally flat. If we leave now, we should make the midnight sailing."

We held one last family vote. And for once we were unanimous. We were heading to Sweden!

Sweden

*Posted by Yvonne**

Dear Readers:

Right now I'm in Sweden and I love it. The food is great, the weather is great, and I love it all. I especially like the people's history. They were Vikings. Viking things are everywhere: old stones here, an ancient Viking king's tomb there. The Vikings were ruthless coast robbers of Holland, Germany, and England. But they weren't just ruthless robbers. They had a culture no one could forget. The Vikings made amazing stone carvings and structures, and they were the best sailors in the world for centuries.

I think the best part of Sweden is the ancient ruins. For example, at the top of a hill on the southern coast of Sweden there is a structure made of about twenty boulders put into the shape of a Viking ship. This is called Ales Stenar.

Another cool ruin is a Bronze Age king's tomb built over three thousand years ago. It is seventy-five by sixty-five meters long and wide, all made of millions of stones piled into a mound. All in all, I think Sweden is my favorite country.

---

* Yvonne wrote essays for homeschool as she biked around the world. The essays were posted on the World Bike for Breath website for our sponsors and followers to read. These essays have been lightly edited for grammar but otherwise remain in her direct words as an eleven- and twelve-year-old girl.

World Bike Bits

Bits and stories about World Bike for Breath. A Bulletin for sponsors. Volume 3

One Elephant, Two Children, and 7¾ Books

Paula

TWO FLOPPY FUZZY EARS AND THE LONG GRAY SNOUT OF AN ELEPHANT are poking out of Lorenz's left front pannier. La La, Yvonne's well-traveled stuffed elephant, and Oinks, her little pink pig, have a front-row seat today because Yvonne's pannier is overly full and La La's head, quite honestly, does not quite fit in. La La seems to be pleased, however, as he bobs his head contentedly at the rocky coves of the Swedish coastline, dotted with colorful fishing villages and the cries of cormorants, seagulls, and swans.

Balancing out the elephant and pig, in the front right pannier of Lorenz's tandem are four books in English—Anya's treasured possessions. As we are now leaving the somewhat familiar languages of western Europe and heading east to the Cyrillic alphabets and Asian characters of Russia, Mongolia, and China, these books—like Yvonne's elephant—have successfully evaded our cycling rules of traveling light.

Indeed, since our family began our world cycling tour for asthma four months and four thousand kilometers ago in Greece, we have been waging, rather unsuccessfully, an ongoing "battle of the bulge" (in this case with our panniers, not our waistlines). Despite monthly weight-reduction programs, our panniers appear to have amazing reproduction properties similar to the magic cooking pot of folklore: always full regardless of the amount of food, or possessions, removed.

The battle began innocently enough with my purchase of a set of Greek worry beads. They became so popular with our family that, ten countries later, they are still traveling happily along in my handlebar bag. In the Alps of Austria, we bought a three-pound, hardcover English version of *Harry Potter*, which was squeezed daily into various panniers for almost one thousand kilometers to France. Upon the book's completion, however, it was immediately replaced by two bottles of expensive skin lotions for Anya's tender complexion along with another six books purchased in England.

Meanwhile, in Germany, reveling in the flatter landscape and the appearance of his family's traditional foods, Lorenz carried along one-kilogram glass jars of sauerkraut, *rotkohl*, and *wurstchen*. And in Sweden, as the burning temperatures of a record hot summer in Europe have finally given way to brisk fall winds, we have added fleece shirts and pants, plus two sets of knitting needles and four skeins of wool. The girls insist that by the time we reach Russia, they will have been transformed into hats and scarves.

To be fair, we have made repeated attempts to gain the upper hand in the weight wars. Weekly trips to local post offices have scattered packages covered with colorful stamps and filled with gifts, mementoes, and photos across our American friends' households—their space wars being, so we think, far less dramatic than ours. And a few items, such as my asthma medications (which provide both the purpose and the physical ability for me to undertake this sixteen-month ride), have dropped significantly—in the case of my inhalers, from thirty-six to twenty-four. Likewise, although our current total of whole books is seven (Anya, four; Lorenz, one; Yvonne, one; Paula, one), I have become skilled at transporting decimated pieces of various travel guides: carrying three more quarters of books held together with tape and packed carefully in Ziploc bags.

As we now head into the former Soviet Baltic states, friends have warned us to be prepared for customs searches through our bags. Although the prospect of customs examinations at first seemed daunting, I am currently beginning to relish the idea of a Lithuanian border guard pulling out the five bottles of shampoo, conditioner, liquid soap, dishwashing liquid, and clothes detergent currently stowed in the outside pockets of our rear panniers. Perhaps the guard will do us a favor and confiscate a few bottles, settling the battle of the bulge—at least until Latvia.

Route Update—England to Poland

Hi, dear friends and sponsors,

We are finally cycling into fall and the uncharted territory of Poland and the former Soviet Bloc. After a much-needed break from foreign-language stress in England (plus, more importantly, the opportunity to buy books in English at a reasonable price) and a wonderful excursion to Saint Malo and the coast of Brittany in France, we took a boat from England to Hamburg in northern Germany. There we spent five hectic days at Lorenz's parents' house tuning up our bikes, gearing up for our journey eastward.

Our preparations were none too soon. Alas, our days of telephone calls and emails from our cell phone while cooking dinner in a farmer's field are numbered. After this route update (and perhaps one newsletter from Poland), until we arrive in Australia, we will be mailing all of our newsletters by the trusty old-fashioned method of the post office. Brett Thackray, World Bike for Breath's president, has kindly offered to type our updates and then email them. In any case, there may be a two- to three-week time warp between our actual location and our newsletters. But that's just part of the adventure!

Here's our route so far:

- Kilometers for asthma and clean air: 3,993
- Miles for asthma and clean air: 2,410
- New countries cycled for asthma: England, France, Sweden, Poland

We are now heading east to the Mazuri Lakes and then Lithuania. Thanks to all of you for your sponsorship and encouragement.

—The Ebers

Cherishing Little Comforts

Posted by Yvonne

"WE'RE STAYING IN A HOTEL." THESE WORDS ECHOED THROUGH MY head. Along with these words came thoughts of a warm bed, a pillow, and the many small amenities that come with hotels. Lately I have come to cherish little comforts that don't come with packable rooms that can barely fit me and my thirteen-year-old sister. Since I have been biking around the world for four months now, I have begun to love a bed that doesn't have to be stuffed up in a bag every day and stuck on a bike. I have learned to appreciate a room that has insulation, so in the middle of the night you don't have a small ice rink at your feet (because water came in your tent somehow and froze in the zero-degree temperatures).

There are many other things I cherish, and one of them is my own space. Considering that my sister and I have to sleep in a three-by-six-foot space for one whole year and a half, and considering that my sister loves to spread out when she sleeps, it is very hard and uncomfortable to get to sleep—especially when you are squished at the bottom of the already too small tent with your sister's elbow stuck in your back.

Perhaps most of all, however, I cherish eating food I recognize. I don't mind eating beaver or slimy pickled mushrooms that leave a jelly-like goo over your plate getting all over your other food. But I can't help getting excited about eating a real American hamburger without coleslaw in it. (A coleslaw hamburger is a Polish favorite.) I really love this trip, but there's nothing better than having a few small comforts along the way.

Müügil

Paula

Day 148—Near Parnu, Estonia

September rolled in to the Baltic states with ice frosting our camping
dishes in the mornings, crisp red- and orange-leafed birches and aspens
lining the road, and colorfully kerchiefed women bending over to pick
the harvests in the fields.

The morning had started out sunny with a sharp bite to the air—the kind that made the lungs startle awake and the legs pump extra hard on the pedals to get the blood flowing. As we swung the tandems back north onto the Via Baltica—the main road from Kaunas to Tallinn—I took a deep, wonderful, sharp breath, filling my lungs with the scent of damp fallen leaves, wood smoke, and the salt of the ocean nearby. I loved the smell of autumn. Finally, the deadly slow, sultry laziness of hot summer was over. And the fresh, crisp air felt full of energy and promise as if something tantalizing and unexpected was being carried in on the chill wind.

As designated leader of the day, I had planned a long but easy ride north toward Tallinn, on the northern coast of Estonia. I could barely contain my enthusiasm as I envisioned a fabulous autumn ride through flaming forests, a tour of the historic town of Parnu on the way, and maybe, if we were lucky, stopping at a small roadside farmstand to buy locally fresh-picked apples, wild mushrooms from the forest, or even freshly collected eggs.

Following the long, sandy Baltic coastline, the road was flat and the pedaling easy. We had whizzed through Lithuania and Latvia in less than a week—a good thing since we had nonrefundable tickets on the Trans-Siberian Railway. We had to be in Saint Petersburg by the third of October—three days from now—or we'd lose $2,200 worth of train tickets. That was almost our entire budget for a month!

Our pedals clicked quietly past a seemingly infinite, silver-trunked birch forest, the leaves bright ochre, scarlet, and magenta. Occasionally a steep-roofed wooden farmhouse would break a clearing in the forest. Its cheerfully painted walls and geometric carvings provided the only relief from the deep, endless woods surrounding us. As usual, our family lapsed into one of our many never-ending debates to make the distance pass more quickly.

"How can you wear that itchy thing?" Lorenz grimaced on the tandem next to me, pointing to my beloved but bedraggled black-and-white wool sweater. Limited to one warm item per person, we each had our own pet theories as to the most appropriate clothing for fall cycling. Lorenz, who had terrifying memories of being stuffed into wool clothes as a child, was wearing a synthetic beige knit sweater topped by his yellow Patagonia raincoat.

"It's so warm and cozy," I countered. "If you don't want to be itchy, wear a long-sleeved shirt underneath."

"I like wool too. My jacket is the best in the world," Yvonne chimed in. In the cobblestoned old town of Kaunas, Lithuania, she had fallen in love with a beautiful handmade maroon felt jacket. Trimmed with bright orange piping and deer horn buttons, the traditional Baltic jacket had looked charming, if a little impractical. "Please, oh please!" She had jumped up and down hopefully, her big round blue eyes pleading. Yvonne had grown at least two inches since we began cycling in May, and the warm clothes she had packed when we left were now all too short. I had expressed my doubts that a traditional Lithuanian felt jacket was really a practical choice for cycling, but Yvonne had prevailed.

"We know! We know!" Anya laughed. "You haven't taken that jacket off since you bought it. You even try to sleep in it!" Behind me on the tandem, Anya was bundled in her white fleece vest over her black Lycra jacket. Like her dad, she could not stand anything that even looked like it might be scratchy or tight.

"But it's so BEautiFUL." Yvonne stretched her arms up in the air in delight and twisted around to show it off.

"Hey, hands back on the handlebars!" Lorenz called back to his dancing stoker. We all laughed. It was hard not to smile at Yvonne's enthusiasm.

The rain began slowly, insidiously. At first I brushed it off, hopeful it was just a short sprinkle. However, the drops continued to fall faster, larger—icy splashes running down the back of our necks and into our shoes. We stopped to pull on our rain pants and coats, tightening the bright yellow hoods under the helmets to ward off the now thick, pelting drops. I glanced around for shelter, but stuck in the middle of a long, lonely stretch of never-ending forest, we had no choice but to get back on the bikes.

"Sorry, girls," I mumbled as Anya and Yvonne glared at me balefully, clearly unhappy to be cycling in the pouring rain. "I'm sure the rain will let up soon." I tried to sound like an encouraging leader of the day, inspiring my little team to press forward, but the angry glares from my daughters were proof enough that I was not succeeding.

Very quickly my fingers became numb as the frigid rain seeped into my gloves. Behind us on the tandems, Anya and Yvonne looked completely miserable, their shoes now sodden with freezing, seeping water that sprayed up from the road and dripped down into their socks from the rain pants. The cheerful banter, which had made the previous miles pass quickly, suddenly evaporated. There was only teeth-gritting silence as our wheels swished round and round, spewing rain and mud onto our legs, shoulders, and faces.

Finally, after almost an hour of bone-numbing cycling, Yvonne glimpsed a break in the forest.

"Look, a picnic shelter!" Yvonne called out in excitement as a set of wooden A-frame shelters appeared out of nowhere in a clearing on the side of the road.

"Pull over," I shouted, relieved to finally find somewhere to escape from the deluge. My beautiful, crisp autumn day was rapidly degenerating into a soggy mess. Everyone was soaked through and cold. I felt irritable and frustrated. Somehow, as leader of the day, I was expected to keep everyone happy and solve all problems. If only it were that simple.

The "leader of the day" plan had sounded like an excellent solution to our family's constant bickering over decisions when Anya had proposed it back in Wismar. I had looked forward to the chance to make decisions the right way—that is, *my way*—every other day as I alternated leadership with Lorenz. But now I was not so sure. Being the leader and taking full responsibility for decisions was so much harder than it looked. And keeping up morale on a wet, freezing day in the middle of nowhere seemed downright impossible.

"Why don't I fire up the camp stove and make some hot soup?" Lorenz suggested helpfully. It was only ten o'clock. Too early for lunch. But as we stamped our wet feet, chilled to the bone now that we were no longer cycling, I knew we had to get something warm down quickly or run the risk of hypothermia.

"Thanks. That's a great idea." I reached down to the water bottle holder on my tandem and pulled out our aquamarine Aladdin thermos. "While Dad's making soup, we should all drink some hot chocolate," I added as I twisted open the lid and began pouring.

The thermos had been a gift from Mori's in-laws, the Palinsky family, whom we had visited in Poland. Yvonne had fallen in love with the big white bunny decorating the side. The next thing we knew, we were pedaling off with a large one-liter thermos that barely fit in the water bottle holder on my tandem. At first I had been annoyed.

"What do we need a heavy thermos for?" I had complained about the extra weight. "We carry that much weight in a loaf of bread each day," Lorenz pointed out.

"And it's a present. You can't just give it away," Yvonne added protectively. "I like the bunny. He makes me happy."

Ironically, the thermos quickly turned out to be one of our most prized possessions. As the days became progressively colder, we began to count on a cup of hot chocolate or tea to warm us on our breaks. Equally important, boiling water for the thermos each morning before we pedaled off also gave us a clean, sterilized alternative to buying bottled water every day. In theory, eastern Europe was catching up to its western neighbors, but as we pedaled through the countryside, watching stocky horse teams plow fields filled with animal dung, it was clear that modern sanitation and mechanization was still far behind. I didn't trust the water for a minute.

I poured the steaming hot chocolate into a Sierra cup, wrapping my fingers gratefully around the warm metal. I had to admit I had been wrong about the thermos. Looking at Yvonne snuggling on the picnic bench in her warm wool Lithuanian jacket, it seemed that perhaps I had misjudged that too. I sighed in frustration. In the classroom, as a professor, I was in charge and rarely wrong. But watching the rain streaming over our little shelter and my bedraggled family huddling around the camp stove, I felt discouraged and unsure of myself. Maybe I should stick to books and theories, I thought despondently. They are far more predictable and easy to understand.

Our motley, soggy group splashed unhappily into Parnu around noon. The rain had not stopped. Any other time, I would have loved to explore the quaint cobblestone streets lined with yellow, pink, and blue houses built in the traditional step-roofed style of the Hanseatic League.* But all we wanted was to bolt for the nearest café. The polite, formally dressed customers in the café pretended not to stare. However, it was obvious that a muddy, dripping family peeling off their filthy rain pants and coats in the doorway was not quite, well ... proper. Still, the waitress smiled sympathetically as we placed our orders by pointing to the delicious-looking pastries and coffee cups on the counter.

"I don't want to bike anymore," Yvonne complained as she munched on a sticky kringle—a type of twisted Estonian cinnamon roll. Although she had put on a clean, dry shirt in the bathroom, her wet hair was still plastered to her head, and she looked rather like a drowned rat.

"Me neither. I'm soaking wet," Anya piped in. "Can we just get a hotel and stay here for the night? It's such a pretty town."

"I'd like to do that too," I began, "but we need to get to Tallinn tomorrow. And I really don't think we can bike a hundred and twenty-five kilometers in one day, even if it is flat."

I looked over to Lorenz for confirmation.

"Don't look at me. *You're* the leader."

He was right. I was supposed to be making the decisions. But somehow this leadership thing was not quite working out the way I had hoped. I had imagined that being the leader meant that I would pick the museums I wanted to visit, choose the nicest campsite, and plan pretty cycling routes. Fun stuff. Instead, I was worrying about hypothermia, keeping my family dry and warm, and figuring out how to make it to Russia in three days.

---

* The Hanseatic League was founded in northern Germany as an association of merchant guilds to fight off pirates and protect trade among the Baltic and North Sea coastal cities. It flourished from the eleventh to fifteenth centuries and, at its peak, spanned the Baltic from Belgium to Russia. Hansa towns are easily recognized by their unique houses, which have tall pointed (often step-roofed) fronts with storage areas at the top of the house. A rope was lowered from a trap door in the steep roof front down to the water below to pull up cargo from incoming trading ships.

Sighing, I took a sip of coffee and bent over my map to calculate the route one more time.

———◆———

I glanced nervously at the time on my bike counter: 6:05 p.m. The sky had that wan, gray, milky look that suggested the sun was going down soon, although I could not see it behind the thick dark clouds. As winter approached, days at this northern latitude became drastically shorter and shorter. I felt a tightening sense of panic in my chest as I stared at the clock once again. We had pedaled out of Parnu four hours ago. My plan had been to cycle about thirty or so kilometers north and then to find a small hotel or inn where we could dry out for the night. But so far, the road had been almost desolate, with few towns or houses along the way.

The rain had not stopped. The fields alongside the roads were overflowing with mud and puddles. Camping in those fields was the last thing I wanted to do. However, according to my calculations, we had at best half an hour of daylight left. Then the night would roll in—bitterly cold, wet, and dark. So if we were going to pitch a tent, it had to be soon.

"What's the plan?" Lorenz looked at me in concern. Although I was the leader, it was clear he was not confident that I was making good decisions. I had lost all support from Anya and Yvonne way back in Parnu, as soon as I explained we needed to pedal onward. My promises of finding a hotel up ahead had been met with disbelief. And from the looks of the empty road in front of us, they were probably right not to trust me.

"I don't know. I don't see anywhere practical to camp," I answered. "The information I picked up at the tourist bureau in Parnu showed two hotels along this road. I don't know why we haven't found them."

"Are you sure we didn't miss them?"

"No," I answered miserably. "You were looking too. There's been nothing."

We continued pedaling in silence, the sky getting progressively darker. My wet feet and hands started to cramp with the cold as the water in my shoes and gloves turned icy. What have I done? I groaned silently. We can't camp soaking wet like this. We're halfway to hypothermia already.

Twilight was rapidly setting in, and the lights of the cars passing by glowed eerily in the misty fog rising from the cold, wet road. A car skimmed dangerously close to us in the semidark. If we don't die of hypothermia, we'll be hit by a car in the dark, I thought gloomily. This is a total disaster.

Ahead was a muddy lane that fronted what I hoped was a flat, grassy field where we might be able to pitch two tents. I pointed to the lane. I refused to look at the unhappy faces of my family as we pedaled closer. Suddenly, in the gloom, a car's lights shone on what looked like a large wooden board hanging in front of a long building with a parking lot in front of it.

"Wait. Up ahead. There's a sign," Yvonne cried out. "Maybe it's a hotel."

As we drew closer, my heart sank. A large white-and-red-striped message ran from one corner to the other, covering the name of the business. "Müügil," it stated.

"What's that mean?" Anya asked.

"I don't know. But the parking lot sure is deserted," Lorenz replied.

"I'm going to check it out anyway." I parked the tandem in front of a green wooden door. The building was two stories high, with a steep, red-tiled roof. The walls were crisscrossed with dark wooden beams in traditional northern European style. It looked like a guest house. But even in the fading light, it was clear the white stucco between the beams was peeling. The place definitely appeared abandoned.

I peered into one of the dusty windows, still framed with white lace curtains, shining my flashlight inside. The light beam jolted eerily up and down over a neglected restaurant. Neat rows of dark, square wooden tables and chairs still stood around the room, as if waiting for guests. Sitting on the bar at the back, I could barely make out a dusty stack—maybe tablecloths? At the end of the bar, the flashlight lit up two shot glasses. One appeared partially full of some amber liquid. Someone has been in here recently, I thought.

I tried the door, but it was locked. Night had already fallen. Unless we could find a way in, we would have to pitch our tents on the abandoned gravel parking lot. The prospect of sleeping in a cold tent in wet clothes in the pouring rain was not inviting. But at least the ground would be relatively dry and flat.

Then I saw a dim yellowish light in one of the windows at the other end of the building. Someone must be in there! I hesitated, trying to summon the courage to knock on the door. Part of me just wanted to jump on my bike and bolt away, but it was too dangerous to continue biking in the dark and the rain. And we clearly could not camp here without talking to whomever was inside. Maybe they were watching us right now. I felt my skin crawl and shuddered, trying to brush off the fear.

Tap. Tap tap. I waited patiently at the door. There was no answer. Maybe the light is just left on to keep away burglars, I thought hopefully. I knocked one last time. Harder. Just to be sure.

Suddenly, the wooden door burst open. I could smell the alcohol even before I saw the short, stout, red-eyed woman. She stared at me suspiciously, listing oddly to one side. How was I going to explain what I wanted? I doubted she spoke a word of English. Few people did except in the cities. And she looked a bit too sloshed to understand anyway.

I quickly grabbed our Langenscheid's picture phrase book and flipped the pages, looking for an image of two beds—the standard European symbol for a hotel room. The woman stumbled forward and peered hostilely at the book.

"*Nyet.*" She shook her head fervently.

I glanced down the hallway to what appeared to be an apartment in the back. I could see the glow of a warm fire flickering around the corner. I started shivering, unable to fight off the cold and exhaustion any longer. I would do anything for a warm, dry bed. Anything.

Desperately, I shone the flashlight on my two daughters and Lorenz, standing miserably behind me, next to the tandems in the rain. The woman peered out in surprise, her large bosom protruding from a red-and-brown patterned dress hanging over a pair of old slippers.

She squinted suspiciously at the peculiar image of two dripping girls in yellow raincoats on a double bicycle, scrubbing her eyes as if to make sure this was not a hallucination. An odd look came across her face—a mixture of astonishment and pity. And then she nodded, her wide ruddy face softening. I quickly reached into my pouch and pulled out four hundred

Estonian kroons—about twenty-five US dollars. She leaned forward, breathing heavily with the stench of alcohol, and grabbed the money.

We had a deal. But I was not sure what I had bargained for.

～

The stairway was narrow and unswept. In the dim light of a lonely bulb on the landing, we dragged our drenched panniers down a wooden hallway behind the sickly sweet stink of alcohol still pouring off the woman. She opened a door to the right and tried to turn on a light, but the room remained dark. She nodded to Lorenz, pointing at his flashlight, which he immediately flickered over two beds and a nightstand.

"*Siin.*" The apparent proprietor gestured to the beds and pointed to Anya and Yvonne.

"We're going to sleep *here*?" Anya mumbled in horror, staring at the bare mattresses and a windowsill full of dead flies. "There's no light."

Yvonne clung to Anya. "Maybe it's haunted."

"Shh." I gestured furtively. "Don't make her upset. We don't want to make her change her mind."

"It's a bed. And it's dry," Lorenz added pragmatically. "I'm sure we just need to find some light bulbs."

Down the hallway on the left, the woman opened a second door to a room with a double bed. On the rickety wooden nightstand next to the bed, she turned on a light. Like Anya and Yvonne's room, there were no linens on the bed, and the floor had dust piles in the corner. I could see my breath in the chill air.

As Lorenz, Anya, and Yvonne began to unpack, unfurling our sleeping bags onto the beds, I followed the unsteady owner to a small bathroom and shower. She fiddled with the taps for a moment, and finally a gush of rusty water spit out. She let it run until the water became clear. I put my hand under the water, which was icy. I had hoped, unrealistically, for a hot shower. But at least we could rinse the mud off our faces.

Stumbling to a closet next to the bathroom, the proprietor pulled out two electric space heaters.

"*Aitah.*" I nodded, offering the one word I knew in Estonian. "Thank you." I truly meant it. Twenty minutes ago I was contemplating a frigid night in a tent in the rain. And now we had dry beds and even heat. It was a miracle.

The woman nodded awkwardly, then turned and disappeared down the hallway.

Within half an hour, the abandoned hotel sprang to life. Lorenz located not only light bulbs but also lamp shades and even a picture or two to hang on the wall of Anya and Yvonne's room. Yvonne tucked Oinks, her pink pig, on top of her sleeping bag, and the room looked almost cozy—well, at least not completely derelict. Anya was busy washing our muddy clothes in the bathroom sink and hanging them over the space heaters. Lorenz found a way to turn on the stove down in the kitchen of the restaurant, and the delicious smell of hot vegetable soup wafted up the stairs enticingly as I swept out the rooms and piles of dead flies.

"OK, so I was not a perfect leader of the day," I admitted half an hour later as we sat around a wooden table in the kitchen. I munched on a thick slice of brown Baltic bread and butter, dipping it into Lorenz's steaming soup. "But it could have been worse." I was beginning to feel warm and relaxed as the soup's heat spread down to my frozen toes.

"Well, you did find us a hotel," Anya admitted grudgingly. "Even if it is closed."

"And I'm glad I don't have to make us bike a hundred and twenty-five kilometers to Tallinn tomorrow," Lorenz added, looking thoughtful.

Thank goodness I was handing over the leadership baton to Lorenz tomorrow. It was exhausting being responsible for a family of four, traveling on bicycles deeper and deeper into strange, unknown lands. I was in complete awe of the American pioneers who had dragged their families across oceans on leaky ships and faced untold dangers crossing the US in covered wagons—without maps, hotels, hospitals, or even stores most of the way.

"It's OK, Mommy." Yvonne cuddled next to me. "It's like Alexander," she said, thinking of the doomed hero of one of our family's favorite children's books. "Everybody has a terrible, horrible, very bad, no good day sometimes."

The "R" in Russia Stands for Ruble

Lorenz

Day 150—Russian Border

Deceived by the relative civility of the Baltic states, I had been lulled into believing that countries belonging to the former Soviet Union really weren't as bad as the Western media had made us believe. As we crossed into Russia, via night train from Estonia, we were slumbering in our bunks when suddenly the compartment door was torn open by two armed border guards wearing shabby green uniforms.

"*Vstavat!*" Get up!

One of the guards was shaking my arm so roughly it hurt.

"*Vstavat!*"

When I managed to open my eyes, I saw a stocky, stubble-faced guard two inches from my face, screaming at me in a torrent of Russian. I understood absolutely nothing and stammered confused syllables, trying to reply and wake up at the same time.

Seeing my bewilderment, the guard let go of my arm and slung the strap of his assault rifle over his shoulder. He pivoted around, picked up Yvonne's pannier, unzipped the top, and poured the entire contents, stuffed animals and all, onto the compartment floor. Seeing nothing of value in the pile, the taller, lanky guard grabbed my pannier, reached in, and pulled out everything, dumping it all on top of Yvonne's sad pile. Meanwhile, his superior began strutting around the compartment, poking at our possessions at random with the muzzle of his gun. The younger guard was rummaging through Paula's pannier, tearing open the zippers and pulling out socks and underwear in a great flurry. Suddenly he stooped and triumphantly held out a string of plastic amber-colored worry beads, which Paula had bought in Greece for just three dollars. He handed the find to his superior, who held it appraisingly up against the dim, flickering dome light.

"Undeclared jewelry," he pronounced gravely, suddenly in excellent English. He looked at me with his sharp gray eyes and motioned me to leave the compartment. I grabbed my neck pouch to leave, but when Paula also made ready to go, the older guard roughly snapped up his hand, signaling her to stay behind.

Both guards pushed me out of the compartment and down the dingy corridor to the greasy, unlit accordion section between cars. The place was deserted; not a soul around. The head guard leaned against the oil-splattered wall, pulled a toothpick from his breast pocket, and clamped it nonchalantly between his teeth.

He held up Paula's worry beads again and drawled, "Undeclared jewelry."

I was scared and shaking but gathered the nerve to say, "Those are cheap plastic. They are worth nothing."

"Undeclared jewelry," the guard repeated, now a little more menacingly.

"They cost three dollars. They are tourist junk," I said defiantly.

The guard's gray eyes flashed, and he leaned forward so close to my face that the toothpick in his mouth dug into my cheek. Through gritted teeth he snarled, "Undeclared jewelry."

I was frantic, racking my brain. What crime could we have possibly committed by bringing worthless souvenirs into Russia? How could these ignorant guards not tell the difference between a tourist trinket and a costly piece of jewelry?

"Must pay fine!" grunted the young guard. Suddenly and miraculously, he too could speak English now.

"For what?" I asked.

"Undeclared jewelry."

Suddenly it hit me. This was all a charade. These brutes wanted a bribe. All along I had been thinking they had a legitimate reason for this interrogation. But no, this was just good old-fashioned corruption and intimidation.

"Unbelievable," I muttered and pulled three hundred rubles from my wallet, holding it out to the guard. "Here is your 'fine.'"

"Too small fine," came the reply, and I added another two hundred rubles.

"Still small."

I added yet another two hundred rubles to the pile of notes, bringing the total to the equivalent of about seventeen US dollars. Slowly, a wide grin spread over the head guard's face. He spat out his toothpick and clapped me on the back with his pudgy hand.

"That is good fine," he said, pocketing the notes with a big smile.

The young guard was also smiling as he shouldered his AK-47 and helpfully guided me back to my compartment. As we entered, the guard pressed the worthless worry beads back into Paula's hands. He waved to the white-faced girls and said, "Welcome to Russia."

Russia Is a Bear

Lorenz

Day 154—Moscow

"Anya! Hit them! They're swarming us!"

"Dad ... How?—Watch out!"

By inches, I missed a melon-sized pothole in the massive six-lane Moscow thoroughfare. Our tandem swerved, out of control, into a queue of stacked-up cars, which were jockeying to squeeze into an enormous clogged traffic circle. I narrowly missed a brown Lada sedan, snagging my shirt on the rusted ends of a twisted coat hanger that held the car's dented trunk shut. Angry drivers honked their horns as our two bicycles and the mob on foot pursuing us dodged, helter-skelter, through the rolling mass of cars and trucks. Trembling with fear, I yanked the handlebars around and shouted, "Anya, grab the flag. Hit them with the flag!"

"Dad, that's a weapon! The steel point could kill them."

"Hit them with the blunt end then, for heaven's sake."

"Dad, they're *kids*! I can't just stab them."

A grimy-faced boy, perhaps thirteen or fourteen, was now running alongside my handlebars, grabbing my left arm and digging his black fingernails into my skin. With his other hand, he yanked on my Casio watch in quick short bursts, trying to break the watch band. Another eight or ten street children were swarming around the bikes, pulling off anything they could lay their hands on. A girl in a tattered orange sundress plucked one of our water bottles from its holder, and I saw the bottle bouncing across the crowded pavement, just missing Paula and Yvonne's front tire as they followed pell-mell behind us.

"Hit them, Anya!" I yelled again in desperation. I felt our tandem tilting precariously under the tall, disheveled boy's vicious pull.

Instead of hearing the whoosh of Anya wielding our steel-tipped bicycle flag, I suddenly felt a fierce jolt in my pedals. Anya had chosen flight over fight and was pushing us forward with all she had. I took the hint and also stomped furiously into my pedals, shooting down a gap that had just opened up between two lanes of cars. The bike lurched forward, and the boy's grip miraculously released. We shot down the corridor of vehicles and zig-zagged back toward the curb as the gang of street children fell back, one by one. Taking a hard right, I dodged into a grimy alley and glanced back, relieved to see that Paula and Yvonne had also escaped the horde of street children. Without warning, the kids had materialized out of nowhere and had suddenly swarmed us just minutes after we left the train from Saint Petersburg in downtown Moscow. Looking back one more time, still trembling, I realized gratefully that we had shaken those menacing street urchins. I zig-zagged around three or four more corners to put as much distance as possible between them and us. Then, finally, I stopped.

Without getting off my bike, I put my forearms on my handlebars and just focused on breathing. Panting, I observed the deep indentations in my forearm, where the street boy's fingernails had dug into my flesh. In a couple of spots, he had drawn blood.

"You guys OK?" I asked between gulps, knowing full well they weren't because I could hear Yvonne's muffled crying.

"Yeah, but they got the food bag I'd tied on top. Lunch and dinner are gone," said Paula.

"They made off with one of our water bottles," I said.

"At least they didn't get a pannier or the money pouch," wheezed Anya.

"One girl snarled at me like a mean dog. She was really scary, like in a nightmare," whimpered Yvonne.

"They scared me too. We're all scared," I said, feeling bad for her.

I could see Paula's hands still shaking as she pulled out the Moscow city map and said, "Let's find out where we are and get to our Moscow homestay. I can't wait to get off these damned streets. I feel like a giant target out here."

—◆—

Twenty minutes later we pedaled up to a dilapidated, graffitied, pre-war high-rise with a stairway that reeked of cat piss. The outside was discouraging, but I was still hopeful. In Saint Petersburg, our homestay had also been in a dilapidated concrete high-rise, but once we stepped inside the apartment, it was beautiful. It was a Russian practice, we learned, to hide one's wealth behind an ugly facade—so the mafia and other greedy people didn't prey on you.

Unfortunately, Gayla, our frumpy Moscow homestay matron, had no need to hide her wealth; she had none. Inside, her home was horrible. Five cats lived with us in the gloomy high-ceilinged room that Gayla assigned to us. Once we discovered that the bedspreads on our beds were thickly covered in cat hair and were crawling with fleas, we let the cats have the beds and set up camp in our sleeping bags on the scuffed linoleum floor. We had prepaid for the room from the US and were stuck with it. In Russia, it seemed, there was also no such thing as a refund policy. Once you handed over the money, it was gone forever.

After quickly unpacking, we left Gayla's and spent as much time outside of her disgusting apartment as possible. The first afternoon, we visited Saint Basil's cathedral with its twisted, jumbled, carnival-colored onion domes. Stepping into the church felt like falling into a kaleidoscope, so intense were the colors swirling around us. The inside of the church was so beautifully decorated, so colorful, it looked edible. We felt as if we had been dropped into Candyland. Saint Basil's was such a wonderful contrast to Gayla's gray, drab, and dirty apartment that we stayed until closing.

The next day we toured Red Square and saw Lenin's tomb. Dark and gloomy, inside a modern monolithic building, Lenin lies pale and perfectly preserved inside an imposing glass tomb. Stone-faced Russian guards stand vigil. Yvonne was not impressed. She said she felt queasy around the dead guy and wanted to leave. That night Yvonne came down with a terrible bout of food poisoning, which she most likely acquired from us cooking meals in Gayla's unsanitary kitchen. The grease on the tiles over the stove was so thick that, one night, I mischievously carved my initials into it.

The following morning, Paula's mom, Nana, called unexpectedly on our Blackberry phone. Appalled by Yvonne's illness and our living conditions, Nana immediately booked us a room in the Moscow Marriott so that Yvonne could recover. After a night in the hotel, Yvonne was better but still looked very green and could not eat one bite of the scrumptious all-you-can-eat breakfast in the elegant Marriott dining room. It irked her no end, seeing the rest of us shoving away eggs Benedict and yogurt with fresh raspberries while she could only watch. Good food meant everything to us on the ride. Paula, Anya, and I felt sad for her. After checking out of the Marriott at about nine, we briefly returned to Gayla, claimed our bikes, and headed for the Trans-Siberian Railway station.

⁓

"What do you mean there are *three* train stations?"

In Paula's neck pouch were $2,200 worth of Trans-Siberian Railroad tickets for the three o'clock train from Yaroslavsky train station. I had hoped to quickly duck inside the relative protection of the Trans-Siberian station, but instead we stood out in the open on a massive city square with train stations on three sides. We looked lost and confused, targets again. Unconsciously, I began scanning for gangs of street children.

"OK, let's not panic. I think I can figure this out," said Paula, taking out her laminated Russian language card.*

---

* For the languages that we did not speak, we carried laminated language cards, which gave us the basic vocabulary and pronunciation to survive. The Russian card also showed the transliteration of

Each of the three railroad stations had a huge sign mounted on its imposing facade, but like everything in Russia it was written in the Cyrillic alphabet. I had never managed to figure out why *pectopah* actually spelled *restaurant*, but Paula, the linguist at heart, had a better grip. She used her laminated alphabet chart to transpose the Cyrillic rail station signs into something that was pronounceable.

"YaROSLAvsky!" spelled out Paula triumphantly as we pushed our tandems underneath the massive sign of the station that would take us to Siberia and then, thankfully, out of Russia to Mongolia. The station clock over the entrance doors read 11:15. We had given ourselves almost four hours until the train's departure at 15:00. From our "no refund" experience with Gayla, we understood that if we missed our train, the $2,200 in prepaid tickets would be lost. We were taking no chances—we thought.

We wheeled our tandems through the center of the cavernous, vaulted main hall, which teemed with hurried travelers flowing around us, as if we were rocks in a stream.

"Paula, I can't disassemble the bikes in these crowds. We'll get equipment and luggage ripped off for sure," I said.

"Over there looks quieter," said Anya, pointing to an alcove near one of the station's side entrances.

We moved our bikes into the alcove, and even though the space was dark, cold, and uninviting, it offered enough room to disassemble the tandems safely. I pulled out my tools and began breaking apart the bikes and shoving the pieces, one by one, into the red, white, and blue woven tarp bags, which we had bought from a street vendor to replace the bike suitcases we had lost in Greece. I love Russian tarp bags! They cost only a few hundred rubles and are huge and tough as nails. They are sewn together from the same nearly indestructible, fiber-infused plastic tarp material that you would cover your wood pile with at home. Fabulous stuff. Having to choose, I would say that Russian tarp bags are probably the one thing the Bolsheviks did right.

"I'm going to scout out where the train platform is," said Paula, our day's leader, as she trekked off toward the far side of the vast building.

---

the Cyrillic alphabet—a lifesaver in a country where, without it, we could not read anything.

Anya and Yvonne spread out their yellow pannier rain covers on the dirty granite floor next to me and settled down to read. Two young fur-capped security guards, shouldering their AK-47s, stopped by, inspecting our curious gear. They joked with Anya and Yvonne that they looked just like their Russian girlfriends back in Kiev and not like Americans at all. They asked a few more questions out of curiosity, but meaning no menace they soon trotted back to their posts near the main station doors.

I had nearly packed up one of our bikes when Paula returned almost thirty minutes later.

"The platform hasn't been announced yet, but a conductor told me that the Trans-Siberian usually arrives at one of the far platforms. I looked. They're really far. Almost a quarter mile away!" said Paula, glancing uneasily at my growing pile of equipment. "I don't like relying on porters, but it looks like we might need one with all this stuff."

I kept working, and by one o'clock I finally zipped closed the last Russian bag. I went to the grimy station bathroom to scrub my grease-stained hands. When I returned, I saw Paula with a porter and his cart in tow. The porter was huge and bald. His shoulders were as wide as a bear's.

We loaded the porter's huge luggage cart, just managing to fit all fourteen bags onto it. Besides the three humongous Russian bags that now held our bikes, the four tandem wheels, and six panniers, we had also gained three bags of food for the train ride. Using her language card and some hand waving, Paula began the negotiations. She showed the porter our tickets to Irkutsk.

"*Skol'ko*—how much?" She swept her hand across the pile on the cart.

Pulling a pen from behind his ear, the porter wrote "500 RUB"— about fifteen dollars—on the palm of his hand.

"*Khorosho*—good."

The porter waved at the board announcing the tracks. Irkutsk was not up yet.

"*Ya vernus*—I will be back," he replied, pointing at 2:00 on his watch.

At two o'clock, an hour before the train, the platform was announced. It was platform 14—the farthest one. We looked around for the porter. Many other porters were hurrying passengers through the station, but no sign of ours. Fifteen minutes later, Paula began getting nervous. By 2:30 she was pacing back and forth across the hall anxiously.

"It's 2:30. Where's the porter? The train is leaving in thirty minutes. It's at least a ten-minute walk from here. It's a really long way."

I tried to move the cart but couldn't. The porter had put a lock on one of the wheels. We watched the station clock tick off another ten minutes and still no porter. At 2:40, twenty minutes before departure, we were in a panic, pulling luggage off the cart, when the porter finally strolled in, smiling. Paula rushed over to him and pressed five hundred rubles into his beefy hand.

"Quickly please, the train leaves in twenty minutes," she pleaded.

The porter turned the notes over in his hands and shook his head.

"What's wrong?" asked Paula. "I thought we agreed on five hundred."

"*Tri tysyachi*," said the porter.

"How much is that?" Paula looked surprised. "I don't know that number."

The porter took the pen from behind his ear and roughly wrote the number "3,000" on Paula's hand. Then he pointed at his watch, smiling.

"Three thousand rubles! That's a hundred dollars! That's total extortion!" Paula shouted. "*Nyet! Nyet!* We said five hundred!"

The porter just stood there, smiling broadly, and pointed again at his watch. He knew that he had us over a barrel. Either give him three thousand rubles or miss the train and lose $2,200 in train tickets.

"You are a very bad man!" Paula yelled in the reverberating hall.

Furious, she spun around and called, "Guys! This guy wants to rip us off for a hundred dollars! Get everything off the cart. We are running for it!"

People were starting to stare at us, wondering what the heck was going on. Looking at the station clock, I was certain we couldn't make it, but since Paula was "leader of the day," the girls and I started ripping bags off the cart as if pursued by demons. I heaved bag after bag onto the girls until they nearly buckled under the weight.

"Go! We've got fifteen minutes! Go!"

---

* Three thousand rubles was the average *monthly* income for Russians at that time.

The girls shot off. Paula was just running back to me when she suddenly halted, spun around, and strode menacingly back to the porter.

"You still have my five hundred rubles!" she screamed.

Grinning, the porter raised his arm and held the money high over his bald head.

"Give me that, you bully!"

"*Bully*, what that?" asked the porter with a bit of English, still smug, taunting her.

"A mean, unfair, cheating jerk, picking on people weaker than them," Paula said, her voice cracking, near tears.

For a moment, I thought she was going to turn away crying when the most extraordinary thing happened. Something snapped, and Paula suddenly charged the porter, screaming, "I'm sick and tired of being cheated, ripped off, and pushed around by thugs like you!"

She ran full-tilt at the porter and smashed into his enormous chest.

"I want my money!" she yelled, her fists pummeling the porter's ribs. "Drop it!" she screamed, her voice echoing in the vast hall, attracting the attention of bystanders all around.

The porter, who had been smug so far, suddenly paled as the screaming, apparently insane American female came for him. He sputtered and reeled around awkwardly, with one arm in the air, trying to get away from the small, surprisingly strong American devil. Alarmed by the commotion, the armed security guards left their posts at the entrance doors and moved toward the crowd of onlookers that was quickly gathering.

"Give me my money!" Paula shouted again and jumped on the porter's back, reaching for the notes in his outstretched hand.

The porter had not expected this and slumped in surprise halfway to his knees. Quick as a cat, Paula rolled from his back onto his outstretched arm, pinning his hand painfully down to the hard granite. The porter groaned, and his hand opened automatically with the pain. Paula snatched the money and was already bolting back toward me when I heard the crowd cheer. The security guards were laughing and poking each other in the ribs. Apparently, they knew the porter's unscrupulous ways and were delighted to see that he had finally met his match in the petite, fiery American.

"Paula, we have ten minutes. Maybe," I shouted over the din of the crowd.

We grabbed five huge bags each and started running through the crowded train station toward platform 14. Besides the heavy bike panniers, we were dragging the food and water for the seven-day train ride that we would almost certainly miss. After just a couple of minutes, my thighs and quads were burning. Paula was stumbling and wheezing, having difficulty running with her asthma. I could hear her breath coming out in ragged gasps. She no longer carried her load but was dragging it across the dirty pavement. A hundred yards ahead of us, I could see the girls dragging their bags the same way.

"Guys, seven minutes and we are screwed," I called as I passed the girls.

"Dad, we can't," yelled Anya.

"Keep going. I'll try to come back."

Just then a small bearded porter with an empty luggage cart came rushing toward us.

"Help you . . . ?"

Still clutching the five hundred rubles in her hand, Paula thrust the money at the porter and pointed to the girls running behind us.

"*Spaziba*," he answered with a quick nod and dashed back to the girls.

A minute later they shot past us with the porter running all out, pushing the overloaded cart at full speed, the wheels clattering so loudly I feared they would come off. Paula managed to quickly throw one of her most cumbersome bags on top of the tottering pile as the cart passed. Paula and I ran on, sweat pouring off our faces.

"Four minutes. Four platforms to go."

When we finally turned onto platform 14, we stared in horror at the moving train. The porter and the girls were running alongside the train, yelling.

"Mom, the tickets!"

Paula lightened her load by dropping two of her bags and leapt forward to catch up with the running girls and porter. A pretty *provodnitsa*, a Russian train stewardess, stood in her trim light-blue uniform at the open door of the moving train, holding out her hand for Paula to thrust her the tickets. While the *provodnitsa* hurriedly clipped the tickets, the girls jumped onto the moving train, squeezing in beside her. The porter kept shoving bag after bag between the *provodnitsa*'s long, bare legs into Anya's and Yvonne's hands, who piled the bags in the narrow space behind them.

Last in line, I was running full speed past the bags that Paula had dropped onto the platform, realizing that I had no way to retrieve them. I had only the slimmest chance to still make the train. I pushed forward with the last bit of my strength and began throwing my bags at the *provodnitsa*, who grabbed them, shaking her head disapprovingly. Completely spent, I snared the oval steel handle beside the receding door and vaulted myself onto the running board.

I looked back at the honest porter standing perplexed on the deserted platform next to Paula's dropped bags. I motioned to him to keep the bags as a tip—both bags were stuffed full of food that we had just bought that morning.

As I turned around, the *provodnitsa* grabbed my arm and pulled me on board. Wagging her finger in front of my face, she scolded me. "You very bad at managing time. Very irresponsible!"

"Yes," I said, panting.

"Your nice children will learn very bad habits. Promise you never do such thing again!"

"I promise," I said. It was futile to try to explain to her what had happened, and besides, I was much too happy to be leaving Moscow to argue.

Compartment 25

Paula

Day 165—Irkutsk Russia

I rubbed my hands jerkily, trying to warm them in the freezing October air. Only a handful of other passengers lurked in the shadows on the gray, concrete train platform in Irkutsk. Hunched silently in the early-morning darkness, a passenger coughed, puffs of his frosty breath wafting under the eerie yellow platform lights. I stamped my feet impatiently. Where was the Trans-Siberian? I tried to peer into the dark, past the massive stone train station, desperate to catch a glimpse of our final train away from Russia. Away, finally, from this godforsaken, depressing, and scary country.

After leaving Moscow, we had rumbled past more than five thousand kilometers of spindly, stunted fir trees, punctuated by occasional lonely ramshackle villages, their only connection to the world the Trans-Siberian Railway from Moscow. Five days later, we had tumbled out onto the Irkutsk platform, a pile of bicycles and panniers stacked in front of us.

Now, waiting for the connecting train to Ulaanbaatar, I counted the minutes until we'd finally leave Russia. Only sixteen more hours on the train, and we'd be crossing the border into Mongolia. So what if Mongolia was the country of wild horseback Mongol raiders and Genghis Khan? That was centuries ago. *Anywhere* else had to be better than Russia!

A sharp whistle pierced the dark winter sky. Shaking the ground as it bellowed smoke from its coal stoves, the Trans-Siberian shrieked and shuddered in front of the platform. Suddenly, the train doors slammed open, steps unfolded below the doors, and a row of conductors, identically clad in gray overcoats and black fur hats, stepped onto the platform. Blowing shrill whistles, they stood at attention along the tracks like a series of toy soldiers, each guarding the entrance to their personal caboose.

Practically hopping with impatience, I grabbed a heavy red-white-and-blue-striped Russian bag containing the dismantled frame of one of our tandems and strode down the tracks. In front of the metal steps to our carriage, a thin Chinese conductor shivered, his pinched shoulders hunched grimly against the biting wind. As he peered at our ticket stubs, the conductor's bloodshot eyes flickered with surprise. He hesitated. A strong unpleasant odor wafted from his breath. Vodka? Then, almost reluctantly, the slightly swaying man motioned us up the stairs.

I climbed up the steps to our carriage and straight into the eighteenth century. Standing in front of me was a tall, silver Russian samovar, boiling water steaming from its top. Below the samovar, I could see the glow of coal flickering through the metal door of the old-fashioned furnace that heated it. Set on a counter nearby, an assortment of teas, sugar, cups, and napkins offered all the necessary accoutrements for the enormous traditional tea urn.

The four of us dragged our heap of panniers and bicycles down a long, narrow, wood-paneled corridor. Above the paneling, blue velvet curtains framed the windows, and below, a floral-patterned carpet led to our compartment. I half expected Anna Karenina and her friends to sweep behind us in rustling gowns.

Lorenz slid the door to our compartment open with a jerk, flipping on the light to the eight-by-six-foot cubicle that would be our room for the next day and night. Two blue velvet-covered bench seats ran the length of the compartment, separated by a narrow walkway. At the far end of the compartment, a large window in the wood-paneled wall provided a view outside—at the moment revealing nothing but the pitch-black early morning.

"OK. Hand me the gear!" Lorenz said, stepping into the compartment. "Tandems first." He lifted one of the blue bench cushions and stared into the luggage storage space below the seats.

"Oh, shit!" Lorenz's face turned ashen. He dropped the cushion suddenly, as if he had grabbed a hot poker. In a flash, he scrambled up onto the bench cushion. Straddling the narrow space between the two long benches, he grabbed the metal bar above the seat and peered into the overhead luggage rack. "Shit! The stuff's everywhere!"

"What? What is it?" I asked, pushing into the compartment, alarmed by the edge in his voice.

"Look!" Lorenz lifted up the blue bench cushion again.

"What the—?" I stared at the sharp metal tip of a hypodermic needle poking out from the partially opened zipper of a red-and-blue bulging Russian bag. No, not one bag. A stack of bulging bags and suspicious brown cardboard boxes filled the entire storage area below the bench seat. Lorenz leaned over and yanked the zipper open. My heart pounded rapidly as the contents spilled out. Small packages wrapped in brown paper and string. Tiny vials filled with yellow liquid. Plastic containers of strange pills.

"Drugs!" I croaked. "It can't be. No. No," I practically sobbed. "This is *not* happening to us!" I dropped the bench seat, shaking. "No! We must have the wrong compartment!"

I stepped out of the door and shoved a trembling hand into my coat pocket, feeling for the tickets. "Compartment 25," I read the ticket again, then looked at the number on the door. In bold, clear numbers, on a label next to the door, our compartment number stared back at me. Number 25.

"What's wrong?" Anya elbowed Yvonne as they both pushed inside the door to stare at the luggage storage area. Yvonne's blue eyes widened like saucers.

"Let me off. Let me off the train. I want to go hooooome," Yvonne wailed as she backed away from the door.

"Get this stuff out of here!" Lorenz commanded, paying no attention to Yvonne's cries. "If the Russian border guards find drugs in our compartment . . ."

I tried to swallow, but my mouth was dry. What would happen if the border guards found these bags under our seats? A terrifying picture flashed in my mind of Lorenz screaming in agony as Russian border guards beat him to a pulp in the corridor. Last time we had gotten off easy—a few hundred rubles for some plastic Greek worry beads at the border of Estonia. But what would we have to pay for smuggled drugs as we crossed into Mongolia? A thousand dollars? Ten thousand? A hundred thousand?

And if we didn't have that much? I shuddered as I imagined a burly border guard carting Anya and Yvonne off the train, locking them in some horrible concrete cell. I bent over gasping, trying to breathe. We had to get rid of this stuff. *Now.*

I swallowed hard, trying to think straight. "I'm getting the conductor," I said, willing my shaking legs to move. Crap. All we had to do was take *one last train, one stupid little train* out of here. This train was supposed to get us out of this hellhole, not straight into some Siberian jail. "Crap, crap, crap!" I muttered as I hurried down the long, narrow train corridor to the conductor's cabin at the end. Why did the drugs have to be in *our* compartment? And why did *I* have to be the leader today? I froze as I realized that if I screwed up, I could kill my family. This was way too much responsibility!

The conductor followed me back, looking highly irritated. A strong whiff of alcohol surrounded the thin man as he just stood there, impassive, saying nothing. He knows, I realized with a shock. He knows! He's in on this. Someone must have paid him to keep the bags in our compartment, and we're screwing up the plan. Well, to hell with his plan! We were *not* getting mixed up in this! I grabbed a Russian bag and tossed it firmly to Anya outside the compartment door. "*Nyet!*" I shouted.

The bag burst open, spilling its contents on the floor. The conductor's eyes narrowed with disapproval. A volley of completely unintelligible

Chinese words cascaded from his mouth as he pointed to the scattered syringes and brown paper packages in the corridor, clearly displeased with the turn of events. Standing steadfastly at the door to our compartment, Lorenz's tall figure looming menacingly over the thin, short man.

"This stuff is not coming back in here," he shouted and heaved another box into the hallway.

Hunching his shoulders in resignation, the Chinese man stared mutely at this strange American couple with a weeping child and heaps of bicycle parts and little brown packages scattered in the corridor. Sensing that debate was futile, he slid off, defeated, along the patterned flower carpet to his tiny cabin at the end of the caboose.

Half an hour later, perhaps reinforced with a second bottle of vodka, the sallow-faced conductor reappeared at our door, swaying significantly more. He smiled at me wanly, deliberately avoiding my husband's challenging eyes, and waved a wobbly arm at the five-foot-high pile we had stacked outside of our door. I followed him as he wove unsteadily down the rocking hallway to the small metal platform connecting cabooses at the end of the carriage. He pointed vigorously to the open metal platform, then back to the stack of brown boxes and bulging Russian bags in front of our compartment.

I was glad to be rid of this dreadful pile! I stared at the wobbly stack we had hauled to the platform at the end of the caboose, puzzled. Were these legal pharmaceuticals? Illegal drugs? Maybe this was a shipment of lifesaving medications? No, there was more to this. Why hadn't the owner put them in his own compartment? Or shipped the boxes via the baggage car? Why didn't he come and claim them? Something wasn't right here. I wished fervently the bags would just disappear.

Back in our compartment, I felt jittery. What if we had overlooked a random syringe or vial hidden between the cushions? I jumped each time a passenger wandered by our compartment, afraid they were the owner of the drugs. Would they throw us off the train? Force us at knifepoint to put the bags back under our seats? I gazed out the window at the undulating brown treeless steppe whizzing by, occasional drifts of snow the only relief in the landscape. We had turned south from Lake Baikal a couple of hours after we left Irkutsk, and except for one sad, gray town with belching concrete smokestacks and muddy, unpaved roads lined with dilapidated wooden buildings, there had been no sign of life in this remote southern corner of Siberia. If they threw us off the train here, we'd surely die.

As the sun began to set, the conductor returned, swaying a little less but looking increasingly irritated with us. Motioning to the latches on the walls above our seats, he dropped the two upper bunk beds. Silently, he laid out linens and blankets for the two upper and two lower beds and disappeared. With a click, Lorenz locked the compartment door behind him as I crawled into a lower bunk. Turning on my side, I pulled the wool blanket up over my head and tried to stop thinking about the drug-filled boxes and bags swaying between the cabooses as the train hurtled south in the night.

<hr />

I woke with a start. How long had I slept? I could not tell. The train's brakes screeched loudly. It lurched. And then stopped. Silence. Dead silence. I looked at my watch. Midnight.

I wrapped a blanket around me and stepped onto the carpeted floor of our compartment, pressing my nose against the outside window. In front of me lay a desolate landscape. The moon was shining, casting an eerie, silvery glow over the silent steppe. Not a house or building or even an animal interrupted the vast, bleak, treeless expanse.

"Where are we?" I whispered to Lorenz, who was fumbling in the pitch-black in his bunk bed across from me. I could hear him slip onto the floor.

"Somewhere near the border, I think. Maybe we're waiting at a switching station. They might be assembling the guards to board the train at the border."

Border guards! I shivered uncontrollably. Suddenly, I heard footsteps. Thud thud thud. Three heavy shapes stomped past our compartment window along the dimly lit hallway.

"Who was that?"

"I don't know. Looked like three men."

Lorenz looked at my terrified face. "I don't think they were guards. They didn't have uniforms." He opened the door and slipped out. "I'm going to see what's up."

Before I could protest, he was gone. I returned to the window, pressing my nose against the icy glass. Looking for—I didn't know—a way out of this horrible nightmare. From the corner of my eye, I glimpsed a strange shadow standing outdoors near the tracks at the end of our caboose. He was gazing up at the platform where we had piled the drugs. In a flash, three bulky figures jumped from the end of our carriage, hauling what appeared to be large bags on their backs. And then, as silently as they appeared, the figures melted into the night.

A few minutes later, Lorenz slid open the compartment door and sat down on his bunk again, breathing heavily. "Did you see those guys jump off the train?"

I nodded. "Where were they going? We're in the middle of nowhere."

"Not sure, but they were carrying the drugs with them."

"How do you know?"

"One of the guys tripped, and the bag on his back fell and burst open. I could see syringes and pills as they spilled out!"

The train suddenly lurched. A thud. Then it swayed as the wheels screeched forward in complaint. We were off again. Barely ten minutes later, a series of piercing whistles woke everyone up. Wheels screeched, and the train stopped again. Compartment doors started banging. I could hear feet shuffling down the hall.

"*Soyti s poyedza!*" someone was shouting. Doors slid open then slammed shut. "*Soyti s poyedza!*" A tall border guard's pinched face appeared at our door as he rapped sharply.

"Why do we have to get off the train?" Yvonne complained, rubbing her eyes, as we joined the line of sleepy passengers shuffling down the corridor. Many of us were still in our pajamas, wool coats and warm hats pulled on hurriedly over green striped cotton pants or blue long underwear.

"I think we're at the border of Mongolia." I put my arm around her as we stood in the paneled carriage hallway. "The guards probably want to check our passports."

She stared at me wide-eyed. She hadn't forgotten our ripped-open panniers and tossed, crumpled clothing after the border guards had "inspected us" the last time.

We shambled behind the crowd in the hallway to the end of the caboose. At the top of the stairs, I peered through the door at the metal platform between our carriages. The pile of drugs was gone.

The passengers stood in clusters on the train platform, whispering nervously. Behind us rose a large, silent brick building, presumably the station. The building was unlit, and its heavy doors were locked. Across the tracks, a high wire fence followed the rails. Trapped outdoors, the crowd shuffled quietly in the middle of the night, stamping feet and blowing into their hands in the frigid air. Waiting.

At the end of the platform, I could see four tall men in thick, gray uniforms, guns sticking out of the holsters on their hips. I reached nervously for the neck pouch with our passports. But instead of walking up to the passengers, the border guards began climbing up the steps to the last caboose of the train. Suddenly, all the steps to the train were hauled up and the doors locked menacingly. Thud. Thud. Thud.

"What are they doing?" Anya asked, shivering in the cold.

"I think they're inspecting the compartments," a young woman's voice piped up next to us. She sounded Scandinavian. "Probably looking for drugs and other illegal stuff. They check everywhere. Under the seats. Even lift the panels off the ceilings and check in there."

My stomach did flip-flops as I thought about the drugs. I prayed fervently that the smugglers had taken everything. That we had not missed a syringe or bottle of pills somewhere in our compartment.

An hour later I stood at the window of our compartment as the train rumbled slowly over the border into Mongolia. For the first time in weeks, I felt the knot between my shoulders ease. Outside the window, the wild, empty Mongolian steppe slipped by under a silvery moon. The formless landscape had not changed, and yet—maybe it was my imagination—Mongolia felt different. Hopeful. Free. I sent up a deep, heartfelt prayer of thanks. We had survived Russia. Barely.

I laid back down on my bunk, pulling the woolen blanket up to my chin. As my eyelids slowly began to droop, I wondered what Mongolia would be like. Anything had to be better than corrupt border guards, thieving street children, swindling train porters, and drug smugglers. I drifted off to sleep with visions of wild, free, dark-haired Mongolian men on horseback, hooves pounding across the empty steppe as they carried a pile of red-and-blue-striped bags of drugs far, far, far away from the Russian border.

PART IV

LOST IN TRANSLATION

Into the Fire

Paula

Day 167—Ulaanbaatar, Mongolia

The train screeched into the station at Ulaanbaatar as the sun inched upward over the vast dry horizon. I peered nervously from the window at the end of our carriage, hoping, praying that Mongolia would not be as dangerous and depressing as Russia. Outside, a throng of shouting, laughing voices lurched toward the train, hands stretching forward to grasp the bags and boxes and passengers descending excitedly from the steps. Brawny men wrapped in calf-length brown woolen coats clasped each other with delight, jabbing each other with affectionate punches.

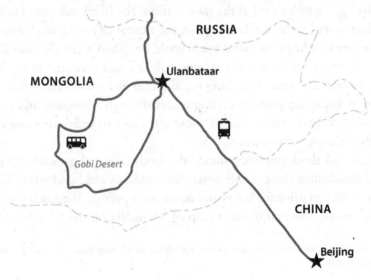

Laughing dark-eyed women in long red jackets swayed with cries of happiness, their long, dark hair swishing back and forth over their blue waist sashes. And laughing broad-faced children darted excitedly between the boxes and the bustling crowd.

I sighed with relief at the brilliant colors and the laughing, smiling people. Mongolia was nothing like Russia! But what was it like? I struggled to recognize the musky scent hanging over the crisp, late-October air. Tobacco? Coffee? Wet soil? The thick, earthy odor permeated the colors, the cries, the very texture of this strange, wild place. This was the rich, pungent scent of camel and horse dung* burning in the thousands of tiny Mongolian *gers* or tent homes surrounding the nomadic city of Ulaanbaatar. This smell was Mongolia's lifeblood—the glowing dung embers providing the flicker of warmth and light in the cold nights, the flavor that seeped into the mutton stew and the boiled herb teas. But I did not know this as we stumbled down the stairs of the train to the bustling platform, gasping in bewilderment as a loud, boisterous crowd of guides clustered around us, handing us cards and brochures advertising their tours.

~ ~

We sat in the lobby of our hotel in Ulaanbaatar, talking to a guide who had given us his card at the train station. The hotel was one of only a few four-story "high-rise" buildings in the capital city—if a small core of permanent buildings on paved roads could be called a city. Surrounding this permanent center was the strangest sight I had ever seen in my life: a ring of nomadic tents stretching for miles on dirt roads around the city. We were discussing possible cycling routes through Mongolia, and I was beginning to have serious doubts about our plans to pedal for a week by ourselves through the country.

"I do not think you understand," the guide repeated patiently. "If you leave Ulaanbaatar, there is only desert for hundreds and hundreds of kilometers. You can drive for hours and never see a person. The roads you see on your map?" He pointed to a map of Mongolia on the table between

---

* In the treeless Gobi Desert, the primary fuel available is dried dung from the herds of camels, sheep, and horses.

us. "They are dirt. They do not have signs. You need to know the country, or you will get lost." He shifted uncomfortably. "And if you get lost, it is very dangerous. There is little water. Even now, in the winter, there is not snow. The desert is too dry."

"There are no paved roads?" Lorenz asked, surprised.

"Paved roads do not work with the sand. And the wind. They are covered quickly in the desert. It is easier if most of the roads are dirt." The guide paused, perplexed. How could these foreigners not understand? "It is not like in your country. Phones do not work in the desert. And we do not have—how do you say—searching people?"

I looked at Lorenz, distressed. We had barely made it through Russia, and now we were talking about cycling with children through hundreds of kilometers of uninhabited desert in a country with no roads or water! Had we just jumped out of the frying pan and into the fire?

"How do people get between the towns then?" I asked.

The guide smiled politely, trying not to be insulted by this ignorant foreigner. "By camels and horses. They know the desert. They don't need roads." He continued quickly, ignoring the worry on my face. "We have towns. Yes. Some. But many people prefer to live the traditional Mongolian way—in tents. They move around, following their herds of camels and sheep. They are called—nomads is the word, I think?"

"Ooh." Yvonne's eyes widened. "They're like us then! We move around and camp in new places. We must be nomads too."

"Really?" The guide's eyes crinkled in a smile as he realized that perhaps we were not so completely different after all. "Even so, I think it would be better if you did not bicycle here. But I think you can still camp." He pulled out a card as he stood up to leave. "This is a name of a friend. He knows the desert very well. He grew up there. He can drive you to the places you want to see in his van. And at night you can sleep with Mongolian families in their tents."

As the guide walked out the glass foyer door, I sighed. After Russia, I'd had enough danger for a lifetime. Forget biking through Mongolia! Maybe we should just get back on the train and continue straight to Beijing? Or—I glanced at the card in Lorenz's hand—why not take a nice, comfortable, easy trip around Mongolia in a heated van instead?

World Bike Bits

Bits and stories about World Bike for Breath. A Bulletin for sponsors. Volume 4

A Light in the Dark

Editor's note: This special newsletter is a bit out of order but one of the best yet!

I am writing this newsletter to you by candlelight from a Mongolian *ger* (yurt) in the Gobi Desert. For the past ten days, we have been traveling along almost nonexistent dirt tracks over the vast brown, red, and ochre Mongolian steppe. Briefly trading in our tandems for a ride in a bumpy, dusty Russian off-road van, we have shared our days with herds of camels, horses, yaks, sheep, and goats led by proud, purple-cloaked Mongolian horsemen pounding down the rolling hills. Each night we share their simple yet beautifully decorated round felt tent homes, cooking our meals on their dung stoves. I am amazed and inspired by a people who live their days fighting the fierce wind and sun and their nights battling the ice and snow in the tiny *gers*, the light from their stoves flickering like tiny stars across the wilderness.

Each evening as I listen to the soft, uncomplaining coughing of the children around the smoky dung fires, I am reminded of my reason for being here. For respiratory illnesses kill more children in the developing world than any other disease. I think of the cheerful Polish farmer, Anton, who smiled and joked between coughs and wheezes as he served us mushrooms gathered from the woods, along with jellied meat and tea. Like me, he has asthma. But unlike me, he does not have access to the medicines that make it possible for me to cycle around the world. So he chokes and struggles to breathe unnecessarily, as do millions of other people throughout the world.

Then there is Brenda, a generous Englishwoman who returned half the price she was charging for her bed and breakfast when she heard the purpose of our ride. Her sister and brother both have asthma (though luckily not herself), she said, and so this was her contribution. Yet as she served us an extraordinary English breakfast of fried eggs, ham, tomatoes, peppers, mushrooms, toast, juice, coffee, and cereal, her high-pitched wheezing made me wonder. Sadly, millions of people with asthma go untreated—misdiagnosed or undetected—each year.

But perhaps my strongest reason for continuing on this journey is a little boy named Tim, who left a message on the World Bike for Breath answering machine a few weeks before we left for Greece.

"My name is Tim. I live in Victoria, Canada," a small voice began. "I'm very excited about your ride." He paused, then continued hurriedly, "I'm six years old and"—adding in a quiet voice—"I have asthma."

Tim is not alone; 10 percent of his classmates probably have asthma too. And this year over 450,000 people, hoping, like Tim, for a cure, will not get to see if our world ride succeeds. They will die from asthma before we return.

For the past few nights, before snuggling up in my sleeping bag in the *ger*, I have stood in the snow under a brilliant sky filled with so many stars that the limitless expanse of the desert seems insignificant. Yet as I gaze at the tiny solitary *ger* in the wilderness, its firelight bravely glowing among the stars, I am humbled by the tenacity of the human spirit. If here, in one of the most remote and inhospitable environments of the world, life is not defeated, then it seems that nothing is truly impossible. And no matter how small we may sometimes feel, like the *ger* in the desert night, it only takes one dream to light up the sky.

Route Update—Poland to Beijing

Dear friends and sponsors,

Hooray! We are now in Beijing, China, and connected again to the world after a long and challenging stretch through the former Soviet Union and Mongolia. Our family has been on the road six months, cycled over five thousand kilometers, traveled halfway around the world from Greece to China, camped over 120 nights, and visited sixteen different countries. Throughout it all, Anya and Yvonne have been amazing—overcoming physical and emotional challenges that would daunt even the most courageous and hardy adults. And our family has become closer and more tight-knit as we face and survive each new adventure together.

But we still have a lot of distance to cover in the next six months before returning to the US. Our goal is to be back in Seattle, ready for our major fundraising and asthma awareness push across North America, by World Asthma Day—May 9!

With each passing day, I find a growing faith in the need for this ride. As we pedaled through Polish towns suffocated with the black smell of burning coal (to heat their homes), as we choked from the clouds of exhaust from the Russian buses, as we gaped at the hundreds of people walking the streets with masks to protect themselves from the smog in

Beijing, and as we met person after person suffering from asthma on this trip, I have become convinced that asthma and air pollution are issues that we must address within our lifetimes. I am proud and thankful that you are each part of this adventure—helping to make a difference that could change the entire world!

The route update is as follows:

- Kilometers for asthma and clean air: 5,203
- Miles for asthma and clean air: 3,134
- New countries cycled for asthma: Poland, Lithuania, Latvia, Estonia, Russia, Mongolia,* China

---

* We traveled through Mongolia by Russian van.

Snowstorm

Paula

Day 182—Beijing, China

Snow fell in thick heavy flakes, covering Beijing in a carpet of white. Overnight the bustling royal city had transformed into a glittering maze of frosted willow trees bending over twisting snowy alleyways. Colorful storefronts proclaimed their wares under snow-rimmed red-and-yellow banners. And green corner street signs, etched with unintelligible Chinese characters, stood proudly over tall mounds of white.

Our tandems leaned at an odd angle in the drifts of snow behind the Beijing Youth Hostel, handlebars and seats covered with a thick white crust.

"Maybe we should stay another day," I suggested, gazing uneasily at the honking stream of cars, carts, and bicycles sliding and swerving down the street in front of us.

"It's just a freak early November storm. It'll be gone in a few hours," Lorenz pronounced confidently. "Look. The sidewalks are almost clear already." I stared at the swarm of laughing, pantalooned shopkeepers busily sweeping the nearby sidewalks with palm brooms. Perhaps he was right.

"Well, if you're sure." I tried to swallow my apprehensions. "You're the leader today."

I walked reluctantly up the hostel stairs to collect the panniers. Really! What's a bit of snow? We'd biked in snow plenty of times to get to classes at Northwestern during grad school. Still, I couldn't shake the nagging feeling that Lorenz was a little too hopeful.

━ ～

The snow continued to fall thickly as we clipped into the toe cleats on our tandems. Within minutes, large wet flakes iced our eyelashes and created frothy mounds on our gloves and helmets. Wobbling through a pile of icy slush, we skidded onto the main road. Suddenly, we slid into a churning sea of bicycles. Undaunted by the early November storm, an uninterrupted stream of intrepid morning bicycle commuters flowed past us down the enormous eleven-foot-wide bicycle lanes on each side of the road. On my right, a jet-black-haired girl in a smart red jacket and mittens pedaled alongside us. On our other side, a cyclist in a thin gray jacket and pants slowly pulled a wooden wagon laden with snow-covered guava and persimmons, probably headed for the morning market. Ahead a businessman wearing patent leather shoes and a tie suddenly swerved to weave around a three-wheeled bicycle food vending cart—its purple and red bean buns bouncing temptingly on the metal shelves behind the frosty glass panes.

Biking through the heavy white drifts in this teeming city of twenty-one million people felt like skiing a hazardous slalom course. Ahead a stalled car blocked the center of the road—angry, honking cars jockeying for position in the slick, sliding mass swarming past it. Trapped in the crowd, a cyclist towing a cart piled high with slippers rang his bell frantically. *Brrring brrring*, it shrilled as an ashen-faced elderly man slid precariously past the cart, skidding on a hidden patch of ice. The churning, frothing mass of bicycles, cars, mopeds, and carts swept forward, pulling us with them. Onward, onward the jumble of shouting voices, screeching brakes, and clanging bells pushed us. Onward to the busy stores, onward to the bustling offices, onward to China's bright future.

By noon we finally reached the outskirts of Beijing. Pedaling out of the gigantic, sprawling, twisting city had taken hours. Here the roads were less chaotic, laid out in planned straight lines. In contrast to the ancient, picturesque, narrow alleyways of Beijing's historic center, these enormous thoroughfares were lined with stark steel-and-glass high-rise buildings. I shivered in the dark canyons under the silent skyscrapers, suddenly missing the noise and laughter of the bustling inner city.

Lorenz had been right. The thick morning snowfall did end—only to be replaced by a slow, icy drizzle of sleet and rain. The roads transformed into a dirty, freezing slush. Icy water sloshed around my soaked toes. My gloves clung soggily to my aching hands, fingers so cold they barely felt the handlebars. Black, gritty spray flew up from the bicycle tires onto our faces, jackets, and rain paints. The quaint picturesque scene of historic Beijing in winter melted in my mind into a muddy, endless, frigid metropolis.

I slogged forward, working hard to breathe as the old familiar band tightened around my chest. My lungs rasped, angry and irritated by the icy, dry air mixed with Beijing's ever-present gray smog. No wonder most residents wore masks outdoors. I slowed to a crawl and pulled my turtleneck up over my mouth, trying to put a barrier between my lungs and the freezing daggers piercing them.

"Are you OK, Momma?" Anya asked as she pedaled behind me.

I lifted my arm up, nodding OK. With the collar of the turtleneck covering my mouth, a moist cushion of warm air was now flowing into my lungs, calming them down. A simple trick—one of the many little adaptations I had learned to manage my asthma and keep it under control over the years.

"I'm *soo* cold. My feet are frozen," Yvonne moaned, shivering as we stood waiting miserably at yet another asphalt six-laned intersection for the light to turn. Her hair lay plastered in icy clumps onto her cheeks. Her bright red nose contrasted starkly with her cheeks, ashen and white in the frigid air. "Can't we stop?"

Captaining the tandem in front, Lorenz gritted his teeth in irritation. Yvonne had been complaining behind him in the stoker's seat for the past hour. Cold and wet and, I suspected, not half so confident about his decision to pedal off in the snow this morning, Lorenz looked sullen and angry.

"Look, here are some plastic bags." He thrust a handful of large Ziploc bags into her hands. "Tie them around your feet. It'll help keep them dry."

With stiff, unbending hands, I helped Yvonne and Anya wrap the plastic bags over their socks. With a set of plastic bags tied around my own feet, I squeezed them into my wet, soggy, cold shoes. Within minutes, icy water had seeped into the bags again. This time, the plastic bags held the water in, sloshing against my toes each time I turned the pedals.

"Everyone's cold, Lorenz." My tandem slid to a stop at the next stoplight alongside Yvonne, who looked like she was ready to cry. My hands were so numb and heavy I could barely grasp the brakes. "We can't go on. We need to find somewhere warm to dry out."

Lorenz looked over at me, clearly annoyed at my complaints. Sure, he was leader of the day, but dragging us out into this snowy, icy mess was—well, honestly—a dumb idea. We should never have left the hostel! I glanced around the canyon of towering steel high-rise buildings looking for a store, a restaurant, any place to warm up.

"Over there!" Yvonne pointed to the corner of a busy intersection. "A restaurant! Can we eat there? *Please?*"

"Where?" I asked, puzzled, gazing at a sign displaying unintelligible, bright red characters.

"No, Mom, across the street. Look. At the bottom of that black skyscraper. See the picture of the noodle bowl?" I peered again, still unable to see anything that remotely looked like a restaurant. At last I saw it. A sign with a picture of a bowl of noodles and chopsticks hanging above a steamy window filled with people huddled at tables.

We found a tiny table in the noodle shop, crammed among the throng of slurping customers. The soupy noodles, decked with unrecognizable but tasty green floating vegetables, soon warmed us up. But Lorenz was determined to visit the emperor's Summer Palace today. Half an hour later, we were out in the cold again. At least the rain had finally stopped.

I pulled on my soaking wet gloves, muttering under my breath. This whole trip was a goose chase. What were the odds the Summer Palace was even open? I was close, very close, to mutiny, but I'd already learned the hard way that running this trip by committee was a disaster. I bit my tongue and pedaled angrily ahead.

***

"So you were right. The Summer Palace *is* open," I admitted grudgingly to Lorenz as we pulled our tandems up to a frail chain-link fence in the parking lot in front of the emperor's Summer Palace.

The waning winter sun cast a weak yellow glow over the ornate, red-pillared entrance gates. I looked in surprise at the palace gate's colorful tiers, surrounded by snow-covered trees and gardens. This was such a stark difference from the Forbidden City, which we had visited several days earlier in the center of Beijing's old city. There, the massive, intimidating pink brick walls that surrounded the imperial palace closed off the inhabitants of the emperor's permanent court, only allowing special guests in through small doors in the imposing walls. The Forbidden City was clearly intended to keep people out. In contrast, the Summer Palace almost beckoned visitors into its beautiful gardens behind the gate. No wonder the emperor and his court liked to spend summers wandering through the intentionally natural landscaping of this ornate, almost playful palace set below a magnificent backdrop of unspoiled mountains, far from the heat and intrigue of the Forbidden City.

Lorenz stared uncertainly at the chain-link fence, looking around the parking lot for a safer spot to lock the tandems. When we had tried to enter the palace gardens, the guard's wild hand and facial gestures had made it quite clear that the tandems could not come with us. But we couldn't just leave the tandems unprotected out here, piled high with all our clothing and gear!

"May we help you?" a polite voice in English interrupted our deliberations. I turned to the voice, surprised to see a kindly, well-dressed Chinese couple smiling at us. "We are English teachers. My name is Chao." The gentleman bowed slightly and graciously opened his arms. "And this is my wife, Jia. Perhaps we can assist you?"

A few minutes later, thanks to Chao's interpreting, Lorenz and I were wheeling the tandems into a locked compound behind the guard's gate. The next thing I knew, Jia and Chao were escorting us through the palace gates, chatting away happily to Anya and Yvonne.

I gasped at the breathtaking winter wonderland of snow-covered trees as we stepped into the garden together. Before us lay a gently rolling landscape of white-capped pagodas guarded by frosted statues of dragons. The snow made everything so beautiful! For the next two hours, we strolled together under the richly decorated seven-hundred-meter promenade of the Long Corridor while Chao explained the mythical stories depicted in the hundreds of scenes painted above us. Reaching the boathouse on the shores of Kunming Lake, Jia narrated the story of the ornate stone boat that demonstrated that the emperor had infinite power—for who else could keep a stone boat afloat on water? Finally, we returned under the snow-covered roofs of the colorful Suzhou Market Street, which, according to Chao, provided an opportunity for courtesans to "play shop" since, in real life, all their necessities were purchased for them by servants.

With the last of the sun's rays spreading crimson across the incredible backdrop of jagged mountains shimmering in the palace gardens' lakes, the six of us finally stepped back through the gates of the Summer Palace.

"Where is your hotel?" Chao asked as we stood shaking hands, awkwardly saying goodbye. "Perhaps we can show you the way."

"We were just going to look for a small pension around here," Lorenz replied. "Do you have any suggestions?"

"It will be difficult. There were many small hotels here once. But"— Chao pointed to a string of empty lots between a set of dilapidated row houses—"as you can see, everything is being torn down for new build-ings. The Olympics will be soon. And China wants to show the world a modern city."

I stared uneasily at the darkening streets and shivered. My feet were still wet and cold, and the air had taken on a decided chill now that the sun had set.

Chao spoke quickly with Jia in Chinese, then turned back to Lorenz. "If you would like, we can walk with you. To help you find a hotel. You may need help translating perhaps?"

We most certainly did!

The massive building towered above the little maze of icy, muddy streets behind us. We had been wandering for over half an hour now, looking for a pension with no success. Without warning, we had spilled into a wide, open plaza in front of this gigantic structure. One entire side of the plaza was overtaken by the modern three-story metal-and-concrete edifice. Hanging across the front of the building was a stupen-dous iron chain, each link at least ten feet long. And under the chain, a twenty-foot-tall statue stood guarding the entrance. The entire scene was surreal. Was this a modern art museum? A crazy billionaire's mansion?

I turned to ask Jia and Chao about the statue and iron chain, but the couple had disappeared, leaving us to cower in the building's deep shad-ows, shivering as the wintry wind whipped across the empty plaza. It had been bad enough biking in the snow and the slush. Now, with the sun already down and our hopes of finding a bed for the night dwindling by the minute, I was feeling increasingly worried. If I had to grade Lorenz's leadership today on a scale from one to ten, I'd say he deserved about a minus five. And that was just being generous because of the visit to the Summer Palace.

Suddenly, our hosts reappeared. "You can spend the night here," Chao said, pointing to the bizarre chain-wrapped building. "They have sleeping rooms for guests."

"But you must first pay for the baths," Jia added. "It is a—how do you say—bathhouse?"

Our tandems standing on the hotel roof in Athens after Lorenz had assembled them there in secret.

We often camped in farmers' fields. At this German farm, the friendly farmer and his wife not only let us camp but also let us use their shower and gave us breakfast!

We never saw or had a bicycle accident, but we witnessed five car and motorcycle accidents firsthand, like this one in Germany.

Paula with her bike in the town center of a medieval German town on the Romantic Road. We sewed country patches onto our bike panniers so that we could explain to curious folks where we had been, especially in countries where we could not speak the language.

Not all of our route was picturesque. The air quality in the German Ruhrgebiet was so bad we were covered in soot at the end of each cycling day.

Studying in unorthodox locations was Yvonne's and Anya's life. Here they are doing homework in a field by the sea in Sweden.

Much to the detriment of our bicycle wheels, dirt roads became more and more common as we entered eastern Europe. Carved wooden poles by the side of the road were a common sight in Lithuania.

Remember, whenever you use a hammer to repair your bike, you're doing it wrong. The roads in the former Soviet countries were so bad the bikes started to routinely break spokes. Replacing them was a major chore without large tools.

We stayed in this Latvian farmhouse on a cold October night. It had a large tile fireplace that heated the entire house beautifully, but there was no running water, and Yvonne had to fetch water from the icy well in the morning.

The entirety of our gear sitting on a luggage cart to go onto the Trans-Siberian train. This photo was taken minutes before Paula's showdown with the Russian porter. Paula is looking worried.

The Ebers in front of a ger they shared with a Mongolian herdsman family for the night.

Biking on China's congested streets was a challenge, but Chinese drivers are used to lots of bikes on the road. Lorenz calls this image "Grandma's worst nightmare" since he can just see Anya and Yvonne's grandmother waking up in a cold sweat with this dream image still fresh in her mind.

This Japanese couple served us a hot breakfast at six in the morning in a school playground.

When we were lost and had to ask directions, the girls would break out their books and read while the adults figured out where we had gone wrong. In this image, we had accidentally cycled into a remote Japanese mountain valley at dusk.

Taiwan's east coast has stunning scenery: tropical ocean views, tunnels, and bridges crossing craggy mountain gorges.

Some Australian wildlife is benign if not approached, but then there are the more deadly species like funnel-web spiders, sharks, and saltwater crocs that you definitely want to stay away from.

Bicycling on Australia's coast was extremely grueling; it is the world's most challenging combination of heat and monster hills.

We had some miserably rainy days. Here we are in the bush of Australia, where you would least expect it.

In Seaspray, Australia, we rented a cabin and celebrated Anya's fourteenth birthday. Gifts were very small and light.

Pristine tropical beach pictures usually don't show the ever-present biting insects so common in the tropics. However, during our stay in the island kingdom of Tonga, a bug managed to crawl into Lorenz's camera and started to appear in different places on every image of the entire roll of film (here in the upper left corner). Not until Eric, our photography friend, had developed the roll of film and called us frantically from the US did we realize the bug was in there.

A group of Tongans preparing a giant Easter pig roast for the entire village.

Anya and Lorenz prepare lunch as we stop in the Columbia River gorge in eastern Oregon.

In the western United States, most towns allow you to camp in city parks and at fairgrounds.

In North Dakota, the wind finally became a tailwind, and we were able to enjoy the stunning vistas along the Missouri River.

On the home stretch, along the beautiful 184-mile-long Chesapeake and Ohio Canal into Washington, DC.

It was an odd, if somewhat enticing, proposition. I would give anything to get into a warm, dry bed. And given my muddy, frozen state, a warm bath was worth every extra penny! I nodded a definite "yes" vote to Lorenz. No point in asking complicated questions about bathhouses that rented beds. We wouldn't understand the answers anyway.

I had hoped that once we got through Russia, that would be the end of our difficulties. But China and Mongolia had come with their own challenges. Ever since we had stepped off the train in Ulaanbaatar, my brain could barely handle the sensory overload. Traveling on a bicycle, interacting with local people who had never even seen a blond-haired family in their lives, we were plunged deeply and rapidly inside the local culture. Each day brought a new, strange, unexpected experience—sleeping with nomads in a *ger*, cooking over a dung fire, cycling in a throng of noisy, colorful cyclists pulling wagons of fruit and buns. It was exhilarating, exhausting, and overwhelming. Looking at the bizarre looming building with the chain in front of us, I worried about what we had signed up for this time.

I'm sure this culture shock is just temporary, I thought hopefully. Really, how strange can things get? We'll stop being surprised sooner or later. Asia just *has* to get easier.

⚬

Fifteen minutes later, Anya, Yvonne, and I were standing in a sleek, modern dressing room. After taking off our muddy, frozen shoes at the front door, handing our luggage to a polite uniformed porter, and sliding our feet into plastic sandals, our family had parted ways. Lorenz had been escorted by a silent young man in a starched blue jacket to the men's part of the building. We three females had followed a petite young Chinese woman in a beautiful silk *quipao* (high-collared dress) to this room. Shyly, she held out three soft white robes, then backed away politely.

Alone in the room, we stared at our horrifying images in the mirror. Dirt-spattered jackets. Stiff hair plastered to our heads. Bright red noses. Woodenly, I tugged off my muddy jacket, my fingers aching as the blood slowly tried to return to my hands. Next to me, Anya peeled off her soggy rain pants while Yvonne struggled with her sweatshirt, pulling hard to disentangle the wet cuffs clinging to her wrists. My Lycra cycling tights were almost painful to remove, plastered to my legs like sticky wallpaper. I dropped them on the filthy pile accumulating on the bench. Below the pile, a little stream of mud dripped down to the floor of the sparkling room of gleaming white countertops and polished wooden benches. Feeling embarrassed, I quickly scooped the clothes up and hid them in our cupboards. Finally, I slid my arms into the clean white robe, savoring its thick warmth and soft scent of soap.

The three of us opened the door at the end of the changing room, unsure what to do next. We stepped into an enormous glistening blue-and-white-tiled room filled with a series of sweet scented bathtubs, steaming showers, and—in the center of it all—a swimming-pool-sized jacuzzi hot tub. A handful of naked Chinese women lay in the tubs or reclined on the lounges, talking softly to each other. I stared down at my muddy feet, trying to wiggle them farther into the plastic sandals to hide them.

An attendant led us to a wall of steaming hot showers. For a moment, I hesitated, embarrassed about the idea of standing in the nude in front of her. Then, unable to resist the enticing misty warm jets for even one second longer, I threw away all modesty, handed her my robe, and jumped into cascading, steaming ecstasy.

Ten minutes later, leaning back against a soothing jet of hot water in the jacuzzi pool, I waved contentedly at Yvonne, who was soaking in her own private milk bath. Next to Yvonne, Anya was playing with the rose petals in her own separate tub, delighted to be soaking in the favorite bath of Cleopatra. Fleetingly, I reconsidered my harsh grade for Lorenz's leadership for the day. I had struggled to lead some very tough days too. Come to think of it, I couldn't think of a single easy day since Sweden.

I shifted my position so that another jacuzzi jet could massage my aching toes as they gradually thawed out. OK, maybe Lorenz deserved at least a score of four or five—or even six—I conceded as I slowly melted into a blissful state of pure and utter contentment.

Burial at the Great Wall

Paula

Day 184—Beijing, China

"The rose petal bath was the *best*!" Anya bubbled as she filled her bowl with a rice soup from the breakfast buffet at our spa-hotel the next morning. "Feel how soft my skin is!" She held out her arm in delight.

Following behind her, I topped my soup with some strange-looking pickled vegetables and something I hoped was seaweed. Stopping at the gleaming metal tea urn, I filled our bunny thermos with

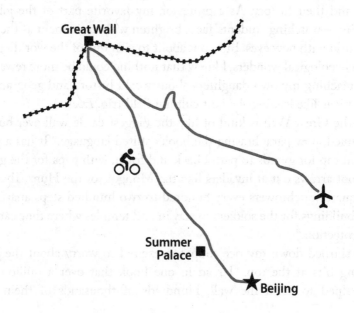

steaming hot tea for the ride ahead. Ahead of me, Anya paused at a clear, round small fruit in syrup, debating. Tentatively she put a scoop in another bowl before walking back to our table at the window, overlooking a sweeping panorama of Beijing and the surrounding countryside.

"The Great Wall is in that direction, I think." I set my rice bowl down at our breakfast table and pointed north out the window to a horizon of brown, jagged mountains dusted in snow. I strained to catch a glimpse of the famous twenty-one-thousand-kilometer barrier between China and Mongolia in the snowy outlines of the Badaling Mountains. No luck. We were too far away.

I sat down and tasted my rice soup. Interesting. Definitely not something I would order for breakfast at home, but the tangy, salty taste wasn't bad.

"It's not just a wall, you know," I explained to Anya and Yvonne while I browsed through the maps and torn pieces of my China guidebook that I had brought with me to breakfast. I pulled out a ragged chapter on northern China. "The book says here that the Great Wall is actually the world's longest fortified complex."

I read out loud, thrilled to be sharing my passion for different cultures and their history. As a professor, my favorite part of the job was teaching—watching students' faces brighten with excitement as they saw the world with new eyes. But now, about to visit one of the world's greatest archaeological wonders, I knew that nothing could be more rewarding than teaching my own daughters about world history and geography in situ. It was like leading the best cultural field trip. *Ever.*

"The Great Wall is kind of like the biggest castle wall ever built," I continued, now paraphrasing the book's stilted language. "It has a walkway on top for guards to patrol back and forth, with gaps for the guards to shoot arrows out at invaders like the Mongols or the Huns. There are big square watchtowers every hundred to two hundred steps apart. And even buildings for the soldiers to stay in and temples where they can pray for protection."

I slurped down my rice soup, too excited to worry about the green floating bits at the top. "I read in one book that over a million people helped to build the wall. Hundreds of thousands of them died.

Supposedly some of them fell into the wall as it was being built. They just continued building on top of them!"

"No kidding!" Anya stared up at me, fascinated. I was delighted with her enthusiasm. For the past week, she had been playing the soundtrack from the Disney movie *Mulan* over and over on the MP3 player, driving us all crazy as she hummed "I'll Make a Man Out of You" for the sixtieth time. When the movie had come out several years earlier, Anya had been mesmerized with the story of a brave Chinese-girl-cum-warrior-maiden. She especially loved the scene where Mulan fought the invading Huns as they swept over the Great Wall of China. Now, less than a day's bicycle ride away from the Great Wall, I suspected that I was not the only one who was struggling to contain her excitement.

Impatient to get on the road quickly after breakfast, I hurried everyone back up to our strange bedroom—an eight-by-eight-foot windowless box, filled from wall to wall with a single mattress on the floor. We dragged our panniers down the sweeping, grand entry staircase of the spa and clambered back on the tandems, happy to be pedaling in dry shoes. Onward we cycled, past market stalls of slippery fish, Chinese slippers, and squawking chickens. Northward we pedaled, along narrow cypress- and willow-lined canals. Upward we biked, around snow-dappled fields filled with bok choy and pungent manure and laughing kerchiefed women in thick sweaters bent over their crops.

And then it appeared. Amid the chickens and the snow and the colorful kerchiefs, a faint black line emerged along the snow-dusted peaks ahead. Twisting and winding its way along the crests of the mountains, up and down valleys, over jagged points, the Great Wall expanded so far across the horizon that it seemed to stretch past the sky, far beyond history or time into infinity.

For hours we pushed in rhythm, pedaling the tandems higher and higher up the rising terrain. The dirt, the noise, and the smell of manure disappeared, and all I could see was that undulating, swirling line, growing, moving toward me. I do not think there is a more awe-inspiring bicycle ride in the world. Approaching this monumental barrier, slowly, at the pace of a human or horse, as it would have been viewed by the ancient Mongols or Chinese peasants, I could hear the sound of long-dead hooves, smell the dust rising, feel the overwhelming power of a people who could build a wall so enormous it seemed to stretch to the ends of the earth. Our tandems flew over the ground as the long black line slowly became a towering rampart, crenellated walls, a series of steep rectangular watchtowers with thin, slitted windows. We had arrived at the Great Wall of China!

I stared up at a towering, thirty-foot, gray stone building as we wheeled our tandems up to an intimidating arched gateway at the entrance to the Great Wall at Badaling. A yellow-and-red-roofed guard house watched over the plaza where we stood below. I leaned my tandem against the wall below a towering double parapet. Crash! The Russian bunny thermos popped out of my water bottle holder and fell to the ground, rolling into a drift of snow. I thought I heard a tinkling sound as Lorenz reached down to pick it up.

He shook the thermos, concerned. "That sounds like glass."

Yvonne's face fell. "It isn't broken, is it?"

Lorenz opened the lid and peered inside. "It's hard to tell with the tea." He lifted up the thermos and began to pour out the steaming brown liquid. The tea gushed out with an ominous clinking sound.

"Oh no!" Yvonne moaned as we stared at a heap of broken glass on the ground. "Can we fix it?"

Lorenz shook his head. "Sorry, honey. Once the glass inside is broken, you have to throw it out. You can't drink from it. It's dangerous."

"But the bunny was our friend! He was a present from the Palinskys in Poland." Yvonne looked close to tears. "We can't just throw him away!" She reached for the aquamarine thermos and cradled it in her arms. "Can we just keep him anyway?"

I looked at Yvonne's stricken face. I had no intention of dragging a broken thermos around the rest of the world. But only a heartless mother could just throw the precious bunny thermos on a trash heap. I began grabbing at straws. "I think the Great Wall of China is a pretty cool place for the thermos to end its journey. Not many things have traveled so far."

"He's not a *thing*." Yvonne clutched the thermos fiercely.

Standing behind her, Anya reached over to Yvonne, putting her arm around her shoulder. "Don't cry, Vonnie," she said. "Maybe we can just hide the bunny in one of the guard towers on the wall, not throw him out."

"But what if a guard finds the thermos and throws the bunny away?" Yvonne looked unconvinced.

"I have an idea," Lorenz said, rummaging in his pannier for a Sierra cup. He knelt on his hands and knees and began scooping up piles of dirt with the cup, digging a makeshift "grave" for the thermos.

A few minutes later, the four of us stood in front of a little mound of dirt covering the interred bunny thermos at the foot of the Great Wall, bending our heads in memorial to Yvonne's lost friend. Perhaps a thousand years from now, some archaeologist will dig up the thermos and wonder what strange religious ceremony had led to the bunny's burial—nestled next to the ancient stones, the arrows, and the bones of long-dead Chinese workers and warriors.

Madame Butterfly's

Lorenz

Day 192—Osaka, Japan

We had just arrived in Japan from China. I was standing in front of a cash machine in the Osaka airport, pondering how much to withdraw. China had been cheap. With a satisfied smile, I remembered the night in China, near the Ming tombs, where we had found a local hotel that had charged

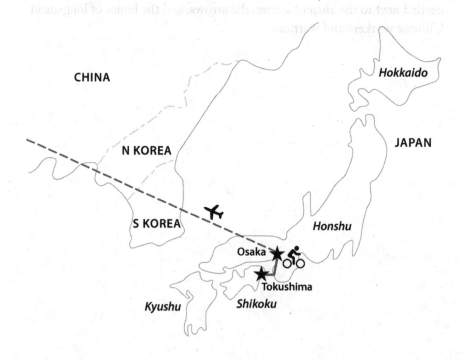

CHINA

Hokkaido

N KOREA

JAPAN

S KOREA

Honshu

Osaka

Tokushima

Kyushu

Shikoku

us only three dollars (!) for the night. For thirty dollars per day, the four of us had lived like kings in China. How much cash should I take out for highly developed Japan, I wondered. I decided to be on the safe side, tripled the budget, and typed in $360 for the next four days. Diligently the ATM spit out thirty-six thousand yen in colorful cash. Grabbing the large notes, I thought to myself that one hundred dollars per day had to be massive overkill.

The first shock came when we decided to take a quick day trip to nearby Kyoto,* the ancient capital city of Japan. After a lovely day visiting the temples, formal gardens, and imperial palace, we discovered that we had spent eighteen thousand yen. Half our four-day budget! Clearly, Japan was not China. We would have to spend much more carefully.

The second shock arrived when we biked out of Osaka and stopped in a small suburb to take out more money from a bank machine that staunchly rejected our card. We tried a second and third card and then four other ATMs. None of them even gave out a single yen.

At the fifth machine, near panic, we met a nice bank teller lady who was just locking up the bank lobby as we stood in the foyer. Luckily, the bank lady spoke English. She explained that except for a handful of ATMs at the large international airports, Japanese ATMs were on a different banking system and did not accept European or US bank cards. She kindly exchanged fifty euros that I had in cash by withdrawing money from her personal bank account. Having only about ¥12,000 left, and trapped in a seemingly infinite suburban sprawl, we snuck into a children's playground after dark and camped "wild," trying to make no noise so that we wouldn't attract the police. Camping in the playground was surely forbidden.

The next day I used the cash the nice bank teller had given us and took a train back to the Osaka airport, seventy kilometers away. I found the well-behaved airport ATM and pulled every cash card I owned from my wallet. I spread the cards in a fan on the counter of the ATM and went to town. Take it to the limit, baby! I pulled ¥40,000 from the red card, ¥80,000 from the yellow one, ¥30,000 from the blue card, and

---

* Kyoto was the capital of Japan for more than one thousand years (from 794 to 1868—when the emperor moved his family to Tokyo). It is considered the center of Japanese culture and Buddhism, housing some 1,660 Buddhist temples and another 400 Shinto shrines across the city.

another ¥40,000 from the second red card. Self-consciously, I looked around for prying eyes and quickly stuffed the two-inch-thick wad of bills, totaling nearly $2,000, into my breast pocket. The train ride back to the girls was nerve-wracking. I carried a twenty-day supply of cash—our only usable money until we reached Taiwan—in the pocket of my rain jacket. My fellow passengers on the train instantly became the world's most conniving group of pickpockets in my mind, but no one attacked me, and to my surprise I made it back to the girls OK. We had messed up but thankfully had managed to recover.

<hr>

Two days later, we really screwed up. When our ferry from Honshu Island docked in Tokushima, on the island of Shikoku,* it was already 8:00 p.m., and the streets of the bustling metropolis were dark and nearly deserted. The relatively inexpensive youth hostel we had scoped out in our guidebook turned out to be seven miles up a steep, dark mountain road. Unattainable by bike at this late hour. Frustrated, Paula tossed the map of Shikoku into one of the empty plastic chairs of the ferry terminal and said, "I'm just not taking the risk of biking through pitch-dark, hairpin curves and getting us all killed. We're taking a hotel."

We were in the right area for hotels all right. The choices were numerous and enticing. For the discerning business traveler who prefers a central setting with traditional Japanese decor, there was, for instance, the Great Dragon Hotel located along the picturesque central canal and competitively priced at ¥52,000. For the customer who prefers more Western surroundings with modern accents, The Windsor across the way was a sensible and fashionable choice at ¥40,500. The thrifty budget traveler, on the other hand, was well served by The Pearl, which offered traditional tatami mat accommodations for a mere ¥20,500. Tatami mat rooms consisted of a rice straw mat on a hard wooden floor. No furniture. Asian austerity at its best.

---

* Japan is actually an archipelago consisting of over 6,800 islands extending over three thousand kilometers from Hokkaido near Russia in the north to Okinawa near Taiwan in the south. Ferries run regularly between the major islands. We cycled four of the five largest islands: Honshu, Shikoku, Kyushu, and Okinawa. (We did not cycle Hokkaido, the fifth major island.)

Standing in the foyer of The Pearl for a long time, counting our combined cash, we stubbornly ignored the fact that we had never paid the equivalent of $190 to sleep on a floor. Anywhere. Ever. Finally we conceded that we just did not have enough money to sleep inside on the floor in Japan. Dejectedly, we had returned to our tandems when the landlady of The Pearl came running after us with a gift of six mandarins. She had quickly realized that bicycle-riding foreigners were obviously too poor to sleep in Japan and required immediate charity. We accepted the gift eagerly. By now we had also learned that bicycle-riding foreigners were also too poor to eat in Japan.

Back in the street at 9:00 p.m., we headed for the nearest park and devoured the mandarins for "dinner" on a park bench.

"I wonder what Madame Butterfly's is," said Yvonne, pointing with her half-eaten mandarin at a small sign that radiated the only English characters in a sea of oriental neon.

"Probably just another outrageously priced hotel," said Paula, dejectedly.

"Let's give it one more try, Mom," Anya nudged. "I'm really tired."

A beautiful, slightly older Japanese lady greeted us in the courtyard of Madame Butterfly's. When I asked about a room, she shook her head from side to side, causing her straight shoulder-length dyed-blond hair to twist around her head like a miniature carnival carousel. In broken English she asserted, "Room not now. Come later, still use."

For some inexplicable reason, we could not come to terms on renting a room, but she had obviously taken a liking to us. Anya's and Yvonne's rosy cheeks and naturally blond hair fascinated her no end. When the girls let her touch their hair, she squealed with delight and immediately summoned her coworkers to join in the fun. Instantly, like a flock of colorful birds, six tiny, young, and chattering women were fluttering around us, touching the girls' hair and cheeks, shrieking with joy. We knew that we had stumbled into something good when our hostess announced that for "such nice family," she would drop the room price from ¥17,000 to ¥12,000.

Thinking that we had come to an agreement, I unsnapped my panniers from the bike and began carrying them up the stairs when with outstretched arms our hostess jumped in front of me and barricaded my way. Spreading the folds of her kimono like the wings of a beautiful butterfly, she announced again, "Room not now, come later."

"Later? When, later?" I inquired.

"One hour!" pronounced Madame Butterfly with a confident smile.

A little confused, we headed back to the park, set up our camp stove, and prepared a scrumptious dinner of four plain packs of ramen noodles. We had already resigned ourselves to the fact that ramen noodles, at two dollars a pack, would be our one culinary chance of survival in Japan.

Exactly one hour later, we reappeared at the hotel and were immediately surrounded by Madame Butterfly and her giggling flock of girls, who must have been patiently lying in wait for us. Armed with sheets, pillows, and blankets, they bustled us from the courtyard, up the narrow outside stair, toward our room. Three of the girls wrestled a humongous mattress up the stairs behind us. Madame Butterfly opened our room door, which had a strange, complicated lock with a digital clock on top and a coin slot below. Once inside, Anya, Yvonne, and their young escorts screamed excitedly like teenaged girls at a sleepover.

"You like Milke Mouse?" one of the girls asked Yvonne.

Yvonne emphatically nodded her head and said "Yes!" with conviction.

It was a good thing that she liked Mickey Mouse, because if she didn't she would have gone insane by the morning. Surveying the room, I quickly came to the conclusion that Walt Disney's personal interior designer must have escaped Hollywood and decorated this room during an unfortunate episode of mental instability. Mickey Mouse was everywhere. An eight-foot-high, back-lit mural of Mickey and Minnie Mouse rambling through the countryside in a Model-T Ford dominated the room with penetrating fluorescence. Two mouse mirrors with large black ears, one of them with a polka-dot bow in the center, hung on opposite walls. A "his and hers," I surmised cleverly. The king-sized Mickey Mouse bedspread touted Mickey hugging Minnie, a giant heart floating midair between them. Millions of Mickey Mouse throw pillows covered the rest of the bed. The crown jewel of the room was the Mickey Mouse clock prominently placed as the focal point of the room. Not only was the clock in the shape of our favorite mouse, but Mickey's tail ingeniously formed its moving pendulum. To top it off, the ears above the face of the clock moved back and forth in the same mesmerizing rhythm as Mickey's behind. In case all of that that wasn't enough, a smiling three-foot-high Mickey statue, holding a tray with colorful candies, stood by the door to greet bedazzled visitors. The room was clean and comfortable but definitely mouse infested.

My décor-induced trance was interrupted when the oversized mattress, propelled by the three young women outside, suddenly hurled past me and deployed with a loud *plop* in the middle of Mickey's paradise. Giggling, our escorts descended on the mattress with their sheets, blankets, and pillows and made up Anya and Yvonne's bed on the floor. Madame Butterfly dug through the mountain of throw pillows and triumphantly emerged with two soft Mickey dolls that she lovingly snuggled beside Anya's and Yvonne's pillows.

After a lot of bowing and "*Arigato!* Thank you!" our feminine entourage waved good night, one by one, and only Madame Butterfly remained to give us final and puzzling instructions.

"Door not open, automatic lock. Cannot get out. You want things, you knock on wall. Must leave eight o'clock. New customers."

With a wave of her kimono wings, Madame Butterfly was gone, and the door shut with an electronic whir behind her. A bit perplexed but too tired to care, I got ready for bed.

When I shuffled into the bathroom, Paula had already taken up residence in the oversized jacuzzi bathtub and was smiling contentedly while mountains of bath foam rose in a geotectonic time warp all around her. Brushing my teeth and only half awake, I noticed that the unusual jacuzzi touted a waterproof TV screen built into the wall over the tub. Ready for bed, I walked out of the bathroom and passed Yvonne in front of the smiling Mickey Mouse statue.

"Dad, can I eat a candy before bed?" she asked, picking an orange one from Mickey's tray and waving it before my bleary eyes.

"Sure, but brush your teeth and get into bed right after that," I responded automatically.

I clambered across Anya, who was already snuggled up in her cozy bed on the floor, reading Japanese comic books that she had found by our bedside. Suddenly I froze. Something about Yvonne's orange candy wasn't right. Twisting around painfully, I hurled myself across Anya and hit the floor with a hard, painful thump. I just managed to grab Yvonne by the ankle before she disappeared into the bathroom.

"Give me that," I wheezed as the air rushed from my lungs.

"No. It's mine. Get your own."

I pulled back on Yvonne's foot, but she grabbed the bathroom faucet with her free hand and hung on, screaming.

"Mom, Dad's gone nuts! He's trying to steal my candy."

"It's not a candy!" I grunted as I finally wrestled Yvonne onto the bathroom floor and clawed the condom package from her hand.

"Mom, he stole my candy! Do something! Tell him to get his own!"

With that as encouragement, I jumped up and snatched the remaining condoms from Mickey's tray, giving him an accusing look and mumbling something about childhood idols gone bad. Trying to irritate me, Mickey smiled back impassively. I was about to hide the condoms on a shelf when Anya called out, "Wow, these comic books are weird. Why don't any of the characters have clothes on?"

Whirling around again, I inadvertently hit three-foot-tall Mickey (served him right), dropped the condoms on the floor, and hurled myself onto the mattress, snatching the comic books from Anya's fingers. As suspected, the whole lot was triple-X and beyond graphic. The confiscated comic books in hand, I jumped back on Yvonne, who was now darting around the room snatching up "candies" as if she were at a Fourth of July parade. The battle raged fiercely for a while, but with failing strength I regained control, gathered Mickey's condoms and Madame Butterfly's enticing house literature, and dumped the whole pile in the bathroom next to the jacuzzi. Burned out, I slumped against the wall.

"Hard day at the office?" Paula asked with a smirk, picking up a catalogue from my pile of confiscated sin. The catalogue depicted Madame Butterfly's exotic toy and movie collection that could be bought or rented at the front desk for just a few thousand yen. Lifting her leg enticingly above the foam, Paula winked and queried, "Interested?"

In mock-exhaustion I grinned and collapsed on the bathroom floor. That night Mikey saw no action, just well-deserved deep sleep.

At 6:30 the next morning, the motion sensor alarm on my tandem was making an ear-piercing racket in the courtyard below our window. Opening the shutters, I looked outside and found Madame Butterfly dancing around our tandems with her hands over her ears, looking extremely embarrassed. When the alarm finally stopped, her cheeks red with shame, Madame Butterfly explained that she just wanted to touch Yvonne's soft sheepskin seat cover. Laughing with her, I waved from the window and promised that we would leave by eight o'clock sharp, if she would just release us from our lovely prison.

At twenty minutes to eight, the door to Mickey's love haven was opened from the outside by Madame Butterfly and her girls. Smiling and laughing, all seven of them swooped down on our luggage and carried it down the stairs for us. In the courtyard we loaded our bikes, and Madame and the girls missed no opportunity to touch our daughters' hair and rosy cheeks. Even Yvonne's sheepskin seat cover received its lifetime quota of petting during the occasion.

When it was time to leave, Madame Butterfly brought out four bento lunch boxes that she and her girls had carefully packed for us. The boxes were decorated with beautiful bows and contained scrumptious food that we knew we would not eat again in Japan, on our budget. It was a moment of true kindness and love. Just what you would expect in a Japanese love hotel.*

---

* At the time, we had no idea that we had stumbled into a Japanese love hotel or even what that was. Love hotels are a Japanese phenomenon, pay-as-you-go accommodation reserved for any conceivable kind of intimate liaison. The hotels are largely not for prostitution, even though some of that does occur. Married couples use love hotels to get privacy from their children, lovers come to play out fantasies in rooms equipped with swings and vibrating beds, and businessmen take their coworkers for a "quick lunch break." In a love hotel, you can sleep in a cave full of stuffed animals, meet your lover in a pretend prison cell, or order rentable fantasy outfits and even rentable people from the front desk to wear them. The rooms are usually very clean and tidy, but there are no chocolates on your pillow. Instead, you get an XXX comic book.

Step Up to the Tub and Don't Be Afraid

Lorenz

Day 195—Shikoku Island, Japan

"Hey, you want to come?" Paula stood, her head wrapped in a white towel, on the porch of our cozy tatami mat cabin, a look of relaxed satisfaction playing across her face.

Just an hour ago, we had been bicycling up a lonely Japanese mountainside on the island of Shikoku, with sleet pelting against our rain

jackets and slush seeping relentlessly into our cycling shoes. By sheer luck, Yvonne had spotted a campground nestled in a misty river valley off the winding mountain road. Miraculously, the campground had still been open this late in November. Via a comic pantomime act, the friendly husband-and-wife proprietors made us understand that they had two small cabins, heated with kerosene heaters, for nearly the same price as two frigid campsites. Delighted at the prospect of a cozy night, I blew on my frozen fingers protruding from my cycling gloves, thawing them just enough to scribble our names onto the booking sheet. Not only did the cabins turn out to be clean and beautiful in their Asian simplicity, but the entire establishment boasted amenities we had never dreamed of finding in such a remote location.

"They have a bathhouse down there, and Yvonne and I are going," said Paula, our local bath addict.

"No kidding," I mumbled as I unrolled my sleeping bag onto the rice straw mat, which covered the entire cabin floor. I still felt the chill from our icy ride in my bones and replied, "Yeah, I'll come. Should be an experience."

We rambled downhill through the completely deserted campground, heading toward the picturesque bathhouse, its curved wooden gables rising through the cold valley mist. Secretly, I was already convinced that the bath was closed, since there was not a soul around who would have warranted the extravagance of large amounts of hot water.

"Mom, look at all the steam coming out of the bathhouse. I feel warm all over already," exclaimed Yvonne, who was obviously looking forward to her well-deserved reward. I did not have the heart to tell her it was icy mist from the river and not steam that engulfed the picturesque structure.

When we came to the front of the building, we found two sets of double doors that, to my surprise, yielded when I placed my hand on their rough, half-round bamboo slats. Paula and Yvonne excitedly scurried into what appeared to be the women's entrance and left me alone outside. Tentatively, I pushed through the other set of doors and found myself in a well-lit but empty changing room. Except for steam hissing from somewhere in the interior, the place was absolutely quiet and deserted. I was alone and certain that no one had been to this place all day, since it was uncommonly clean and picked-up, almost stark. I peeled off my sweaty clothes, unceremoniously dumped them on an hourglass-shaped plastic stool, wrapped a towel around my waist, and proceeded through another set of heavy metal doors that promised to reveal the interior of the bath.

As the massive doors swung shut behind me, I felt as if, through a fluke in time-space, I had landed in another world. Before me lay a giant raised pool that spilled cascades of hot, steaming water over its rims onto a black tile floor. The wall behind the pool was built of gigantic basalt boulders from which two waterfalls cascaded into the frothing water below. Dozens of naked men were bathing noisily within the spray. On the remaining walls of the bathhouse were showers and odd-shaped basins occupied by yet more very naked men, who were in the process of washing and scrubbing every imaginable body part. The din in the place was mind-boggling.

Suddenly the entire room became completely quiet, and it seemed even the waterfalls reduced their volume, attentive to what was going to happen. Thirty pairs of eyes focused on a single black slate floor tile in the room. It happened to be the one tile I was standing on. Finally the lonely hissing of steam was accompanied by an awestruck "Ahhh" emerging from every mouth except mine. After the longest pause of my life, a short, fat man stepped out of the hot pool and advanced, bowing, his hands folded in front of him, toward me through the billowing steam. He too was completely naked.

"*Sianara*."

"*Sianara*," I stammered in shock.

"*Sianara*. What are you?"

"Good, how are you?" I tried for an answer.

"No, *what* are you?"

Confused, I answered tentatively, "American?"

"American!" the man exclaimed, squeezing my hand in admiration.

The entire room erupted in an admiring "Ohhhh," followed by excited chatter.

"You Arnold Schwarzenegger?" he asked.

By now a number of other men had gathered and stood in a half-circle before me.

"No, I am not Arnold Schwarzenegger," I said with a wry smile.

"Why, but you so big," said another diminutive gray-haired man who was already squeezing my chest with his hands from the front and back. Setting his arms immobile, like a pair of machining calipers, he moved away and displayed the gap between his hands to the awestruck group.

"Ahhhh," was the unanimous response, billowing from the steam.

I have never thought of myself as a very big guy, but looking down at the crowd of fully grown Japanese men, none of whom were taller than five foot eight, I must have looked like a giant.

"You weigh much a lot . . . you do?" asked the first man, who seemed to have appointed himself as my bathhouse host. Being admired for being six foot tall was one thing, but now this chap was getting a bit personal, I thought.

"Much meat; ninety kilos, maybe, I think," continued my host, squeezing the side of my hip and turning me around appraisingly.

"No, seventy kilos," said another.

"Eighty," said the gray-haired human caliper.

"No, ninety kilos," said my host with conviction.

At once, the men around me plunged back into Japanese, apparently discussing the magnitude of my stupendous weight. Finally, my host addressed me again.

"How much kilo?" he asked.

I shrugged my shoulders and responded honestly, "I don't know."

I had not weighed myself for months and could not remember how to convert 180 pounds into kilos. I started to think I had walked into every teenage girl's nightmare, so surreal was the scene.

"He no know," said my host to himself, shaking his head. Then in Japanese he addressed the others and scurried away into the fog. Moments later, a triumphant cry could be heard through the open doors of the changing room, and an old man, grinning toothlessly, came shuffling back, holding a bathroom scale high above his silver-haired head. My host carefully positioned the scale on the tile floor in front of me, and the men behind me began prodding my back with their fingers, urging me onto the scale as if I were a condemned pirate faced with the plank. There was no escape, and I knew that I was completely at the men's mercy in this place, where chaos and pandemonium reigned unabatedly. I was a very tall, very heavy captive of thirty naked men in a Japanese bathhouse.

The scale's pointer swung up dramatically, finally coming to rest near the peg at eighty-two kilograms. The impact of the measurement was impressive. The crowd whooped, clapped, and cheered. To make the measurement exact, the human caliper pulled my towel from my hips and watched the scale drop only half a kilogram.

"Eighty-one point five kilos," he cried, swinging my towel triumphantly over his head in a giant circle. He had obviously won the bet. Then he stared at me, standing completely naked on the scale, and said admiringly, "You are very big."

"Thank you," I responded as humbly as the ludicrousness of the situation allowed.

"You Arnold Schwarzenegger brother? You live Hollywood?" asked my host now, after the weight question had been scientifically settled.

"I am not Arnold Schwarzenegger's brother. Arnold Schwarzenegger weighs at least one hundred thirty kilos and lives in California. I am from Seattle."

"One hundred thirty kilos . . . impossible! Only cow weigh one hundred thirty kilos!"

I knew Americans (and Austrians) better but kept quiet, since I did not want to get involved in yet another weighty debate with this unpredictable crowd.

"Settle . . . Settle Malinas. Settle?"

"Seattle, the city on the West Coast," I said in clarification, at the same time sensing a new emotion rising in my host.

Suddenly my host grabbed me by the arm and jumped up on the rim of the hot pool. He screamed at the top of his lungs, "Settle Maliners! Ichero!"

"Ichero!" went up a cry.

My naked friend yelled one more time "Ichero!" and then fell, arms flailing, backward into the pool.

The weight thing had been just barely comprehensible to me, but now the man had apparently lost it altogether. I watched stunned as the bathhouse erupted anew in chaos. Men jumped into the hot pool and began to chant, "Ichero, Ichero, Ichero."

"Settle Malinas, Settle Malinas!"

"Ichero!"

Mayhem was all around me, and I must have looked quite shell-shocked because my host climbed drenched out of the pool, took me by the arm, and looked me in the eye.

"Settle Malinas, Settle Malinas, Ichero!"

The first part of the message made no sense, but somehow I had heard the Japanese word *Ichero* before.

"Settle Malinas, Ichero," my host repeated.

I am not much of a sports fan, but suddenly it dawned on me. He was saying "Seattle Mariners, Ichiro!" Ichiro Suzuki is the Japanese power-hitter phenomenon who plays for my hometown team, the Seattle Mariners.

"Ichiro, the right fielder for the Seattle Mariners!" I said in recognition.

"Ichero, Ichero, Ichero," began the chant again.

My host grabbed me by the arm, and we danced naked and happy together through the bath shouting, "Ichero, Ichero!"

There is nothing as satisfying as skin-deep international understanding.

Persimmons

Posted by Yvonne

My, my, another Persimmon,
Another Persimmon oh deary me.
Orange and bright
Yet still a plight
when offered to me upon my bike.

Japanese
always trying to please
taking off their trees
pounds of this tasty fruit.
A beautiful gift
is this loot
but will this help me up the
mountain of my route?

Note to the reader: While I was biking through Japan in November (the persimmon season), I made up this poem. For no apparent reason other than pure generosity, Japanese people kept giving us pounds of persimmons. We really love this gift. But hundreds of pounds of persimmons in one week is an awful lot of weight to carry over a mountain pass.

The Breakfast Club

Lorenz

Day 202—Kyushu, Japan

We were climbing up a steep hill overlooking the large urban sprawl along the coast of Hakata Bay on Kyushu Island when the derailleur on my bike suddenly made a sickening crunching sound. Abruptly, the chain jammed, jolting Anya and me to an instant halt. Inspecting the damage,

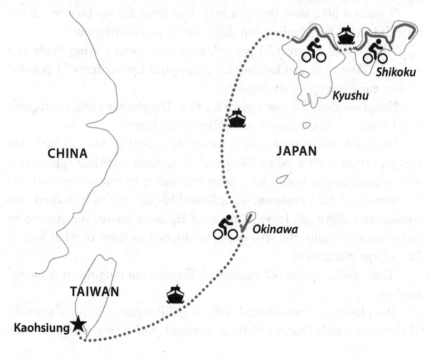

I found that the derailleur cage had come apart and that one of the two plastic cogs, which guide the chain, had gone missing entirely.

"Damn," I said as I wiped my greasy hands on my somewhat less greasy pants. "I can only fix this to last a couple of kilometers, and it's going to make a hell of a racket as we pedal. We definitely need a bike store."

Paula had already unfolded the map from her handlebar bag and was assessing our options. "It's almost four o'clock. Catching the ferry to Okinawa today is out. And I don't see anywhere in Fukuoka where we can camp for the night."

As we debated back and forth, we didn't notice a man stop his car and come up behind us.

"Are you having trouble with your bicycles?" He bowed politely. "My name is Naoki. I am a cyclist too. Maybe I can help you?"

"I'm not sure that you can," I replied. I explained our predicament carefully, though I sensed this man's English was quite a bit better than that of the average Japanese.

"I know a bike store that can help. I go there for my bicycles all the time. It is a bit far. Maybe I can drive one of you to the store?"

"That would be great." I paused, uncertain about leaving Paula and the girls. "We were also looking for a campsite for our tents." I pointed to the gear piled up on the tandems.

Naoki nodded. "I know a place for that. The place is a bit . . . irregular. But I think . . . Yes, it may work. Follow me, please."

He drove slowly in front of us down the mountainside and back into the populated coastal valley. We pedaled through suburban sprawl that was so confusing it would have been impossible to exit on our own. At the bottom of the mountain, we followed his tiny car as it ducked into equally tiny alleyways. It was a maze of Japanese houses surrounded by cedar fences. Finally, the stranger's car stopped in front of what looked like a large playground.

"Dad, look . . . so cool!" exclaimed Yvonne, jumping down from her tandem.

The playground was dotted with large fiberglass climb-on animals. There was a panda bear, a rabbit, an elephant, and even a giraffe. Yvonne bounced from one sculpture to the next until she finally settled on the giraffe to climb onto.

"Best Japanese campground ever," she chimed out from her lofty perch.

Naoki walked up to me and said, "This is a school playground. I think if you are quiet you can stay until the morning and leave before the school starts at seven thirty. Now you and I must go. It is getting late to find the bicycle repair shop before the closing."

Half an hour later I walked, smiling, out of the bike store with a brand-new Shimano derailleur in my hand. However, I was not smiling anymore when we walked back into the playground, which was now bathed in flashing white-and-blue light. I could see at least three police cars and one fire rescue truck. The playground was literally swarming with police. Most of them had gathered around our tandems and Paula, who was trying to explain things and gesticulating wildly. As I pressed through the throng of police, I saw two younger policemen straddling our silver tandem. One of them was ringing Yvonne's "I love my bike" bell. The place was in pandemonium. I shouted at Paula over the heads of the last row of policemen, "What in the heck is going on here?"

"I have no idea!" called Paula. "First one police car showed up, and then they just kept coming. It has something to do with the bikes, I think."

Trying to get to Paula, I pushed past the last pair of police officers, who were lifting our green tandem, apparently assessing its weight. Naoki touched my arm and stepped in to exchange a few incomprehensible sentences with an older silver-haired officer who was obviously in charge.

Finally, Naoki came back to me and explained, "They say you broke the law. In Japan it is against the laws to ride with two people to one bicycle. The police want to take away your bicycles."

"What? But that's what tandems are made for—two people. We've biked almost around the entire world and now in Japan, of all places, they want to impound our tandem bikes? That's nuts!" I said and pulled our World Bike for Breath brochure from my handlebar bag to show Naoki our route.

"It is an old law to stop people from riding on luggage racks and handlebars. They never thought of tandem bicycles. Wait . . ." He suddenly focused on the brochure. "You are bicycling the whole world! Incredible! Please give these papers to me. This is a big help!"

I handed him the brochure, which he quickly took back to the gray-haired police officer. Even though I could not understand a word, I could sense the mood of the assembled crowd shift as Naoki explained, pointing out things on the brochures. I started hearing names of some of our bigger sponsors.

"T-Mobile! Oh!" and "Patagonia! Ah!"

Suddenly, the whole scene broke into a party. Policemen came up to us, shaking our hands, ruffling the girls' hair, and wanting pictures taken with us. The bikes were prodded, lifted up, and rolled around. Then some of the more adventurous policemen requested backseat rides on the tandems, which Paula and I obligingly gave, since anything was better than getting our bikes confiscated. The festivities lasted a good half hour, after which the police slowly cleared out, shaking our hands and wishing us luck. Naoki was the last to leave.

"Naoki, you saved us!" I said as I shook his hand. "You found us a place to camp, fixed our bike, and saved us from the nice policemen. You are our hero!"

After Naoki left, we had a quick yet filling dinner of five packs of ramen noodles. Yvonne petted her newfound friend, the giraffe, good night, and we all sank exhausted into our sleeping bags for a few hours of badly needed slumber.

It was just gray in the predawn sky when I heard a voice outside our tent say, "Good morning! Anyone awake?"

I rolled over, nudged Paula, and whispered, "I think the police have come back and want us to move on."

"Oh, damn!" mumbled Paula as she extracted herself from the sleeping bag and threw on some clothes. We both exited the tent, bleary-eyed, and stood in shock at what we saw.

Naoki stood behind a fold-up table covered in a red-checkered table-cloth. The table was set with delicious breakfast treats and a large carafe of coffee! Next to Naoki stood a beautiful petite woman with jet-black shoulder-length hair, a shy smile on her face.

"Good morning. I am Miki, Naoki's wife. Naoki and I thought that it was a very cold night and you might like a hot breakfast."

I wanted to say something, but nothing came out. Paula's mouth stood open too.

"I am an English teacher and have to get up early to teach my English class anyway. So Naoki and I thought we would get up a bit ear-lier and make breakfast for you," Miki added. "Here, have some wet, hot towels. You can wash up a little since there is no bathroom."

Miki handed us bamboo tongs and a covered wicker basket that held four hot, steaming towels. Hearing the voices, the girls emerged from their tent, their breath steaming in the freezing morning air. We all washed our faces, hands, and arms with the luxuriously hot towels and felt like we had landed in heaven. The breakfast was equally delicious. Naoki and Miki handed us hot sugar rice, warm chocolate chip muffins, eggs, hot chocolate for the girls, and coffee for us. Lots of food for every-one, and it was wonderful!

World Bike Bits

Bits and stories about World Bike for Breath. A Bulletin for sponsors. Volume 5

Cherishing the Christmas Chaos

FOR THE PAST THIRTEEN YEARS, SINCE THE BIRTH OF OUR DAUGHTERS, Anya and Yvonne, the holiday season from October to January has tended to resemble a crazy roller-coaster ride—climbing to the top of one American holiday to whiz far too rapidly down and around to the next big celebration. Indeed, I must humbly admit that, by the time December approaches, I have occasionally felt positively Grinch-like: complaining about my aching feet after a long day of traipsing around Seattle searching for gifts, getting frustrated at the long lines in the Town and Country supermarket, and exhaustedly hurrying the already harassed-looking barista at Bainbridge Bakers before rushing off to yet another holiday event.

Yet this fall, as our family continues our world cycling tour for asthma through Asia—spending Halloween in China, Thanksgiving in Japan, and Christmas (a few weeks from now) in Hong Kong—I have begun to look back with nostalgia on the hustle and bustle of our American holidays and to realize that perhaps I (like many of my fellow holiday grumblers) have judged the tinsel and glitter of the season a little too harshly. After two months of pedaling through the drab, solemn, colorless poverty of eastern Europe and Russia, where store shelves all carry the same limited monotonous supply of basic living goods, I confess that the tawdry lights and commercial holiday shopping bustle of American stores seem an amazing luxury.

Indeed, this Halloween we were more than a little delighted to arrive in colorful, lively Beijing, streets filled with every kind of imaginable and unimaginable toy, gadget, and gizmo. Trick-or-treating consisted of our girls knocking on the door of our hotel room, dressed in scarves, hats, and various assorted souvenirs collected in the past month. But at least we were able to provide a basket of (admittedly strange) Chinese plum, jelly, and fish candies. As Anya and Yvonne observed the time-honored Halloween tradition of sampling candy after candy in their bags, I was grateful they had never faced a childhood in Communist Poland, where once a month each family was given a coupon allowing them to purchase one—and only one—chocolate bar per child.

By late November, after a month of being constantly hungry as we attempted futilely to fuel our rides over three-thousand-foot mountain passes in Japan and China with a diet of fish, rice, seaweed, and bok choy, we found a new meaning to the tradition of an abundant meal at Thanksgiving. In previous years, like many of my waistline-obsessed fellow Americans, I had listened to radio broadcasts proposing menus for low-calorie desserts and tips on how to avoid the holiday appetizers. This year, desperately hungry and more than a tad homesick, our family sprang for Thanksgiving dinner at a Japanese hamburger joint on the southerly island of Okinawa. Luckily for us, the menu had photographs of the various entrees. Oddly enough, the menu also listed the caloric value of each meal. For the first time in our lives, instead of worrying about whether or not to have that second slice of pie, the four of us spent half an hour figuring out how to order combinations with the highest possible caloric value.

That evening, I curled up on my tatami mat in the Naha youth hostel feeling more than a little sorry for myself. Focusing on previous Thanksgiving dinners spent at a table piled high with food, surrounded by laughter and friendship, I am ashamed to admit that I had already forgotten how fortunate we were. Our night camping in the field of a poor Lithuanian farmer just two months ago—sharing the only loaf of bread from his completely empty cupboards—was far from my mind. It was Yvonne who set me straight.

The next day, as we set out our evening meal of tempura vegetables, rice balls, and fried fish, Yvonne remarked that we had failed to observe one of our most precious Thanksgiving traditions: giving thanks before the meal. And so, as we sat cross-legged on the tatami mat around the simple Japanese meal, she began the ritual, stating, "I am thankful for my friends and my family."

One by one we continued, expressing thanks for our good health, for the opportunity we have to travel, for the many warm and generous people who have helped us along the way, and for the countless blessings in our lives.

Next December, as I sit with my feet propped up on the ferry after a busy day of Christmas shopping, I hope I remember the simple lessons of an eleven-year-old: to be thankful that I live in a country and community where the store shelves are filled with an amazing chaos of choices; where despite the lines in the Town and Country supermarket, I have always returned home with more than enough food; and where I can order a single tall latte, medium foam, and know that the barista, although frazzled, will not serve me a bowl of worms instead!

Biking in Robes

Lorenz

Day 208—Kaohsiung, Taiwan

"Those are very interesting bicycles," said a voice in impeccable English behind me as I watched golden koi snap up morsels of food from the glassy surface of the placid pond. Expecting to address the rare British

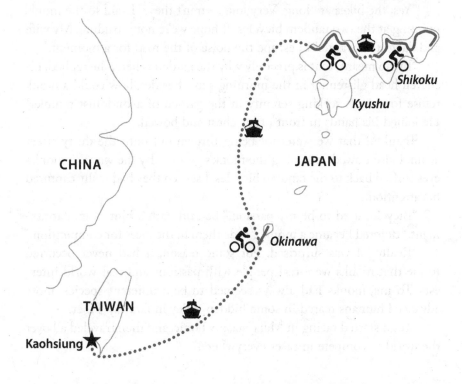

tourist in industrial Taiwan, I turned and was stunned to see a Buddhist monk standing in flowing gray robes in front of the smog-obscured sun.

Just yesterday, our family had stumbled off a terrifying, rust-bucket freighter from Okinawa, Japan. We had endured two days in gale-force winds with twenty-foot waves washing over the freighter's deck. Overjoyed to arrive in Taiwan alive, we had docked on dry land in Kaohsiung, Taiwan. Unfortunately, our joy had quickly disappeared after a day of bicycling through a landscape of billowing smokestacks, putrid industrial lagoons, and rusting manufacturing plants that stretched endlessly south from the dilapidated metropolis.

In an attempt to escape the relentless noise and pollution, Paula had steered our bicycle caravan into a gated garden she had glimpsed by the side of the road just moments ago. We had no idea who the garden belonged to or if we were even allowed inside. All we hoped for was to stop the sensory overload and to escape into the oasis of temporary serenity that had divinely materialized.

"Yes, the bikes are long. Very long—aren't they?" I said to the monk, pointing at the two tandem bicycles. "I hope we're not intruding. My wife and daughters wanted to escape the noise of the road for a moment."

"By no means, that is precisely why the garden is here," he replied, his shaven head glistening in the morning sun. "Besides, how could a monk refuse four souls seeking serenity in the garden of a Buddhist temple?" He joined his hands in front of his chest and bowed.

Thankful that we were not being thrown out onto the dusty street again, I also bowed, returning the monk's gesture. By the way the monk's eyes shifted back to the tandem bicycles, I sensed they had really captured his attention.

"Bicycles used to be my passion," he said with a hint of embarrassment. "Before I became a monk, I rode them in the races for competition."

"Really?" I was surprised. For some reason, it had never occurred to me that monks were real people with passions and real-world interests. To me, monks had always seemed to be a different species, more advanced humans reared in some hidden valley in faraway Tibet.

"Yes. I started racing in Malaysia, my home, and then traveled all over the world to compete in races everywhere."

"Is that why your English is perfect?" I asked.

"No, no, perfect it is not. But yes, I have traveled many places, and by the look of your bicycles—how do you call them—twin bicycles, you have traveled far also."

"We have. We're bicycling around the entire world. We're about half done now. Eight thousand kilometers to go."

"Incredible!" gasped the monk. "With the children? I must tell my master immediately! Don't go away!"

With that, the monk ran down the path toward the temple, his robes billowing in the morning air. A couple of minutes later he returned, out of breath. "You must stay for tea. The master requests it. The master would like the honor to share the tea ceremony with your family."

I felt embarrassed, but before I could say anything, Anya replied, "I love tea. We would very much like that. Of course we'll stay."

As we removed our shoes to enter the white marble temple, I pointed at my watch and threw Anya a disapproving "what the hell—this will eat up our day" look. Anya just smiled back at me, knowing full well that I was socially trapped and had to go along.

Suddenly the monk paused and said, "I am sorry, I completely forgot. My name is David," and with another little bow he motioned us through a beautiful bright-red arch adorned with raised gold-colored symbols.

David seated us on floor cushions in a clean, plain room where the master of the temple already sat in front of a magnificent lacquered table made from the root wood of an ancient tree. The table was of a design I had never seen before and contained many terraces carved into the wood, on which the master had placed small, ornate vessels holding green tea leaves. Billows of steam obscured the master as he poured hot water over the tea leaves, purposefully spilling large amounts of liquid onto the table. The steaming water cascaded off the table's tiers, forming a beautiful miniature waterfall as it finally collected at the bottom. We sat mesmerized, watching the complex ceremony for several minutes. Taking in the sweet tea aroma, I realized that we had stumbled, or rather trespassed, into a beautiful cultural ritual that very few outsiders ever get to see.

Finally, the master collected the tea into a small clay pot and began pouring it into several porcelain tea cups. As he poured, a young monk appeared with a tray containing an extremely strange fruit. It was round, the size of a walnut, and had a thin, hard light-brown shell.

"It is called dragon eye," David explained as he cracked the smooth outside shell to reveal a white glassy fruit inside. "We believe it is very good for your health."

After the tea had been served, the master began to speak. David, sitting cross-legged on the cushion next to him, effortlessly translated each word. Within minutes we were in deep conversation about our trip and our cause to raise awareness and funds for asthma. Time flew as David's words bounced off the tearoom walls, mingling one language with the other. When a young monk appeared at the door, the master was surprised to find that it was already lunchtime.

"Naturally, since it is so late and we enjoy talking so much, you must join us for lunch," he said as David translated, adding, "I hope you don't mind vegetarian food, because we Buddhists don't eat meat."

The master led us into a large, spartan dining room, which was bustling with monks pushing food carts, setting tables, and chatting excitedly. Gray robes and shaved heads were everywhere. We found a spot at one of the three long tables, set with plain china bowls and chopsticks. Over the din, the master motioned us to take a bowl and join the rapidly forming line in front of the food carts. David escorted us, giving us his recommendations for the unfamiliar dishes.

Barely managing to raise his placid voice over the clamor, he said, "Today is going to be especially good, since sister Kira has prepared the lunch. She is a monk from Thailand and an outstanding cook. Tomorrow is my turn to prepare the lunch." With a chuckle he added, "You are very lucky to be here today instead of tomorrow."

"So, there are girl monks too then?" asked Yvonne, gesturing toward a young bald-headed woman garbed in gray helping herself at the food cart. Backlit by the sunlight streaming through the room's clerestory windows, the woman's shaven stubble of hair created a golden corona around her young face.

"Of course. Boy or girl, it makes no difference. A monk is a monk. We humans make too many distinctions. Boy . . . girl. Poor . . . rich. Ugly . . . pretty. The universe is too grand to bother about silly things like that, don't you think?" said David, smiling at Yvonne. "In fact, it seems that the best students at our Buddhist university are often girls." Suddenly David stopped ladling a delicious curry onto the rice in his bowl. "I just had a wonderful idea!"

His bowl only half filled, David turned and whizzed back to the table where the master was mobbed by a throng of young monks. Everyone was undoubtedly quizzing him about the strange visitors with the elongated bicycles. When we returned to our table, we could tell that something was up. David came back to us and said, beaming, "The master is all agreed. All you have to say is 'yes.'"

"Say yes to what?" Paula wanted to know, raising her eyebrows just a little.

"We just finished building a brand-new Buddhist university. It is only thirty kilometers from here and almost on your way to Kenting. It is truly a lovely place, and you have to stay somewhere tonight anyway. So why not stay with us? What do you think?"

I looked at Paula, who shrugged benevolently as if to say, "Well, the day is done for already. So why not? This could be quite the experience."

"There is one problem, though—"

"What would that be?" I asked, thinking that we might have to undergo some exotic spiritual cleansing ceremony or convert to Buddhism before we could be allowed to set foot into the sacred halls of the monks.

"The university is very hard to find. The master and I fear that you will become hopelessly lost. It is in the foothills of the mountains, and there are no signs, you see."

Unbeknown to David, reading road signs had become a luxury of the past for us. Ever since we had entered Asia, the pretty little squiggles on the road signs meant absolutely nothing to us. We had long ago decided to navigate by a combination of compass, reading land features, and trying to match the Chinese characters on our maps to the squiggles on the road signs. Nevertheless, finding this monastery in the foothills of a still-unfamiliar country did pose a problem.

"Could you draw a map?" I inquired of David.

"Possibly, but there are many, many turns where you could go wrong," he said, scratching his shaven head. An extended exchange in Mandarin with the master ensued, and David finally spoke to us again, smiling.

"We might have a solution," said David with a grin. "A solution that would suit me, personally, very well. Monk Chang and Monk Jin just volunteered to drive your daughters in the master's car to the university, and I could ride with one of you on the back of the—how do you say again? Oh, yes! Tandems. That way, I can show you the way *and* I can ride a bicycle again. A special bicycle I have never ridden before." David's smile was wide with anticipation.

Thirty minutes later I was riding my tandem through Kaohsiung's busy streets with a Buddhist monk in billowing gray robes on the seat behind me. Passersby stared and gaped, openmouthed at the spectacle. One wizened man wearing a pointed straw hat was so bewildered that he walked right off the sidewalk, narrowly avoiding spilling his load of fish, which he was lugging in two faded plastic buckets.

David, oblivious to all the attention, was having the time of his life. "This is wonderful! It's been years since I rode a bike. Turn right at the Taoist temple. I can't believe how easy it is with two people. Turn left at the shrine. Look at how fast we are going. Fantastic!"

"I am glad you like it," I said, trying to keep up with the complex directions that were mixed into David's verbal torrent.

"I love going fast. How fast can one go on this?" he nudged.

The curves in the road had just given way to a long straightaway between a swampy pasture dotted with water buffalo and a shrimp farm. Shrimp farms seemed to cover all of coastal Taiwan and consisted of murky man-made lagoons with rickety waterwheels floating on the surface. The waterwheels churn and aerate the lagoons to keep the shrimp thriving. This particular farm must have had a hundred waterwheels cascading water into the air at full speed.

"How fast? Let me show you," I said, stepping hard into the pedals. The tandem surged, and in an instant we were going nearly forty miles per hour. The waterwheels of the shrimp farm became a white blur, and the buffalo, standing up to their bellies in muck, turned into the dirty smudges they really were. David was yelling, ecstatic with the speed. I am quite certain this was my only time on earth that I helped a Buddhist monk enter into heaven.

6.6

Paula

Day 208—Kaohsiung, Taiwan

The morning air wafted into our tent with the sweet scent of hibiscus and tangy salt. I poked my head out of the Taj, perched on a little wooden platform in the quiet campground at Xiaoyeliu just north of Taitung. What an amazing campsite! My eyes swept over a lush tropical garden filled with purple azaleas, pink hibiscus, and tall sugar palm bushes. In front of our tent, a paved stone walkway and wooden bridge meandered to the ocean and Xiaoyeliu's famous rock formations. Above me a graceful heron glided over the waving fronds of coconut palms. It was hard to believe this was December.

"Coffee's almost ready, Paula," Lorenz called from the nearby picnic table.

A picnic table! After cooking and eating on the ground in eighteen countries, we had finally found a campground with a *table* in—of all places—the east coast

of Taiwan. This country was full of surprises! The west coast had been one long industrial slog through heavily populated urban areas, leaving us all with horrible coughs from the smog-filled air. Unexpectedly, the moment we had reached Kenting National Park on the southern tip of Taiwan, everything had changed immediately. Suddenly we were cycling over steep, lush mountains and across cascading rivers; up and down uninhabited tropical valleys; and along pristine, unspoiled beaches. As we cycled north along the east coast toward Taipei, the sprawling modern cities of Taiwan's west coast were replaced by traditional Chinese fishing villages, fleets of colorful flat boats filling the harbors. Tucked in the hills, wooden houses with palm-thatched roofs reflected the culture of the Amis, the original Polynesian inhabitants, who had lived there before the arrival of the Chinese.

"Be there in a minute," I replied as I forcefully stuffed our sleeping bags into their compression sacks and hurried toward the aroma of thick Asian coffee wafting from our camp stove.

Whistling cheerfully, Lorenz set out two metal Sierra cups steaming with coffee, a faded plastic plate piled high with steamed buns, and a Sierra cup filled with slices of freshly cut pineapple.

"So what's in the buns?" Anya asked suspiciously as she strolled up to the picnic table. She carefully eyed the round, white steamed rolls that Lorenz had bought from a Taiwanese street vendor last night.

"It's not that purple bean stuff. Is it?" Yvonne grimaced. "That's awful."

"I kind of like the purple buns." I reached for the top roll on the pile.

"Don't worry. It's pork." Lorenz split open a bun to reveal a mouth-watering meat dripping in barbecue sauce. "Here, try one."

After breakfast, not wanting to leave this tropical paradise, Lorenz and I sat basking in the warm December sun, indolently sipping coffee from our Sierra cups at the picnic table. We lingered happily, listening to the calls of the tropical birds while our ponytailed daughters curled up under a palm tree: Yvonne with pencil and sketch pad in hand, Anya with her nose buried in a book. For once, traveling through Asia felt easy, even fun!

Finally, we loaded our tandems and pedaled down the trail to the famous stone formations of Xiaoyeliu—ancient sandstone and shale rocks that stood in jagged rows in the ocean waves like forgotten soldiers battling the coastal storms. Yvonne jumped and skipped over the rocks and swirling tidepools, with Anya strolling alongside. Next to them, Lorenz invented hilarious names for the bizarre formations, his booming laugh echoing across the silent shapes.

It did not seem that anything could spoil such a glorious day.

Taiwan's coastline glistened below us in the midday sun. Perched above the crashing Pacific Ocean, we wound along desolate tropical bluffs on a road that had been literally chiseled into the steep mountainside. We had been pedaling up and down the steep coastal cliffs for the past two hours, and the calories from the steamed pork buns had evaporated quickly. Below us, a little village of ramshackle huts clustered between the beach and the road.

"I'm hungry. I need lunch soon!" I called forward to Lorenz, our leader for the day, as he cycled ahead of me.

"Me too," Anya said.

"You want to eat *here*?" Lorenz was clearly uninterested in stopping.

"Can we at least look?"

Anya and I peered into the first rickety tin-roofed shack. A bucket of squirming squid stood by the door as we gazed into a dim room filled with red-teethed men and women, the bloodred juice from the soporific betel nut dripping steadily down their chins. A violent shaking of Anya's blond hair urged us on to the next shack.

The scene in the next dilapidated building was no better. In the dim light, I could make out a group of dark-haired men who were sticking their grimy hands into a large communal pot. The men grinned and beckoned to us as they pulled out handfuls of slippery cooked shrimp, cracked the shells between their teeth, and spit the hulls onto the floor. I hurriedly put my hand to my mouth and ran out of the shack.

We pedaled on, my stomach rumbling angrily. Suddenly, the beautiful day had become irritating. The cliffs that had seemed so picturesque earlier now felt like horrible ovens, fiercely radiating the heat of the sun. The calls of the birds in the lush jungle overgrowth were no longer lyrical but grated on my nerves instead. And the peaceful, empty coastline was just plain desolate. Why didn't this stupid coast have more towns where we could stop for lunch? And *eat*.

"Lorenz, we need *food!*" I shouted at his tandem speeding ahead of me.

Oblivious to my rapidly dropping blood sugar, he pushed forward, ignoring my frantic calls. Then, without warning, Lorenz and Yvonne screeched to a halt at the side of the road. I looked around, annoyed that we had stopped on another barren stretch of road for no obvious reason.

"Look! Over there!" Yvonne called out, pointing to the cliff ahead. I wondered what goose chase she was sending us on now. Then I saw it. Tucked under the cliff, a cute white wooden café overlooked a sweeping sandy cove. We parked our tandems in front of the café's open front door, decorated with tall red-painted Polynesian wooden sculptures. Above the bamboo counter just inside the entrance, mouth-watering photographs of roast meat and rice advertised various stir-fried dishes.

"All right," Lorenz conceded defeat. "What do you want to eat?"

Our little restaurant had only a handful of wooden tables and no other guests. Red and white Chinese paper lanterns swung softly from the roof in the fresh salt breeze. I selected a quiet, sunny spot by the window and settled down in a comfortable wicker chair. A few minutes later, the owner's wife appeared with a teapot and set down four tiny china cups on the table.

"Tea?" I asked Lorenz, lifting the pot to pour the green tea into one of the cups.

Inexplicably, the teacups began to shake. Hot tea flew across the table. I stared, stunned, as large green drops spilled from the teapot onto the tablecloth. Abruptly a loud rumble shook the building. Confused, I looked out the window, expecting to see a low-flying airplane.

There was no plane, just a loud ominous roar. Louder and menacing like a hundred semi-trucks, the sound bore down on our café. I pressed my hands to my ears as the roar swept into the building. Above me the roof tilted left and right. My heart beat wildly. Why were the Chinese lanterns swinging uncontrollably above our heads? I jumped, terrified, as one of the lanterns broke from the roof and plunged to the floor, narrowly missing our table.

Lorenz shouted, an edge to his voice I had never heard before. "Earthquake!" He shot up from his seat. "Get out of here! Now!"

An earthquake! That's impossible! I stumbled for the door in shock, swerving drunkenly as the ground heaved under me, undulating higher and higher. Gasping to catch my breath at the door, I suddenly froze. There were only three of us.

"Where's Yvonne?"

"What?" Lorenz turned to me, unable to hear over the crashing, pounding roar.

I scanned the room desperately. Yvonne. Where was Yvonne? A wooden ceiling slat plummeted in front of me. A wicker chair slid wildly across the floor as if on a slalom course. Under a wildly bouncing table, I glimpsed a tendril of blond hair. Of course! She had ducked and covered, following the earthquake drill taught to every schoolchild in the Pacific Northwest.

"Yvonne!" I screamed. Without thinking, I staggered back to our table, floundering as if on a wildly heeling sailboat. Outside of the window, the horizon kept bobbing up and down, dipping and rising above the creaking frame. Shattered glass sprinkled the floor, wet green tea oozing along the cracks.

I stretched my arm out under the bouncing table and pulled on a small trembling hand. I don't remember how we made it across the mountainous hills of the floor and through the flapping and creaking door, but suddenly all four of us were lying facedown on the grass outdoors, holding on to the earth, clinging to it as if to keep it still, to stop it from shaking and shuddering.

From the outside, the restaurant owners and our family watched as the little café contorted numerous times, like a flimsy cardboard box squeezed by its corners. Finally, after what I was certain was many hours, the shaking stopped. I crawled onto my knees, hesitantly, not trusting the ground below me. A few feet away from me, Lorenz was already standing, staring in disbelief up the coast. Every few hundred yards along the shoreline, massive landslides cascaded from the high cliffs, spewing rocks, branches, and mud across the road and into the ocean.

"Oh no!" I gasped, gazing in a confused haze at the route ahead of us. "How are we going to bike through *that*?"

Suddenly, we all turned quiet. After a long pause, Lorenz said what we had all been thinking. "If we hadn't stopped for lunch. If Yvonne hadn't found this restaurant"—he swallowed hard—"we would have been cycling *there*. Under those landslides."

I watched the clouds of dust and rocks cascading from the cliffs ahead, thankful that we were all safe. The smallest of all of us, Yvonne, seemed the least likely person to help our family on this journey. And yet her keen eyes had found this restaurant and saved our lives! I reached over and wrapped my arms around her, squeezing long and hard.

—◆—

We swallowed lunch down in a daze. Despite the chaos, the restaurant owner managed to pull together a meal in a kitchen scattered with tumbledown pots and dishes. I suppose we were all simply on autopilot. Like a chicken with its head cut off, we each kept moving forward despite the lack of any logical thought behind our actions.

Finally, the four of us got back on our tandems and continued north toward Hualin. We cycled slowly, nervously picking our way with care along the hazardous, narrow road below the unstable cliffs. Simply too stunned and shaken to do anything more than tread—right, left, right, left—we turned the pedals, inching mechanically forward. Fallen debris from the landslides punctuated our trail as we wove cautiously around the plumes of dust rising from the pavement.

Fifteen minutes later we came to an enormous crater, over six feet wide, in the middle of the road. I stared in horror at the gigantic eight-foot-high boulder next to the crater. It had bounced—this enormous murderous rock had *bounced*—onto the pavement as it had fallen from the cliffs above, gouging the crater before landing next to it.

"Wow," Anya said, staring in awe up at the massive boulder towering above us. "Good thing we weren't *here* when the earthquake hit!"

My stomach felt queasy as I gazed into the gaping crater. The earth-quake had hit about fifteen minutes after we sat down in the restaurant. If we had continued on instead of stopping to eat, we would have cycled about three to four kilometers. I looked at the counter on my bike. Three kilometers since the restaurant. Right about here! A cold shiver ran down my spine.

I thought the worst was behind us. Far from it. For hours the earth continued to hiccup and tremble with aftershocks.[*] Each rumble increased the lurching in my own heart. Mechanically we twisted and turned above the ocean, warily skirting around the occasional dilapi-dated building along the road, fearful that the partly standing walls and tumbled-down roofs would collapse completely with the next violent shaking of the ground.

Each village brought the same visions of destruction and loss. In one village we dodged a fallen water tank that had toppled from the roof of a nearby house, water streaming rapidly down the road as if in a desperate effort to find a safe crevice in which to hide from the ongoing quivering. In another village we passed a thinly dressed woman weeping next to her tumbled roadside stand, broken jars of homemade preserves and pickled vegetables scattered on the ground. A year's worth of labor lost in one minute! With sinking hearts, we cycled onward.

Slowly the early winter evening began to creep over the shaken and tossed landscape. Finally we arrived in a small town with a cracked plaza lined with crooked buildings.

"We need something for dinner." Lorenz pulled his tandem to a stop in the plaza. He motioned to a peeling two-story building with a market on the ground floor.

I stared uneasily into the unstable structure. No way was I going in that thing! I was relieved that I was not the leader today. How much had changed since the early days of the trip, when we all battled to make the

---

[*] The initial earthquake registered a 6.6 on the Richter scale. However, aftershocks of up to 5.3 con-tinued for twenty-four hours after the quake, adding significantly to the destruction, which would have been much worse if the epicenter had not been in a rural area.

decisions! Now I was happy to let Lorenz be the leader on his day. Being responsible for our family, making decisions that could mean life or death, was *hard*. Sometimes it was great to let Lorenz solve the problems. It would be my turn soon enough.

"We'll stay out here and watch the tandems," I answered quickly.

As Lorenz and Yvonne disappeared into the market building, Anya buried herself in a book, pretending not to notice the little group of huddled children who stared curiously at our peculiar bicycles for two. Abruptly, the earth boomed and lurched again. Up. Down. Up. Down. Sharp and distinct like the cracks of a whip. The children shrieked and clung together as our tandems toppled to the ground.

Below the building where Lorenz and Yvonne had disappeared, the market stalls swayed and pitched. A heap of guava tumbled off the stand. Dark-haired women carrying wicker baskets of food hurried out of the swinging structure. I waited, uneasily, anxiously. An infinite minute passed and then another even longer one. Where were they? I fretted, the tension in my stomach increasing to a heavy lump. Why were they still in there? I gritted my teeth, indecisive. Should I leave Anya alone and go in?

Suddenly Lorenz stumbled out carrying several bags filled with rice, bean sprouts, custard apples, and eggs. Ashen and trembling, Yvonne wobbled behind him.

"Why won't the earthquakes end?" she cried tearfully as I wrapped my arms around her. "Why won't they stop?"

I stroked her hair, trying to offer encouragement, but no words came out. I had expected we would face hardships on this journey, but an earthquake? Never in a million years would I have thought we would cycle into an earthquake. As we stood in this foreign shuddering plaza, unable to talk to anyone and so very far from home, I suddenly felt very, very alone.

Emails to bikeforbreath@hotmail.com

GREETINGS FROM HUALIN, TAIWAN!
It was an unforgettable experience for us to know your family. We have learned much from you, especially the courage you show. Huan's English students always talk about the dinner we ate together. We are honored you accepted our offer to stay the night at our home.

The next morning, when I came back to the room where Anya and Yvonne stayed, I found three words were written on our blackboard there—I LOVE TAIWAN. I was touched and felt very happy. May you have a safe and successful world cycling trip, and maybe someday we will meet in Bainbridge Island. Merry Christmas!

—Jin and Huan, Taiwan

Postcard to World Bike for Breath

Hi, Brett

Happy New Year!! Enclosed are receipts from China, Japan, Taiwan, and Hong Kong. Since I don't read any of their languages, I really can't say what is on them. Thankfully the Hong Kong receipts are easy. They're the only ones in English. After cycling through five countries with completely different scripts, it's awesome to be able to read road signs (and receipts) again.

I've also enclosed an article about us in the *Taitung Daily* (I think). It appeared the day before the earthquake on December 9. Could you scan it and have Mike put it on the web? (Not that most sponsors can read it, but it's kind of cool.)

I hope you and Maureen and the family are all well and that you had a great Christmas and New Year.

Paula

Route Update—Beijing to Thailand

Dear friends and sponsors:

We wish you a merry Christmas and a happy New Year from Hong Kong and Thailand. We must admit that our Christmas in Hong Kong has been much more festive than Thanksgiving. Hong Kong residents love Christmas, and the city is filled with fake Santas and plastic Christmas trees in all the store windows. We even bought a gold tinsel tree for our hotel room! However, Santa was restricted to a severe weight limit in gifts this year: nothing heavier than two ounces (unless it could be eaten) nor larger than a wallet. But we were all so thrilled that he had a tree to leave the presents under that we didn't mind.

Hong Kong has been a delight in other ways too. After four solid months of communicating with hands and feet while praying that the squiggles on the signs actually mean "north" or "hotel" or "ferry," we can actually read the road signs and menus and—joy of joys—find people who can speak English! Most amazing of all, instead of staring into bowls of brown wobbling things and worrying whether our meal is still alive, we find foods we recognize—of course, still outnumbered by the hundreds of strange Chinese herbal medicine stores selling bird's nests and restaurants specializing in shark fin soup.

A few days after Christmas, my mother and stepfather, John, arrived bearing letters, gifts, and encouragement. Nothing could have raised our spirits more than to be with our family over the holidays! We greeted the New Year together by burning colored papers for good luck in a Taoist temple and watching the Chinese gong ring in the waterfront plaza in Kowloon.

We are now in Thailand. Our bicycles carefully disassembled and packed in large burlap Taiwanese construction bags, we flew to Bangkok with my parents. We are now spending a week on a long-needed vacation on the beaches of Pattaya. (OK, I see some grins—but if you had just spent eight months cycling over mountains, against wind, rain, snow, and fierce heat, camping over 180 nights and eating worms and seaweed, a bed and a beach would sound like a great idea for a week.) Next stop: Australia!

Anyway here's the latest route stats:

- Kilometers for asthma and clean air: 6,633
- Miles for asthma and clean air: 4,132
- New countries cycled for asthma: China, Japan, Taiwan, Hong Kong,* Thailand*

---

* Did not cycle here.

Riding an Elephant

Posted by Yvonne

THE AVERAGE PERSON WOULD BELIEVE THAT RIDING AN ELEPHANT would be a walk in the park experience. But no, that is not how it is. Don't get me wrong, riding an elephant is a very fun way to take a walk down the road and back, but I would not advise you to take more than a fifteen-minute ride on one, since you will soon find the flaws in riding an elephant. I can tell you, when I climbed up on the ten-foot-high Asian elephant's back in the botanic gardens of Pattaya, Thailand, the ride was anything but romantic.

First of all, if you think the seat is covered with pillows, blankets, and an awning from the sun (like they show in books and movies), you will have thought incorrectly. The actual seat has a hard metal frame with a board for the bottom and about a half-an-inch hard foam padding.

Secondly, if you think the conductor will be wearing gold buckle-up shoes and a red cape, you will be wrong again. The conductor wears his normal daily wear, which most of the time consists of a dirty T-shirt and ripped jeans.

Thirdly, if you expect the elephant's walk to be a slow, calm, and undisturbing walk, then you will be wrong for the third time. An elephant's walk is a very disturbing up-and-down, side-to-side movement.

When you are forced to hold the back bar for fear of falling off, it doesn't help that the conductor (who sits at the top of the elephant's neck) starts to chuckle about how weird tourists are, saying, "They're scared of riding ten-foot elephants!"

Fourthly and lastly, if you expect the photographer to wait for you to pose and smile, you will be wrong again. The photographer jumps around you and the elephant while the elephant is still walking and takes about twenty photos while you are hanging on for your life on the back bar and barely thinking about photos. Then, when you finish the ride and the photographer barrages you to buy some photos he took, you are more than horrified at what he shows you.

I now have a horrific picture of me basically falling off an elephant to prove what an Asian elephant ride is like. But if you don't believe me, then go ahead and try.

Part V

Braking Point

Sweating It Out Down Under

Paula

Day 257—Melbourne, Australia

I thought cycling through Australia would be easy. Flat-as-a-pancake easy. I'd seen the photos of Ayers Rock sitting in the middle of endless flat red desert. Plus, Australia wasn't that large, as far as continents go. From my quick glance at the world map, Australia seemed like it could fit into the US about two to three times. Best of all, Australians spoke

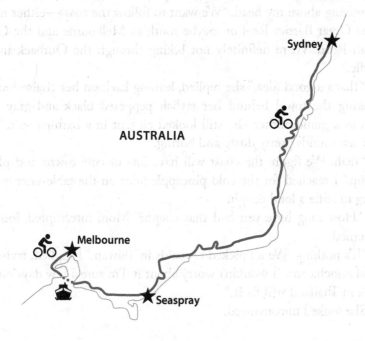

English! Once we could read signs again and stop getting lost all the time, I figured we could easily whiz across most of the continent in a month or so.

"So where do you plan to cycle in Australia?" my mom asked, rubbing some more suntan lotion on her tanned olive legs. My mom and stepdad, John, had given us the best Christmas present ever: a family vacation together in a traditional Thai villa at the lush Rabbit Resort on Dongtan beach in Pattaya, Thailand. I had to admit, this laying-around-on-beach-chairs, rolling-into-the-pool-to-cool-off, iced-coconut-drinks, and flower-decorated-bedroom style of traveling had its advantages.

I'd avoided thinking about Australia for the first few heavenly days of swimming and snorkeling and hot showers and sleeping in a bed in Thailand. Really, what was there to plan? Aussies spoke English. They ate normal, safe food that did not cause dysentery. They had drinkable tap water and hot showers. And best of all, the country was flat and easy. A cake walk after cycling over the Alps and through eastern Europe and Asia.

"Not sure," I answered, gazing lazily up at the green fronds of a palm tree waving above my head. "We want to follow the coast—either north to the Great Barrier Reef or maybe south to Melbourne and the Great Ocean Road. We're definitely not biking through the Outback in the middle."

"That's a good idea," she replied, leaning back on her chaise lounge, adjusting the towel behind her stylish peppered black-and-gray hair. Even as a grandmother, she still looked elegant in a bathing suit. "The Outback sounds pretty dusty and boring."

"Yeah. We figure the coast will have lots of cute towns and places to stop." I reached for the cold pineapple juice on the table next to me, trying to stifle a loud cough.

"How long have you had that cough?" Mom interrupted, looking concerned.

"It's nothing. We all picked up colds in Taiwan," I replied, trying to sound nonchalant. "I wouldn't worry about it. I'm sure a few days on the beach in Thailand will fix it."

She looked unconvinced.

"After this vacation," I continued, trying to turn the conversation back to Australia, "we'll be all rested up to bike most of the coast of Australia. A month should be plenty."

"Are you sure?" Mom counseled in her offhand way. "I think you should check your mileage on that, dear." My mom tried very hard not to interfere in my life, even when I announced crazy plans like cycling around the world with her grandchildren. Still, she had this uncanny way of nudging me, ever so gently, when I headed off in a foolish direction.

I bristled silently, certain I was right. Just to prove my point, I decided to look the question up.

It couldn't be! I stared at the web page on our Blackberry in disbelief as I laid on the luxurious, freshly made, traditional teak bed in our room, listening to the cries and whistles of tropical birds outside my window. How could Australia be *larger* than the US? According to the website, the distance between east and west Australia was 4,030 kilometers and 3,685 kilometers from north to south. In comparison, the longest distance across the continental US was 4,500 kilometers and a mere 2,660 kilometers from north to south. It would take months to cycle across Australia—even if we took the direct route through the central Outback. Cycling Australia was starting to look a lot more challenging than I had anticipated.

⸻

We should have caught on when we ran into a gibbering German cyclist in Melbourne on our first day cycling in Australia. We were on our way to Geelong on the coast and still debating which way to head after that: go east to Sydney or take the Great Ocean Road westward.

"Mann, nimm nicht die Oceanstrasse!" Hey, man, don't take the Great Ocean Road! The gaunt, sun-scorched cyclist grimaced with pain. "I just came from there. Two weeks of the worst hell you can imagine." His calloused hands gesticulated in an agonized wave as if he had just escaped from a medieval torture chamber. "It's nothing but climbs and descents, climbs and descents. *Ja*, it's beautiful. But by the time you get to the top of these horrible hills, you're in so much pain you don't care about the scenery. I cried. Honestly I cried!"

Lorenz and I stared at his bike, worried. He didn't look like a novice. He was traveling light—all his camping gear and clothing neatly packed into two compact rear panniers. Not like us, with clothes, books, and stuffed animals bursting out the seams.

Seeing that we were still unconvinced, he urged, "This was the toughest long-distance ride I've taken in my life. Ever! Listen, three months ago I cycled the Balkans—from Croatia to Greece. That was *ganz einfach*—so easy in comparison."

"But the Balkans are really mountainous!" Lorenz exclaimed. "Some are almost ten thousand feet tall."

"*Ja sicher.* Sure. But nothing like the Great Ocean Road."

I stared at his Croatian jersey. Yup, this guy was for real. A serious long-distance cyclist.

"Look, you have kids. Do them a favor and just bike to Sydney. It has to be easier." He rubbed a patch of scaly, flaking skin from his peeling nose, clicked into his bike pedals, and reached out his hand to Lorenz. "Go east to Sydney. You won't be sorry."

We decided to bike east to Sydney.

—◦—

"They must have some different engineering standards here," Lorenz huffed as we crawled and sweated up a hill that rose so sharply I could barely even wobble the tandem up. "This must be at least a sixteen percent grade. We would never build a major road this steep in the US."

At the top of the steep three-hundred-foot hill, we stopped to catch our breath. Somewhere down in the valley below us lay Flinders. We had barely cycled sixty kilometers east from Geelong, and I already doubted our decision. For the past six hours, I had crawled up one cruel hill just to slide down and start back on the next. My legs burned, my face was on fire, and every single muscle in my body was hollering to stop.

Worst of all, the hills were killing my lungs—or was it something in the air?* I coughed and gasped for breath as we gazed at the stunning coastline ahead of us. Steep limestone cliffs plunged into the sparkling

---

* In a WHO survey, more than 25 percent of Australians reported asthma symptoms—the highest rates in the world.

ocean. Pristine white-sand beaches dotted the deserted coves below the cliffs. How fun it would be to drive this road in a car—windows rolled down, cooling wind blowing through my hair, listening to the Beach Boys on the radio. Instead, I was swatting flies, dripping sweat, and guzzling down Gatorade* to avoid fainting. I stared at the road snaking ahead and counted the number of times it disappeared down and up another hill. Five more killer hills until I finally reached our campsite and got to collapse in a hot, sandy tent. I understood why the German cyclist wanted to cry. I don't know what the Great Ocean Road was like, but I'm certain we didn't take the easier route. What could possibly be worse than living hell?

I knew we had chosen the wrong route when we ran into a Swiss cyclist and his Olympic cycling partner at the Phillip Island nature park two days later. Anya and Yvonne were browsing the visitor center after a trip to view the penguin parade—the nightly trek of thousands of penguins returning home to nest in their burrows in the sand on the protected beaches.

"We're here for a month of training for the Olympics," the Swiss cyclist explained. "It's a perfect area for hill-climbing stints." I stared at him in shock. What was wrong with hill climbing in Switzerland? Of course, I knew. The Alps were child's play compared to cycling over these excruciating hills.

I was beginning to wish I had never heard of Australia by the time we reached Yarram. After one week of pedaling east from Melbourne in hundred-degree weather over nonstop hills, we had dropped down onto a flat plain. Finally, we're out of the hills, I thought hopefully. Silly me. As if the only challenge Australia had for us were hills!

---

* In most countries we did not consume specialized sports foods or drinks. Gatorade, energy bars, running gels, and tablets simply were not available most of the time. Generally, we found that a balanced diet high in carbs, fruits, vegetables, and simple proteins based on the local food was enough. However, in the extreme heat of Australia, we came dangerously close to sunstroke. Fortunately, sports drinks were ubiquitous in Australia, and we quickly switched to them to help cope with water loss in the extreme heat.

The dust in Yarram swirled along the sidewalks, twisting into tiny tornadoes and bursting around the corners. Gray sandblasted buildings, sagging from years of heat and hopelessness, stood silently as our two dusty tandems pedaled past in the early morning. I shifted miserably in my saddle as we turned down the empty main street, heading out of town. In the extreme heat, I had developed saddle sores. I gritted my teeth and tried not to scream each time the saddle scraped against the painful welts.

Coughing from the dust clouds, I licked my bleeding lips, which were swollen and cracked from the sun. I was not alone in my misery. All four of us were covered in peeling white patches from extreme sunburn. Flaking from head to toe, we looked as if we had contracted some terrible disease—like leprosy or smallpox.

The morning was already warm as we pedaled quickly, trying to make some distance before the worst of the day's heat. After two hours, we turned south from the highway toward the little beach town of Seaspray. For once the road was flat and easy. We whizzed along the quiet lane, Anya humming to the Dixie Chicks on her portable CD player, while Yvonne reread Meg Cabot's *All American Girl* for the third time, leaning her book on the stoker handlebars. There wasn't much to look at anyway—just a long, monotonous stretch of dry, brown fields bordered by an occasional eucalyptus tree.

Lorenz noticed the koala first. Speckled gray and brown, it blended in perfectly with the gray patchy bark of the eucalyptus tree above our heads. He screeched his tandem to a halt, pointing overhead into the dark green leafy branches of the tree.

"Quiet guys," he whispered, pointing overhead.

"Where is it?" Anya stood transfixed under the tree, desperately trying to find the koala in the branches. When it came to people, it sometimes seemed like Anya could take them or leave them, but animals were a completely different story. As a toddler in her stroller, she had cried when I ran over ants on the sidewalk. She rescued wounded birds; spent hours pouring her heart out to her guinea pig, rabbit, and horse; and refused to kill even flies or spiders.

"Up there." Lorenz pointed to a fork in the tree as he pulled out his camera. The furry animal sat completely still, probably a bit stoned from nibbling the tree's narcotic leaves.

"I see it. I see it! It's so cute!" Yvonne exclaimed, jumping up and down and pointing to the Australian version of a teddy bear.

All at once, the dry, brown landscape seemed much more interesting. Maybe we'll find a wombat or a platypus, I thought hopefully. Or at least a kangaroo. We had already seen a couple of kangaroo herds hopping through open fields alongside the road two days earlier. They seemed to be everywhere—almost as common as deer in the US. Hardly any cars had passed us in the last hour. The deserted fields spread for miles. Surely there were other wild animals wandering around here.

Several times I jumped at a motion in the trees above us as we pedaled along the empty road, hoping it was another koala. Instead a few white corellas flew off, their high-pitched whistles and tweets filling the air. In another tree, a green-and-red parrot cried out from above. Even though Australia's trees, lawns, and parks were teeming with at least forty different species of parrots, I still gasped each time I saw a parrot in the wild. We stopped to take more photos and gulp down some water before pedaling onward.

Then, out of the corner of my eye, I noticed a round, brown shape moving in the parched, dry grass at the edge of the road.

"Stop!" Lorenz called out at the very same moment.

"What is it?" Yvonne asked, her eyes widening as she gazed at a strange creature with a long, pointed snout. Its sharp quills bristled, and she instinctively stepped back.

"It looks like a porcupine," Anya whispered in excitement as it started to waddle across the road.

"No, I don't think they have porcupines here. Let me see—" I was rapidly thumbing through my guidebook, which had a photo section on Australian animals. "Here, I think it's this." I held the book up to Anya behind me on the tandem. "What do you think?"

"Yes. It's an echidna!"

"What's that?" Yvonne asked.

"It says here," Anya began reading, "the echidna is a monotreme. It is one of only two mammals in the world that lays eggs in its pouch. The other is the platypus. Sometimes called a spiny anteater, the echidna uses its snout to find ants, termites, and earthworms."

We stood silently in wonder as the odd little animal waddled off into the bushes on the other side of the road. A wild echidna and a koala in one day! As well as parrots and corellas. If we had been driving in a car, we wouldn't have seen any of these amazing animals! Cycling through this seemingly barren country was brutal, but at that moment I was happy to be seeing Australia at ground level at speeds that enabled us to peek below its austere exterior to discover a marvelous hidden world teeming with life.

Kids Care

*Live interview with Radio Disney Seattle**

Christie Thuren: Good evening. Welcome to Radio Disney Seattle *Kids Care.* I'm Christie Thuren, your host. I've been working on this next interview for almost a year now, and I'm really excited about it. We have a phone call specially wired into Radio Disney studios right now. This call is coming from some friends of ours who are from Bainbridge Island, and they are near Melbourne, Australia. This is the Eber family—and they are biking around the world for asthma. We have Anya on the line.

Anya: Hello?

Christie: Anya, I have been trying and trying to get ahold of you for so long! I'm dying to ask—what's the coolest thing about traveling like this for so long? And then I also want to ask, what is the really hard part? What is it you miss the most, and what is it that has been difficult for you?

Anya: The thing I like best about biking around the world is probably getting to experience the different cultures. Because you can always hear about it, like in a textbook, but you don't actually get to be inside the culture and with the people. I think it's also really fun to be at all the historical sites. Like in Athens, Greece, I got to see the Parthenon. In school you hear about how tall it is and see a photo, but I actually get to be up there and see all the statues

* We thank Radio Disney for permission to use this edited transcript from the interview by Christie Thuren on the *Kids Care* program, Feb. 2004.

and stuff. So that has been really cool too. The thing that's probably hardest is missing my friends at home. 'Cuz although you get to talk by email and sometimes on the phone, you don't get to see them. And you hear about how your home is changing. Like my friends will say, like, "Oh, they made a new store" or "They changed this." And I think when I come home it will be a totally different place—

Christie: I'll bet you'll be in culture shock. So—do you guys really get along great? You're with your family 24-7. Does that ever get hard, having to deal with your sister all the time? Just being in cramped quarters.

Anya: Yes, privacy is a huge issue. 'Cuz we only have two tents. And if you get a hotel room, you're usually in the same room. So you never really get to be alone. We always try to set aside time. But it doesn't always work because you're on the back of a bike a lot. And it's really difficult when you're in an argument 'cuz you have to still be with your parents. You have to cook dinner, and you're like "Oh God, I have to deal with them." Back home you could go to your room and lock the door. But that doesn't work here.

Christie: That would be really hard. But I bet it's also really helped your relationships so much.

Anya: You really learn about each other. Like you learn what people's strengths are. So that's definitely a good thing that happens.

Christie: Well, I guess we should let your sister have a go, huh? Thank you so much.

Yvonne: Hello?

Christie: Hi! Hi, Yvonne. This is Christie at Radio Disney! Do you want to tell some of the boys and girls just about the last hour—what you guys have been doing?

Yvonne: OK, well, for the last hour we've been running around trying to find a phone in the middle of Australia. We're northeast of Melbourne, and some really nice people have been driving us around.

Christie: Looking for a phone?

Yvonne: Yes. And we found a gas station that is letting us borrow their phone.

Christie: I wanted you to tell this story because we have literally been trying to set up this interview for eight months. We almost got you in Russia. But that didn't work out. In Moscow, we just missed you. You had just turned your cell phone off to go to bed.

Yvonne: Yes.

Christie: Did you see the Bolshoi [ballet]?

Yvonne: Yeah, it was really fun. We saw the playing of *La Bayadere*. So it was really cool.

Christie: You are in sixth grade. Right? So are you going to go back to school next year? Or do you homeschool?

Yvonne: We're homeschooling right now. And then we're going to go back to school next year. So we have to take a test to make sure we can go up to the next grade.

Christie: Oh, I don't think you're going to have any problem with that test! So, I had your sister tell some of her favorite things about traveling for a year on a bike with your family. And some of the things that she didn't like quite so much. She mentioned privacy as something that's really difficult. You don't get that so much on the road, do you?

Yvonne: No, actually not at all. It's like really hard because whenever you're like angry at somebody, it's really hard to be apart from them. And you can't really go off somewhere because, I mean, you're probably in the middle of some forest or something. Yeah, it's really hard. Especially for Anya because, I don't know, she likes to be alone more. I like to be with my family a lot, so it's not as hard. But it's pretty hard.

Christie: Well, Anya's a teenager, right?

Yvonne: Yeah.

Christie: I was going to ask you one other question before you go. What was it? Oh, what are some of your favorite countries?

Yvonne: Probably my favorite country is China 'cuz it's so different. It's like a really fun, happy culture. They're really different. Like they sell, they eat anything. They eat dog, and they eat scorpions. It's really fun to see the culture.

Christie: So do you feel lucky?

Yvonne: Yeah, I actually do because it's really fun and because some people, they just haven't gone anywhere their whole life. I met kids in Australia, here, and they're like, "Wow you've gone to all those countries. I've never been out of Australia."

Christie: Yvonne, thank you so much for talking today! You have been listening to Radio Disney Seattle *Kids Care* and the Eber family. I'm your host, Christie Thuren, and we're glad you could join us.

Australian Signs

Paula

Day 270—Seaspray, Australia

The signs were Lorenz's idea. After two weeks of hot, sticky, hilly pedaling along the coast, we had rented a cottage in the sleepy beach town of Seaspray to celebrate Anya's and Lorenz's birthdays. That morning as Anya slumbered under a blue, gauzy princess canopy over her bed—an added bonus of luxury we had not anticipated—Lorenz, Yvonne, and I

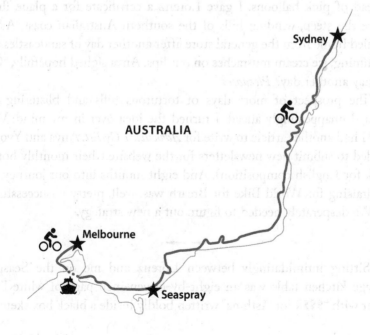

scurried around in the kitchen. We baked a chocolate cake in an oven (definitely an improvement over a camp stove), inflated balloons, and scattered the table with candies and party decorations collected at the tiny Seaspray general store. We laid out a small collection of presents that could easily fit in a twelve-by-eighteen-inch pannier: an Australian face mask made from emu oil and clay, a seashell bracelet, Outback stickers, and a gift certificate for a new book.

The four of us lazed all day on Seaspray's long, empty, sandy beach. We swam (not too far off shore because of the sharks), read, and built sandcastles decorated with bits of coral and even a colorful parrot feather collected on the beach. Happily slurping an ice cream from the general store on the way home, for a moment my chapped lips, saddle sores, and aching legs and back disappeared. I was certain this was how paradise must feel. Warm and contented with a smattering of chocolate chip ice cream on the lips.

The next day we repeated the same routine for Lorenz. This time, I baked a chocolate pudding cake. We reused the party decorations, scattered more gold-wrapped caramel candies on the table, and inflated blue instead of pink balloons. I gave Lorenz a certificate for a plane flight above the steep, winding hills of the southern Australian coast. As we pedaled home from the general store after another day of sandcastles and swimming, ice cream mustaches on our lips, Anya sighed hopefully, "Can we stay another day? *Pleeaase?*"

The prospect of more days of torturous hills and blistering sun loomed unappealingly ahead. I turned the idea over in my mind. Why not? I had another article to write for *Adventure Cyclist*. Anya and Yvonne needed to submit new newsletters for the website (their monthly homework for English composition). And eight months into our journey, the fundraising for World Bike for Breath was, well, pretty unsuccessful so far. We desperately needed to figure out a new strategy.

Sitting intimidatingly between Lorenz and me on the Seaspray cottage kitchen table was an eight-by-eleven-inch page of white lined paper with "$$$$ for Asthma" written boldly inside a black box sketched in the center. Practically bouncing with creative ideas, Lorenz was wildly doodling suggestions on our brainstorming map. Surrounding the box, he had sketched various circles with arrows pointed to the center goal. "Cash donations from ten selected additional corporate sponsors" was a suggestion written in one circle. "Lorenz writes a novel in installments" in another. "Bainbridge fundraising drive" filled a third circle. And "Media—PR firm" stared at us from a fourth.

Below the central goal, Lorenz had written "And then a miracle happens" in black Magic Marker surrounded by a cloud and stars. Yup. A miracle is what we needed. This fundraising stuff was hard. Really hard. Discouragingly hard. Naively, I had assumed that once we started cycling and talking to the radio stations and newspapers about our mission, people would flock to our website and donate thousands of dollars to World Bike for Breath.

But there was one major problem. For the past nine months, we had cycled through twenty countries where the first (or even second or third) language was *not English* (with the exception of England). We had bumbled our way through most of eastern Europe and Asia, barely able to ask for a bathroom or hotel let alone explain what we were doing. I imagine people who drove past us wondered why a family was pedaling with kids and a pile of tents and bags on strange bicycles for two. But I am certain that none of their theories were even remotely connected to asthma and clean air.

It was a miracle that we had even talked to as many newspapers as we had! Or that we had even raised a few thousand more dollars. Sure, we could fund a few scholarships to asthma camp with the money people had donated, but we certainly weren't going to change the world this way.

"I have an idea!" Lorenz suddenly looked up.

"Mmm?" I was feeling rather hopeless at this point. I tried to stifle a cough. "What's your suggestion?" I rummaged around in my handlebar bag, looking for my rescue inhaler. Hadn't I just used it recently? Well, I needed it again. One more puff wouldn't hurt.

"Why don't we put a sign on the back of the tandems? With a donation box saying 'Biking for asthma' or something like that?" Lorenz drew a new circle on the brainstorming map and began scribbling rapidly. "People could see the signs when they drive past us on the road. And when we stop at grocery stores or campsites, people could give us donations."

Two days later, in the town of Sale, we spotted a store that advertised "printing and reproduction."

"What do you think?" Lorenz adjusted the two-by-two-foot white-and-purple sign tied with string around the panniers on the back of our tandems. He stepped back, beaming, clearly pleased with his ingenuity. I had to admit, the plan was pretty clever.

"Around the world for asthma," the sign proclaimed in large purple letters circling the World Bike for Breath logo in the middle. "Donations welcome." Our website was listed on the bottom of the sign just in case someone wanted to look us up and donate.

Suddenly, a ruddy-cheeked man in shorts pressed five dollars into Lorenz's hand. "Good on ya, mate," he called out cheerily as he headed into the store.

"You're doing this for asthma?" A matronly older woman stopped in front of the sign barely two minutes later. "I have asthma and so does my sister. Here you go." She dropped two dollars into the little donation cup Lorenz had attached to the sign.

Amazingly, within twenty minutes Lorenz had collected four donations!

Eight kilometers later, as we pedaled on our way to Stratford, a car pulled over on the side of the road ahead of us.

"Dad, I think that lady is waving something out the window," Yvonne prodded Lorenz on the tandem in front of her.

"This is for you." A slender hand with red nail polish reached out the car window as we pedaled past. "Are you really biking around the world? With these two girls?" the hand's owner asked in astonishment as I filled out a donation receipt for twenty dollars. "That's amazing! Don't you girls get tired?"

"Yes," Anya and Yvonne replied in unison.

"Well, you keep pedaling now! You have lots of hills ahead." The hand withdrew into the car and sped off.

—◆—

"Why didn't we think of this before?" I asked Lorenz as I rolled out of our tent onto a small patch of grass in the Stratford on the River Tourist Park that evening. "Your signs are amazing!"

"I dunno." He looked up from stirring the rice over the camp stove. "Maybe we didn't have the guts. You know, to tell everyone we're biking around the world."

"What do you mean?" I pulled out the metal poles and began crossing them over the tent and clipping on the ties, stifling a cough.

"Well, I don't know about you, but I really wasn't sure we would make it when we started in Greece." He tossed some diced onions into the pot and adjusted the flame on the burner. "I don't think I wanted to advertise what we were doing in case we quit. And looked like idiots."

I hoisted the poles, and the tent sprang to life. "So you think we can make it now?"

"Yes, actually." He paused thoughtfully, his eyes wandering over Anya and Yvonne doing their math homework on the grass nearby. "You know, I guess I do."

While we were shopping in the supermarket in Barnesdale the next day, several more people dropped money into the donation can. Within two days of putting up signs, we had received over $125 in donations. How generous the Aussies were!

I was packing away the last of our food shopping in the panniers when a couple walked out of the supermarket and handed us fifty dollars.

"My sister had asthma," the woman said as she waited for me to write out a receipt in our donation book. She paused, trying to control her words. "She died from an asthma attack on her honeymoon. They were in the mountains, far from any hospitals, when she got the attack. She died in her husband's arms."

I stood there holding the receipt, horrified, not knowing what to say. Should I tell her I was sorry? That I knew how awful asthma was? How you could be well one minute and the next gasping and fighting for your life?

Thankfully, the woman's husband stepped in to fill the silence. "We appreciate what you're doing." He reached for the receipt. "So many people think asthma's just a harmless disease, like hay fever and other allergies. They're wrong, you know. It kills people."*

⌒⌒

The road from Barnesdale to Lakes Entrance should have been easy. The road was flat, skirting a long, wide delta. But instead of whizzing along happily, I felt exhausted, each breath requiring more energy than I could give. Ever since we had arrived in Australia, I had puffed and panted up each climb, struggling to get enough air. I had ignored the constant coughing at the top, telling myself that it was because the hills were so difficult. But today, even pedaling the flat sections hurt my lungs. Something was definitely wrong. I forced my eyes to stare at the front tire as it turned round and round on the pavement. It was the only way I could convince myself to push forward.

At the scenic overlook above the canal connecting the Gippsland lakes to the ocean, I leaned against the metal guardrail, gasping and coughing. Below us, wide, flowing water channels meandered through groves of cypress trees on their way to the glistening ocean in the background. Flocks of majestic white pelicans circled overhead. I closed my eyes and tried to focus on the chirps, caws, and hoots saturating the air around us. But all I could think of was how unfair it was that these birds were flying through gallons and gallons of oxygen that refused to go into my lungs.

⌒⌒

I sat on the bed in our cabin in Lakes Entrance, turning the orange pill bottle round and round in my hand. "Predisone 5 mg," the label said. The miracle drug. It stopped hives, anaphylactic shock from bee stings, inflamed joints. And one good whack of it kicked my lungs back into

---

* More than 450,000 people in the world die from asthma every year. These numbers do not include deaths resulting from asthma-related complications such as COPD, pneumonia, and heart failure.

shape. It was as good as the monster inhaler I'd had as a child. Except—except that I jumped around for days after taking it, edgy and nervous as if I had drunk too many cups of coffee. My skin bruised easily, and I was permanently thirsty. Hell, who cared. I needed to breathe.

I wasn't a doctor—well, except the PhD kind—but I had spent the last forty years with my asthma. We weren't friends. But still, asthma was a part of me, a permanent companion. I knew my lungs. I knew the difference between a rattle and a wheeze. A chest cough and a nasal cough. A shortness of breath I could push through and one that would kill me. I swallowed ten of the little white pills—fifty milligrams should give my lungs a pretty good jolt. Then, exhausted from fighting the tight band around my chest, I crawled into our bed and rested.

I woke up the next day ready to take on the world. I practically bounced around the tiny cabin, tossing clothes and toothbrushes into panniers in minutes. I whizzed around the kitchenette, splashing hot water into cups of dried coffee powder, tossing sizzling sausages in the air, and scrambling eggs wildly in the pan. Anya moaned in the double bed next to the kitchen table and pulled the sheets over her head, trying to escape the mad whirlwind invading our tiny room.

The world was wonderful—amazing. "Look at the sun shining in the window!" I exclaimed as I flipped a sausage onto a nearby plate.

Lorenz and Yvonne stared at me as if I had been invaded by a manic body snatcher. No matter. They didn't know how incredibly wonderful it was to breathe again. Air, gallons of clear, cool air whooshing into my lungs, oxygen pulsing into my toes and fingers. Look! I could jump without gasping. I did a little skip just to prove it. A miracle—that's what prednisone was. I wanted to get on my knees in gratitude to the unnamed pharmaceutical genius who had discovered these tiny white pills. Thank you. Thank you. Thank you.

My lungs cleared up just in time for the hills to turn into wild, desolate peaks. For the next three hundred kilometers, we cycled through five totally uninhabited national parks, each covered in increasingly denser forests of stringybark eucalyptus, myrtle, and kanooka gum trees.

Each day was a never-ending slog through trees, trees, trees, and nothing else—except bugs. Just before Cann River, we crossed a steep pass. The sign at the top announced we had climbed to 290 meters— almost a thousand feet—above sea level. The next day we stopped to gulp down our dwindling bottles of Gatorade at a 310-meter pass. If these were Australian hills, I never wanted to see their mountains.

Finally, nine hundred pedaling kilometers northeast of Melbourne, we burst out of the trees into Eden. It was aptly named. Steep sandstone cliffs plummeted to a coastline of sweeping sandy beaches filled with lush tropical groves and pink-and-white flowering bushes. After five days of cycling through endless Australian bush, it felt like we had died and gone to heaven. Except, of course, for the hills.

The next week was another roller coaster, wobbling, cajoling, and sometimes pushing our bikes up the sadistically steep climbs. But now, in between the hills, we found pristine empty beaches punctuated by cute little towns. As we careened down from the headlands to the next deserted cove, we would dash for the sparkling ocean, tear off our clothes, plunge into the refreshing water, then flop onto the beach, wiggling our toes in the warm sand.

———

We stopped at the tiny wooden clapboard store in Benandarah, hoping for a bit of shade. Eden, two hundred kilometers behind us, seemed a remote memory. I sighed. At this rate it would be another week before we got to Sydney. I had been so wrong about Australia. It wasn't flat. It wasn't easy. And it was anything but a small country. That seemingly short stretch between Melbourne and Sydney on our world map was almost 1,500 kilometers.

"Those your bikes out there?" the burly owner of the Benandarah general store and petrol station asked as he rang up our pile on the counter. One Coke, two bottles of Gatorade, six candy bars, a package of crisps, and a box of biscuits.

"Yes. Do you need me to move them?" Lorenz asked. Our tandems were leaning against the wooden wall of the store under the small petrol awning. They didn't leave much room for a car to squeeze in next to the gas pump.

"No worries. I was just looking at the signs on the back of your bikes." He pointed to our caloric stash. "You want a bag?"

I shook my head. We'd probably inhale all of it before we got back on our tandems.

"So how far have you gone on those bikes then?"

"About eight thousand kilometers. We started in Greece."

"Well, good on ya!" He nodded, impressed. But then the corners of his mouth turned down and a look of pain flashed behind his eyes. "You're doing this for asthma?" He rang up the till and opened it again, pulling out a fifty-dollar bill. "Take this for my brother, Jimmie. He died last year in a surfing accident. It was godawful. We were out there riding the waves together. Having a wonderful day." He handed the bill to Lorenz, shaking a little.

"Then he had one a them asthma attacks. Where you can't breathe and you go all purple-like. I tried to pull him up on the board so I could get him back to the shore, see."

He paused, his Adam's apple moving up and down as he swallowed hard. "I tried and tried. But I couldn't do it. He was just staring at me, his eyes all big, gasping like a fish."

Lorenz stood at the counter, holding the fifty dollars, frozen, not sure what to say.

"Then he sank under." The store owner gulped, his face twisted in grief. "It took an hour for the rescue team to find his body and bring it to shore. It's a good thing you're doing. Fighting asthma. Someone should a done it a long time ago."

Postcard to World Bike for Breath

Sydney, Australia

Hi Brett

Enclosed are receipts for Australia. We have succeeded in collecting $664.80 in Australian dollars from small donations along the road. Hooray! We are enclosing a check for that amount.

We're headed to New Zealand next. And then back to the U.S. after a quick stop in Tonga. See you in a few weeks!

Paula

Goblins and Gremlins

Paula

Day 299—Auckland, New Zealand

"And the winner is—"

A tense hush descended over the crowd assembled in the campground lounge in our "motor camp" just outside of Auckland, New Zealand. Six Kiwi campers, squeezed together on the faded yellow couch on the back wall, leaned forward eagerly, their eyes riveted to the tiny twenty-four-inch television screen suspended from the ceiling. Another twenty-odd viewers were packed in the room, perching on the couch arm-rests, leaning against several scratched orange Formica-topped tables, and even sitting on the rust-colored linoleum floor. A strong odor of sweat, wood smoke, and cigarettes filled the lounge as the campground audience shuffled uneasily, muffling quiet coughs while they waited impatiently.

Billy Crystal, the master of ceremonies for the night, waved his hand dramatically,

then opened the envelope containing the winner for the Seventy-Sixth Academy Awards: "—the *Lord of the Rings: The Return of the King!*"

A huge roar erupted from the jubilant campground crowd. A burly man with a tattoo suddenly hugged the startled man standing next to him. A dark-haired woman in jeans and a flannel work shirt dabbed tears from her eyes. Shouting and cheering, the campers flipped off beer bottle lids, clinking the bottles together and laughing and singing strains of the Maori words to the New Zealand national anthem, "*E Ihowa atua. O nga iwi matou ra.*"

I was thrilled that the third film in Peter Jackson's brilliantly directed movie rendition of J. R. R. Tolkien's Lord of the Rings trilogy had won best picture—along with best director and ten other Academy Awards. But judging from the revelry in the room, you would have thought that New Zealand had just landed a man on the moon!

"Hey, mate. It's a great day for New Zealand, what?" A tall, friendly Kiwi slapped Lorenz on the back. "Have a beer." He thrust a cold bottle in Lorenz's hands.

Lorenz grinned back. "Yeah, it sure is great that the movie won so many Oscars."

"Well, that's not just *any* movie. Peter Jackson is one of *us*—a native Kiwi. He filmed everything right here in New Zealand. You noticed all those white-capped mountains in the movies, right? Took a helicopter up to Mount Cook and the Southern Alps and filmed on location, they did. And Mount Doom with all the bubbling craters? That's not made-up stuff, like with digital images or anything. They filmed that in Tongariro National Park. So you see, that there movie is *our film.*"

"Chur, bro." The friendly beer donor raised his bottle and grinned. "It's not every day *our little country* wins the Oscars."

"Cheers." Lorenz tipped his bottle in reply, happy to be invited to join the national celebrations.

———

As soon as Anya and Yvonne were old enough, Lorenz and I read the entire Lord of the Rings trilogy aloud to them at night. I had loved adventuring to fantasy-book worlds as a girl, and it was almost more exciting to watch our daughters discover these worlds anew. Snuggling in front of the warm fire in our woodstove, we visited cozy hobbit houses, rode across the wild plains of Rohan, and cowered under Mount Doom towering ominously above Mordor. Now, caught up by the country's Lord of the Rings Oscars fever, there was only one logical bicycle route through New Zealand.

"Look, guys! It says here that we can visit Hobbiton!" I held up my copy of *The Lord of the Rings Location Guidebook*, which we had purchased from a tourist shop selling garish rings filled with Middle Earth symbols and T-shirts featuring gray-haired Gandalf. The guidebook listed each filming location across New Zealand, along with a description of the movie scenes and a smattering of tourist information. I waved the book from my spot under a tree at our campground in Thames, at the entrance to the Coromandel Peninsula. The view of the Firth of Thames was breathtaking. Green rolling hills, dotted with white sheep, slid down into a sparkling bay, the three-thousand-foot peaks of the Coromandel Range looming in the background.

"We can cycle round the Coromandel Peninsula, which is supposed to be stunning. Or," I continued, "we can bike to all the cool Lord of the Rings movie sets. What do you think of heading straight south to Matamata? That's where they built the Hobbiton set!"

Two days later we were crawling into round-windowed hobbit houses, strolling under the famous Bilbo Baggins party tree, and taking photos of each other dressed up as dwarves waving broadswords. That night, as the four of us soaked in the bubbling natural hot springs at Opal Springs cabins, we plotted out our next Lord of the Rings destinations.

~

An eight-foot-tall white silica cone steamed and hissed in front of us as we waited for the Lady Knox geyser to erupt promptly at 10:15 at the Waiotapu Thermal Wonderland.

"Hey, Dad!" I waved in excitement as I spied my father and his partner, Sandra, on the edge of the crowd. "You picked an appropriate place to rendezvous." I shouted over the din of the crowd and hissing steam as he squeezed through the crowd to us. "Of course, a passionate geologist like you would want to hang out in a volcanically active place about to erupt anytime!"

"You mean anytime in geological time." He grinned. "A few more thousand years or so."

Dad had been playing leapfrog with our family for the past two weeks, ever since we first met up at Saint Georges Basin, Australia. We had spent two lovely days together there in a cabin, hiking and playing on the long sandy beach. That evening he had come up with an offer too good to refuse.

"How would you girls like a break from bicycling? Join me on a little three-day driving trip to the Blue Mountains?" Dad had asked Anya and Yvonne while we grilled steak and potatoes on the "barbie" outside of the cottage. "Your parents can keep pedaling the tandems to Sydney, and we'll have some fun adventures without them." He waved a greasy spatula cheerfully at Yvonne, who was clearly debating whether this scheme fit within the rules of biking around the world. "I'm sure the kilometers count whether or not you're on the back of the tandem."

I couldn't believe my ears! Three days *alone* with Lorenz? For the past nine months, our family had barely spent a few hours apart from each other. And now we were being offered *three whole days* on our own? My mind reeled with the thought. It was almost as good as going on a second honeymoon!

We spent the next three days pedaling to Sydney in the pouring rain—not quite the romantic trip I had imagined. Still, it was wonderful to finish a sentence, eat an entire pizza without having to argue over who got the last piece, and spend both nights alone in a cabin for *two*— donated each night by generous Aussie campground owners who, glancing at the empty stoker seats, quickly assessed our situation and insisted we could not camp in a tent.

After returning the girls to us in Sydney, my dad leapfrogged ahead of us to New Zealand. Now, a week later, as the Waiotapu geyser erupted, spewing steam and white silica into the air, I grinned at Dad and Sandra. This leapfrog game was pretty fun.

"So what shall we see first?" Dad turned to Anya and Yvonne, pulling out a map.

"I want to see the Champagne Pool!" Anya said, eyes gleaming.

"Oh, you do, do you? I don't think there's champagne in it," he teased. "But I'm sure we'll see some bubbles."

We turned to a path on our right, Dad chatting away to Anya and Yvonne about the origins of the bubbling mud pools, hissing thermal springs, and otherworldly red-and-green metallic-rimmed ponds erupting around us. The friendly Kiwi at the campground in Auckland had been right! New Zealand was a perfect set for a fantasy movie. I could easily imagine the creature Gollum crawling with the ring through the swirling, oozing mud and steam.

For the next few days, the six of us continued to leapfrog south toward Lake Taupo—Dad and Sandra driving off for geological investigations and hikes during the day while we cycled onward through Lord of the Rings territory. Each evening we would sit by the campfire, examining Dad's latest finds—sharp, glistening black obsidian; light air-filled pumice; quartz-flecked andesite. Feasting on grilled green mussels, seared steak, and braised carrots, we discussed the movement of tectonic plates, tried to figure out how the ancient Polynesians had migrated to New Zealand, and debated the location of the Southern Cross in the sky.

<hr/>

"Damn! Another spoke just popped," Lorenz grumbled as he sprang away from my back tire, the broken spoke in question dangling with a menacingly sharp end from the rim.

We had just stopped to view the wildly cascading thirty-three-foot Huka Falls, a few miles north of our next family rendezvous at Taupo Lake Campground. Lorenz had been investigating why my back tire had a wobble. Looking rather frustrated, he pulled out a new spare spoke from the collection duct-taped to his bike frame.

As I helped Lorenz pull off all the gear and extricate the back wheel from the drum brake for the fifth time in two weeks, I wondered, half seriously, if somehow we had offended some goblin from Middle Earth or a local Maori spirit. Since our arrival in Auckland, we had already had two flats, replaced a worn tire, drilled out Lorenz's cleats from his disintegrating bike shoes, and popped two spokes. Most likely the tandems were simply wearing out after ten months and close to nine thousand kilometers of carrying a family of four and their gear around the world.

But still, I couldn't help but feel the presence of the original Maori people, whose culture and beliefs are woven into the landscape of this lush and beautiful country. Large wooden Maori *marae* with high carved columns holding up tall roofs over wide meeting spaces stood sentinel along silent roads, the deep forbidding faces of elaborately carved Maori entryways staring down on us from above.

Back on the road again, I laughed at my silly superstitions. I had been thinking about the Lord of the Rings too much. The spoke was fixed, and that was the end of it. No more equipment goblins or bad-luck gremlins. Or so I thought.

———

"Have a wonderful hike," Sandra said as she dropped Lorenz, Anya, my dad, and me off at the Tongariro trailhead. It was our final day of hopscotching together, and Sandra and Yvonne were taking a quiet rest day at a hostel in Turangi at the southern end of Lake Taupo while the four of us hiked the Tongariro Crossing, one of the most famous treks in New Zealand.

"So what shall we do?" Sandra looked at Yvonne and gave her a hug as we waved goodbye. "I was thinking we might want to go get some muffins at the bakery. And then we could sit outside and draw together if you'd like—"

As we started out on the twenty-kilometer trek below the massive 7,500-foot-high volcano of Mount Ngauruhoe, I knew why Peter Jackson had chosen the Tongariro National Park as the setting for the steaming, hissing wasteland of Mordor. I was certain that the Evil Eye of Mordor was gazing down on us from nearby Mount Doom (aka nine-thousand-foot Mount Ruapehu). All around us lay a wild, desolate, treeless landscape. We climbed past steaming rotten-egg-smelling fumaroles; clambered over jet-black rocky lava flows; and skirted gray, silty, muddy lahars. Was Gollum hiding below? Were orcs on the other side? We wended our way around the otherworldly landscape and climbed slowly upward to a stark, brown saddle. Suddenly, we crested the summit at 6,122 feet and gazed down on a series of fantastic glistening emerald pools—both stunningly beautiful yet also unsettlingly eerie. The spell was broken as we began the downhill slope and the real world finally reappeared—a lush green landscape spreading along Lake Taupo far below in the distance. Still, I kept looking over my shoulder, an uneasy feeling that a goblin from Mordor had somehow escaped this fantasy landscape and was following us.

"Race you to the room! Fifty cents says I win!" Anya challenged Yvonne at the hostel in Turangi that evening. Sprawled on a chair on the lawn of the hostel nursing my sore feet, I was astonished that Anya still had the energy to run after such a long, hard trek. Next to me, my sixty-nine-year-old dad was leaning back in the wide wooden garden chair, contentedly sipping a beer. He had not only completed the hike but had pushed ahead of us most of the time. If only I could be that strong when I'm his age!

"Ready. Set." Yvonne hitched up her blue sarong to her knees, revealing long sun-browned legs and flip-flops. She's growing tall quickly, I thought, admiring the two girls.

"Go!" Yvonne shouted, and they were off, giggling and sprinting as fast as they could to the hostel room door.

Anya, still a head taller and stronger, was in the lead, her brown muscular legs and arms pumping away. Hindered in part by the long blue wraparound skirt bunched in her hands, Yvonne struggled to catch up. In desperation, only a few feet away from the concrete stoop at the front door to our family apartment, she quickly shot her left leg forward, sliding her flip-flops below Anya to hit the stoop. I heard a nasty thwack.

"Ow!" Yvonne cried out. And then, "I won!"

Suddenly, she was curled up in a ball on the ground, cradling her bleeding foot.

"Yvonne, are you OK?" Anya cried out and kneeled to hug her.

All Yvonne could reply was a mumbled "I won" as she clutched her foot, tears welling in her eyes.

The next morning Yvonne's foot had swollen to the size of a melon, purple-and-black bruising running along the edge of her foot where it had struck the stoop.

"Bill, could we take her to the doctor before we leave?" Sandra asked my dad, clearly worried. I glanced up from wrapping a large white bandage around Yvonne's foot and looked over to him hopefully. Judging from the way Yvonne shrieked when I just touched her foot, there was no way she could bike eight kilometers to the nearest doctor. She couldn't even stand up. I was thankful that my dad and Sandra had a car.

I held my breath, hoping he would say yes. With my dad you never knew. He had his schedule: his carefully organized itinerary of exploring the geologic wonders of the north island. After breakfast this morning, we had planned to say goodbye and part ways. From the way Dad was stuffing clothes rapidly into his backpack, I could tell he was in a hurry. They were flying back home in two days, and I suspected he was eager to have some time alone after spending three weeks leapfrogging with our wild cycling family.

The Turangi Community Health Centre was housed in a small, white building. The doctor teased Yvonne about racing her sister while poking the foot gently. He wrapped Yvonne's foot in a fresh bandage and then handed us a prescription for antibiotics.

"It's easy to get infections in New Zealand," he explained. "You need to keep the foot clean and dry." I didn't think it was appropriate to explain that we were camping and traveling by bicycle. *Clean* and *dry* were relative terms for us.

"So it's not broken?" I asked hopefully.

"It could be," the doctor replied evasively. "You need an X-ray." He scribbled an order and handed it to me. "The closest radiology clinic is in Taupo."

Taupo? We had pedaled through Taupo two days ago. It was over fifty kilometers away from us. And Dad and Sandra were headed in the opposite direction.

———

The next morning Yvonne hobbled to the taxi waiting in front of our hostel, her foot still swollen and purple despite a second night's rest. Dad had paid for an extra night for us at the hostel before he left. I had hoped that after a good night's sleep, the foot would be better. No such luck. The Maori spirits seemed to be having a grand time breaking not only our tandems but our bones as well.

"Get better soon, honey." I hugged Yvonne, helping her to slide her heavily bandaged foot onto the back seat of the taxi next to Lorenz.

A lump formed in my throat as the taxi sped off to Taupo. What if Yvonne's foot *was* broken? She looked like she was in a lot of pain. Should we cancel the journey and go home? Call my dad and hitch a ride to the airport with him? Was it safe to fly internationally with a broken foot? And what about insurance for the X-rays? We'd bought international emergency medical insurance, but would it cover all this? Crap. What a mess.

I paced back and forth across the lawn in front of the rooms. Looming overhead, I could see the steep, treeless volcanic cone of Mount Ruapehu. Could it be we had hiked across that range two days ago? How quickly everything could change! Finally, I decided to do something useful. Like calculate our latest "money on hand" numbers. I spent the afternoon adding up every penny we had, including $35 in New Zealand cash and $120 of emergency money hidden inside the frame of the tandems. We had a grand total of $10,866 to our name. Deducting at least $3,000 for extra expenses like plane tickets home to the US, bike repairs—and now doctors' bills—we had barely enough left for two months of cycling. That would just get us back home to the US. And then what? Maybe we should just quit this journey and go home now.

———

Yvonne sat on the double bed in our room, her bandaged foot resting on a pillow.

"So the doctor says it looks like you cracked a small bone in your foot?" I sat next to her on the bed and squeezed her hand. "Do you know where that is?" I lifted the X-ray up to the light, trying to see the spot where the fracture might be.

"Somewhere here." She pointed to a series of long, thin, small bones on the side of her foot. "But it's hard to see." Yvonne had spent the entire taxi ride home studying the X-rays. Rather than worrying about her injury, she had entered the hostel room talking nonstop about the amazing pictures the doctors had taken of the inside of her foot.

Lorenz leaned over the X-ray and added, "The doctor said that in kids the bone is soft and flexible. You can't really tell for sure if there's a fracture until a few weeks later when a white line shows up where the bone has put down calcium to repair the break."

"So is it broken or not?"

"Probably. He said there's very little you can do for it anyway, except keep it bandaged up and stay off it for a few weeks." Lorenz patted Yvonne on the shoulders.

"And biking? I assume that's out."

"Actually, as long as she's not putting any pressure on the pedals, it's probably better for her than walking right now," Lorenz replied.

"What do you think?" I looked over to Yvonne, who was busily studying the X-ray again. "What do you want to do? Should we quit biking and go home?"

"Why would we do that?" She looked up, flabbergasted. "We were going to go swimming with dolphins. And I wanted to see the seals!" She stared over at Anya, who was quietly sitting in the corner reading, deliberately avoiding any discussion of doctors, needles, X-rays, or any other disgusting medical topic. "I'm not going to be the one who makes us quit!"

Email to bikeforbreath@hotmail.com

SAW YOU IN KAIAPOI (JUST NORTH OF CHRISTCHURCH), NEW ZEALAND

We went past you twice. Gosh, you've been riding those bikes so far from home. Just been to your website and been reading through what you've been up to . . . GREAT!

We could see that the youngest girl was enjoying herself . . . she was looking all around and not where she was going. At least, I doubt if she could see past her father's back anyway! Poor thing, I reckon her legs only just reached those pedals, but never mind, you can see she's brave . . . and yes, she was working very hard indeed. I bet she sleeps at night!

The girl on the bike behind her mother looked like she meant business. (You were riding into a head wind "southwester" with a grim set face at the time we saw you, and we could see you intended to catch up with your father and sister, who were somewhat ahead.) I don't know how you manage all the hills, particularly with riding so very far as you've done. I expect it's a case of just putting your best foot forward (laughing heartily). If it was I who was on a bike on a hill, I believe I'd lose patience and hitch a ride in the nearest car.

Wishing you a safe and successful journey.

—Andrew, NZ

Route Update—Hong Kong to Tonga

Hi, dear friends and sponsors:

We are currently cycling in Tonga and will be flying to the US in a week! After eleven months, twenty-three countries, and nine thousand kilometers of pedaling, we are now on the home stretch! When we last wrote to you, we were celebrating Christmas Hong Kong style with a gold tinsel tree and Chinese roast duck. After cycling 1,500 kilometers along the Australian coast from Melbourne to Sydney, we headed to New Zealand, where we had planned to pedal the North and South Islands from Auckland to Christchurch. Unfortunately, however, our plans changed when Yvonne ended a race with her sister at the Turangi hostel by fracturing the side of her foot. So we decided to catch a bus to Wellington, where we could wait until Yvonne's foot had healed enough to continue biking. In Wellington we visited the amazing Te Papa natural history museum and viewed *LOR: The Return of the King* in the Embassy Theater (where the world premier was held). Anya sat in the theater seat with Frodo's name and Yvonne in the seat with Sam Gamgee's name. We then took a gorgeous ferry ride to Picton on the South Island, and after a few more days of laying over, started biking again along the east coast to Christchurch, stopping to swim with seals in Kaikoura.

From New Zealand we flew to the tiny Polynesian kingdom of Tonga. A forgotten island, with little tourism, we have been treated to a true South Pacific experience over Easter. We slept in grass *fales*, drank kava (their traditional drink), attended a pig feast, and biked around the island (a grand total of 150 miles) to visit beautiful coves and ancient tombs and monoliths.

Our route to date:

- Kilometers for asthma and clean air: 8,996
- Miles for asthma and clean air: 5,630
- New countries cycled for asthma: Australia, New Zealand, Tonga

World Bike for Breath is planning several events in the Seattle area, including some great slideshows, before we pedal the finale ride across the US and Canada. We can't wait to see you there!

—The Ebers

The South Sea Bug

Lorenz

Day 340—Nuku'alofa, Tonga

The South Seas fascinate me. I can't exactly pinpoint when it started, but I have been bitten by the South Sea bug for as long as I can remember. Maybe I watched *Mutiny on the Bounty* one too many times, or maybe it was my mom's fault for pulling *Kon Tiki* from her shopping bag one day and handing the book to her bored fourteen-year-old son. That son, me, was severely dyslexic and a terrible reader. Up to that day, the pinnacle of my literary reading achievement had been the painful deciphering of *Asterix* comic books, a couple of pages at a time. But Thor Heyerdahl's journey on his home-built balsa raft, *Kon Tiki*, which floated him four thousand miles across the Pacific to the South Sea islands, had me spellbound with adventure. My dyslexia was swept away by tropical storms,

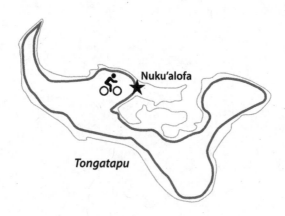

shark attacks, jungle escapades, and poisonous critters that crawled into sleeping bags at night. I knew that one day I too would go.

"You finally made it to the South Seas!" said Paula as we clambered down the rickety aircraft stairs onto the hot tarmac of the Tonga International Airport. The air was sweltering and the asphalt so hot that it stuck to our flip-flops. The airport terminal building was the size of a large garage, and its roof was decked with palm leaves. It wasn't a terminal building at all—it was a terminal hut! I couldn't believe it. I had finally arrived in paradise!

"Cool bicycles! Never seen one made for two," said the baggage handler, his gleaming white teeth shining in his smiling face.

Looking over my shoulder, I did a double take. Was the baggage handler actually wearing a grass skirt? The skirt was light brown in color and frayed at the edges with long reeds hanging down to the ground. The top of the skirt, though, looked more like the tatami floor mats that we had slept on in Japan. Looking around, I noticed that many locals were wearing these skirt-mats. Apparently this was not some show put on for the handful of Anglo tourists who sporadically visited this remotest of nations. This was local dress!

"What? Yes, those are ours," I stammered, taken aback, as I jumped to help him roll our tandems from the belly of the Boeing 737 in which we had just arrived.

"Where are you staying in Tonga?" he asked.

"I think it's called the Heilala Lodge."

"Heilala. You will like it. It's traditional Tongan, three miles up the road from town."

———※———

What the baggage handler failed to mention was that the road up to the Heilala Lodge was unpaved packed dirt. So was nearly every other street in Nuku'alofa (population 19,900), the capital "city" of the kingdom of Tonga. Even the Nuku'alofa town square was unpaved dirt. To my surprise though, the square housed an ATM machine that miraculously accepted my card and spit out colorful bills touting the smiling face of Tupou IV, the king of Tonga. The king had the dubious distinction of being the fattest monarch in recorded history. According to the *Guinness Book of World Records*, he weighed in at an astonishing 462 pounds. While extravagant in his girth, the king otherwise appeared to be very modest. As we biked another mile onward, we passed the king's home, which was no larger than a very nice American house. The king's residence was a picturesque wooden structure topped by a red-gabled roof and a small, square tower with a red egg-shaped dome that had a widow's walk on top. The front of the tower was accented with a flat-roofed entrance portico. It was a beautiful island home but certainly not an extravagant royal palace. If food was the king of Tonga's only excess, more power to the king!

Continuing up the dirt road to the Heilala Lodge, dodging chickens and pigs as they darted from the lush, blossom-laden bushes on the roadside, our nostrils were filled with the pungent smoke from palm leaf fires that seemed to be burning in every local's yard. The air buzzed with insects, and cries from tropical birds echoed from the tops of the palm canopies.

Two Tongan ladies wearing long sarong dresses, exploding with prints of colorful tropical flowers, greeted us excitedly as we unloaded our curious bikes in the hibiscus-filled gardens of the Heilala Lodge. Hiva, the older one, had a face round as a coconut and a broad, sparkling smile. Amipa, the younger one, danced barefoot through the lush Bermuda grass, chattering cheerfully, like a waterfall, as she helped us unload our bags. The lodge was not your average hotel but rather a collection of palm-thatched huts. A larger central hut served as the reception and dining room, while smaller huts dotted the gardens for guests. Hiva and Amipa told us that the huts were called *fales*. On our ride up to the lodge, we had seen that many Tongans still lived in these *fales* instead of Western houses. Amipa and Hiva walked us down a dirt path to our *fale* as dusk settled between the palm trees and the sky exploded into tropical crimson. Hiva shooed away chickens that were pecking for bugs on the path as we walked.

"You girls can help me collect the eggs for breakfast," said Amipa to Anya and Yvonne.

The girls had already hit it off with our new hostesses and were well on their way to making Hiva and Amipa their unofficial Tongan aunts.

At check-in I had spied Hiva sneaking the girls some treats while their parents were supposedly not looking.

"If you wash your hands, I may even let you help in the kitchen at breakfast," said Hiva, waving away mosquitos that had become very thick after sunset. "The islands have lots of bugs. That's why we have these," said Hiva, gesturing at the girls' beds as she swung open the door to our *fale*. Anya's and Yvonne's beds were draped in two snow-white mosquito nets hanging from the thatched ceiling.

"Like two white wedding bells," chuckled Amipa. "Now we just have to find you girls some Tongan husbands to get married to."

"Yuck! No way!" shrieked the girls as they jumped under the canopies. "These are our princess beds! Keep your husbands!"

Before Amipa and Hiva left, they showed us how to work the four incandescent light bulbs that were housed in paper-covered wall fixtures and constituted the entire electrification of the *fale*. We broke out a cold dinner of bread, cheese, and sausage left over from New Zealand and watched in fascination as a family of small lizards, attracted by the warmth of the light bulbs, crawled one by one out from the *fale*'s thatch and settled themselves inside the warming paper wall fixtures.

"I can't believe these lizards want it any hotter than it already is," complained Anya as she picked at one of her numerous mosquito bites. "It's got to be a hundred degrees in here. I also think I have at least a hundred mosquito bites already. I will probably die of dengue fever."

"What's that?" asked Yvonne, suddenly alert.

"Mosquitoes bite you. You start bleeding internally, and then you'll die," said Anya nonchalantly as she shifted her attention to a different bite.

"That's not true," I interjected quickly, but Yvonne had already gathered up her sandwich and was disappearing into her mosquito-net-covered bed with it.

"Just read the *Lonely Planet*, Dad. It's true," said Anya.

"That's just in extreme cases," I retorted, trying to protect my romantic image of the South Seas from my daughter's unsubstantiated assault.

"You are a pretty extreme case, Dad," said Anya, poking me gently in the ribs as she got up from the table.

After dinner, exhausted from a long day of travel and Tongan culture shock, we turned off the lizard lights and crawled into our mosquito-net-covered beds. The girls slept in single beds in the main room of the *fale*, and Paula and I had a double bed in a room off to the side. By eight o'clock we were all fast asleep.

<hr>

"Ahhhhhrrrrrg!"

I shot up in bed, hopelessly tangling myself in our mosquito net.

"What is it?" I snorted, thrashing.

"A lizard bit me!" screamed Anya from the next room.

Ripping the mosquito net off the ceiling, I sprinted to the main room, still draped in the net. Fumbling, I turned on one of the lights and saw two lizards scrambling out of the lamp and ducking into the reed wall. Anya stood in the middle of the room screaming, shoving her hand into my face.

"A lizard crawled into my bed and bit me on the hand!"

"Stay calm, Anya. Lizards don't bite!"

Even though her dad generally knew what he was talking about, Yvonne didn't take any chances. She shot out of her bed past me and jumped, still bleary-eyed, onto the table.

"I'm certain it was just a nightmare, honey," said Paula calmly, giving Anya a hug. "Lorenz, take that off." She pointed at the mosquito net still draped over my head.

"No, Mom. I felt it. It was scaly. It wrapped itself around my wrist and bit me," screamed Anya.

"It was a dream. Now let's go back to bed and get some sleep."

"No way, Dad. I am not getting back in there till you take the whole bed apart," yelled Anya hysterically, shoving her hand back into my face. "Look! It bit me. It hurts."

"Those two tiny red marks? They look like old mosquito bites," I said, unconvinced. Knowing, however, that there would be no sleep otherwise, I lifted Anya's mosquito net and started listlessly pulling apart Anya's bedding.

Suddenly, fast as lightning, a dark-red *thing* covered in mottled scales shot out from under Anya's pillow and slithered on a hundred shiny, scurrying legs off the bed. I jumped nearly two feet into the air, slipped, and fell to the floor. The beast was at least six inches in length and was veering straight toward me. "What the . . . Oh shit!"

Paula and Anya shrieked in unison and jumped onto the tottering table. Joining white-faced Yvonne, they all screamed.

"Kill it! Kiiiiiiiilllllll it!

"Lorenz, kill it!"

"How . . . crap!" I yelped. The thing was making straight for my leg.

I scrambled for my shoe by the door, grabbed it, and started whacking, out of control, my skin crawling. Just as the pencil-long centipede reached my foot, I landed a glancing blow. Now seething with revenge, I lunged forward and struck five hard whacks until the beast finally stopped wriggling and lay prone on the floor.

"What the hell is it?" I asked, standing panting over my vanquished foe.

"I think it's a *molo* . . . *molokau*," said Paula, scanning the *Lonely Planet* guidebook, still sitting on the table. "It says here: 'The *molokau* is a four- to six-inch-long poisonous centipede. The *molokau* bite is not normally lethal to adults.'"

"What the hell does 'not normally' mean?" I wondered aloud.

"Anya isn't an adult! Is she going to die?" asked Yvonne, her eyes as big as tennis balls.

"Should we bring her to the hospital?" I ventured.

"No way! I am not going in there!" said Anya.

On the way up to the Heilala Lodge, we had passed the Tongan "hospital," a moldy green cinder-block building no larger than a three-car garage. It stood on a swampy lot, overgrown by trees and shrubs.

"If Anya goes in there, she will definitely die," said Yvonne with conviction.

Paula took control, pulled out our fat medical kit, and said, "Anya is *not* going to die. We are going to give her two doses of antihistamine and two Advil for the pain. Dad is going to set his alarm, and we will wake her every hour until sunrise to make sure she's breathing."

Since I was still amped up from my mortal combat with the *molokau*, I took the first shift and sat in a chair in the dark, watching Anya's chest move up and down as she slept. My eyes kept darting around the gloomy room, scanning for slithering shadows in all the corners. What if the deceased *molokau* had friends that were going to avenge their departed brother by sinking their fangs into my ankles? I pulled my feet onto the chair.

At sunrise Anya was still breathing. Her hand was swollen but no worse than from a bad wasp sting. She was coherent, and the pain had subsided some. She was going to be all right. Later we learned that, as with scorpions, some *molokau* bites can be deadly. Others you can get lucky with.

I took the dead *molokau* outside in a half coconut shell. The sun was just rising over Heilala Lodge, and the lodge chickens came running up to me, expecting grain for their breakfast. I looked at the *molokau* with loathing and flung him to the chickens. The chickens took one look at the beast and ran the other way. Tongans are very afraid of the *molokau's* awful bite. Apparently, the Tongan chickens are no different and were not inclined to eat the vile thing.

Some South Sea bugs you just don't want to be bitten by.

PART VI

PEDALING ON PRAYERS

Dark Room

Paula

Day 354—Seattle, Washington

Crunch. Whir. Scrape. The new side-by-side refrigerator in Eric and Cheryl's gleaming kitchen in Seattle hummed, then paused. Suddenly, little sparkling chips of ice dropped into the glass I had placed under the ice dispenser. Again, I pressed the buttons on the electronic panel on the fridge door. A whoosh of clear, cold water cascaded on top of the ice. I reached for the glass under the dispenser, felt the cool moisture collecting on the outside, and lifted it to my lips.

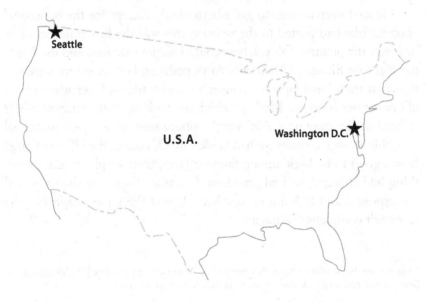

Five minutes later I was back in the kitchen, listening transfixed as the refrigerator crunched more ice chips for me. Oh, the sheer luxury of it! Simply set a glass down on the metal shelf inside the door and suddenly out popped clear, fresh, uncontaminated, cold water! No kneeling by a stream or walking to a campground pump to fill up our bottles. No dropping iodine tablets into the water container to kill the germs. I could do this all day!

"Another glass?" My friend Cheryl smiled. "You must be thirsty."

I nodded. I wasn't thirsty. But there was no way I could explain my obsession with the ice water dispenser.

"Oh wow! That's a nice shot of Paula and Anya on that mountain trail in Japan!" Lorenz clicked the digital photo on the computer screen on Eric's desk to enlarge it.

After arriving in Seattle,* we had first stopped to visit our friends Cheryl and Eric. As we cycled across the globe, they had faithfully developed and digitized all our film. Now Lorenz was eagerly looking through the thousands of photos he had mailed back, selecting the best for our upcoming slideshows and talks.

I leaned over Lorenz to get a better look. Except for the occasional photos Mike had posted to the website, this was the first time any of us had seen the pictures. Oh yes, how could I forget that road and the freezing night on Shosanji? There was Anya pedaling behind me up a narrow trail, past traditional Japanese houses, their clay tile roofs set against trees of orange persimmons. My legs ached just looking at the steep climb. It seemed so far away now. And yet the photo seemed so much more real than this strange country we had landed in. Of course, the US was home! It was good to be back among familiar faces, familiar places. But everything had changed, shifted somehow. It was as if someone had adjusted the exposure and lighting on our lives. It was the same image, but the scene felt completely different.

---

* On our way home to the US, we flew first to Los Angeles, where we visited Paula's parents and family, before returning to Seattle for the finale bike trip across the US.

"So what's this photo?" Eric asked, pointing to a picture of Yvonne and Anya trying to lift up a tire in the middle of the desert. Next to them stood several camels. "Cheryl and I have been debating about it for weeks."

Standing next to Eric, Cheryl laughed. "My theory is that the girls wanted the spare tire for the Russian van. Maybe you had a flat."

"Oh, let me see ... that's Mongolia. The Gobi Desert." Lorenz peered at the photo. "The girls are lifting the tire up to open a well. They are watering the camels." The four of us laughed at the two radically different interpretations.

What had Cheryl and Eric thought as our photos emerged from the dark room? Or our friend Mike as he posted them on the website? Judging from some of the hilarious captions Mike had put under our pictures on the web, he had clearly struggled to make sense of the fragments of our experiences we sent home. Maybe, like us, our friends were also floundering as we each tried to navigate across the enormous journey that separated us.

A few days later, we pedaled onto the ferry to Bainbridge Island. I felt an odd lump in my throat as I watched the Seattle skyline recede in the distance behind the churning water. How great it was to smell the familiar salt air, to see the beautiful Cascade Mountains covered in snow! And yet our visit with Cheryl and Eric had caught me off balance. I was home, but I felt strangely like an outsider. Stop being silly, I chided myself as I watched the large green-and-white ferry pull up to the heavy wooden pilings at the dock on Bainbridge. We just needed to reacclimate. This was only a temporary stop—a short layover to see our friends, check on the renters in our house, and meet with the board of World Bike for Breath. We'd have plenty of time to readjust as we pedaled across our own country over the next few months.

Half an hour later, we were pumping the tandems up New Brooklyn hill, the fresh smell of a recent spring shower rising from the road. We turned left at a small sign tucked under some blooming rhododendrons. The tandems bounced down a dirt track under a canopy of lush cedar and maple trees. Pedaling behind Lorenz, Yvonne wiggled impatiently, excited to be sleeping over at her friend Hallie's. I was looking forward to seeing my friend Robin too. Robin was a professional grant writer, and I was hoping she had some fundraising suggestions for World Bike for Breath. Our next board meeting was in two days, and I could use some ideas.

"So how's it going?" I looked up at Lorenz as he walked into Robin's large, bright kitchen the next morning, his hands greasy from working on the tandems in her garage. I was sitting at the kitchen table under a lovely bay window overlooking Robin's field. And feeling very irritable. A huge stack of envelopes, bills, and bank statements lay in front of me—a year's financial backlog, despite my mom's best efforts to manage our bills while we traveled.

"Bad news. The tandem wheels are shot. We need new ones." Lorenz started scrubbing his hands under the kitchen tap. "And the entire drive-train needs to be redone. Basically, the bikes need a complete overhaul. It's going to cost us several hundred dollars."

"Oh no! Not that too!" I rifled my hands through my hair as I stared at the numbers on the balance sheet in front me. "How are we going to pay for the bike repairs? We barely have thirty-five hundred dollars left in our bank accounts!"

Lorenz wiped his hands on a paper towel and walked over to look at my calculations. I pointed to our dismal figures. "It's going to cost at least eight thousand for the four of us to cycle across America. We don't even have half of that! And now we need to spend hundreds of dollars on the tandems?"

"I'll give Burley a call. Maybe they can send us new wheels," he suggested. "And what about World Bike for Breath? Weren't they going to help out with the US expenses?"

I nodded. Of course they'd help. We'd made it back to Seattle—even returning with some savings to cross America. There was no way they'd let the journey end now.

The board meeting for World Bike for Breath got off on the wrong foot right from the start. Sitting around the wooden coffee table in Brett and Maureen's living room, I stared in surprise at the first item on the agenda in front of us: new director. Brett had worked tirelessly as director for a year with no pay while we were gone. He had done a fantastic job. But who would replace him? Around the table, I saw a sea of silent faces. No one volunteered. I felt a knot in my stomach. Something felt wrong.

Next, the treasurer, Chuck, distributed a sheet with the latest financial data. I glanced down the page. Since our family had left to cycle around the world a year ago, the organization had received another $8,112 in donations. Hey, better than I had expected!

Then my eyes slid over the expenses for the year. They'd funded a scholarship for asthma camp. Great! There were a bunch of office expenses. Our health insurance. And a payment to Jonathan Maus, who was doing a fabulous job as our PR manager.

"Currently World Bike for Breath has a total of four thousand one hundred and seventeen dollars in the bank," Chuck finished his report. My head jerked up as the numbers finally registered. What? *Only four thousand dollars?* My heart thumped loudly in my chest. Crap!

"Well, we've made it this far," I said, trying to be positive. "And the main fundraising push is still ahead of us. We always expected to raise most of the money when we cycled across America." I glanced from Maureen to Tom to Brett to Chuck and Tatiana and swallowed hard. There was no easy way to say this. "We were hoping—um—our family has used up almost all our savings to make it back to Seattle." I twisted the financial sheet awkwardly in my hands, then plunged in, typical Paula style. "We don't have enough money to finish the trip across the country. We need another forty-five hundred to make it across."

Silence. Absolute dead silence. Maureen shook her head, resolutely. "You've done an amazing job so far. But we have to be practical here. Even if the board gave you everything in the account, it wouldn't be

---

* Both Linda and Debbie left on sabbaticals in Europe just as our family started cycling around the world. They were replaced by two new board members—Chuck Veilloux and Tatiana Dudley.

enough. What if someone gets sick or it takes longer than you thought to get to DC? No. It's unrealistic."

Suddenly I felt as if I were holding on to a ball of wet clay disintegrating in my hands. "But if we don't bike to DC, we're quitting at the most important point!" I argued, trying to fight back a rising panic. "The ride across North America is where we talk to the newspapers and radio and TV! How can we raise awareness of asthma and clean air if we don't go?"

Tom shook his head. "What your family has done—biking around the world—is incredible. I think you should be proud of what you have accomplished." He paused, trying to find the right words. "But we can't run an organization on hope. Running a fundraising ride across the country would require all the money we have now. And more. We'll need to hire a new director. And if the point of cycling around the world is to raise awareness for asthma, we also need to pay Jonathan to manage the PR for you. We can't keep expecting you to set up interviews with the newspapers and TV haphazardly on your own while on your bicycles in the middle of nowhere."

Maureen and Brett nodded in agreement. "You're already back on Bainbridge. So why not just stop. Stay home? You've done an amazing job already."

I took a deep breath and tried to clear my head. Were they saying our journey was *over*? That we had cycled three-quarters of the way around the world—*to end now*? Lorenz opened his mouth to speak, then shut it. He could see there was no point in arguing.

I leaned back on the couch in shock. I felt nauseous, and my face was flushed. "What about the fundraising dinner at Island Center Hall this Friday?" I asked, grasping at straws.

"Yes, of course. We'll still hold the event," Maureen said. "At the very least it will bring in some more money for asthma programs."

I felt as if I had just slammed my tandem into a brick wall. My head was throbbing, and I was dizzy. This couldn't be happening!

The next days were a blur. Lorenz stopped by City Hall, entertaining everyone with hilarious stories of our adventures as they begged to know when he'd start back at work again. Anya and Yvonne took their home-school exams and registered for school in the fall.* I finished up an article for *The Encyclopedia of Women in Islam* that was long overdue.

Our old life here wasn't so bad, I reproached myself as I pedaled into town past lush gardens of yellow tulips and pink rhododendrons. What was wrong with returning to our jobs and our friends? Anya and Yvonne seemed glad to be back home again. I had hardly seen them since we returned. They spent every possible minute playing at their friends' houses and going on sleepovers. Come on! We could sleep every night in a warm bed. Take a shower whenever we wanted. Stay indoors when it rained. What was I thinking, even considering going on? We needed to stop this rootless life and give our kids a normal childhood again.

And yet—over the past week, I had occasionally glanced over at Anya to catch a look of exhaustion on her face. Was she struggling, like me, to make sense of this strange new world that we had returned to? To find a way to reconcile two completely separate lives and experiences? I bit my lip, worrying. I doubted we could ever give our daughters a "normal childhood" again.

The line for the fundraising dinner and cycling slideshow wound down the wooden stairs in front of the hundred-year-old Island Center Hall and out into the parking lot. Back in the hall's ancient kitchen, I could hear my friends Mindy, Eileen, and Adrianne hurriedly stirring pots of chili, cutting up salad, and stacking baskets of bread for the dinner. I peered through the large wooden doors of the blue-and-white board-and-batten community hall to the crowd below, both hopeful and worried. So many people had come to listen to our stories and see our slideshow! Would we have enough food? Would we raise enough money?

I glanced down the steps to see Lorenz's colleagues from City Hall laughing and chatting together. Behind them I could see several members of the Bainbridge cycling group, Squeaky Wheels. And then in the

---

* In Washington State, all homeschooled students are required to take an annual placement exam at the end of the year to determine whether they are ready to move to the next grade. Yvonne and Anya ended up significantly ahead of their age groups in most subjects.

back—could it be? The Connors? There was no mistaking the Connor family with their seven children. I waved and hurried down the steps.

"What are you guys doing here?" I asked Julie and Gary as I gave them a big hug. "Corvallis is at least seven hours from here."

"Six. If the traffic's good." Julie laughed, glancing over at Anya and Yvonne, who were talking animatedly to Tyson and Jordan, the two Connor children closest in age to them.

"We weren't going to miss a slideshow about some crazy people who biked around the world!" Gary replied. "Say, when do you guys start biking across America?"

"Well," I began slowly, not willing to go into all the ugly details about our disastrous finances, "we're supposed to leave on May eighth, next Saturday. That's World Asthma Day. We were planning to start in Astoria, Oregon. The beginning of the Lewis and Clark Trail."

"Astoria! That's an easy drive from our house," Gary said. "We're driving back to Oregon tomorrow. We'd be happy to take you along and drop you off on the way."

I shook my head. We'd have to raise thousands of dollars tonight to make that happen.

"OK. But if you change your mind, we could come back up and get you next week. Seriously. We don't mind driving up again. We want to help."

I nodded. No point in spoiling the evening by explaining there was a good chance we were never going. Not in a week. Not in a year.

After everyone left, Brett counted the proceeds from the dinner. We had taken in over $1,460! For one delusional moment, I imagined that maybe the board would change their mind. But reality quickly set in. There was no way an additional $1,460 was going to pay for running the organization and hiring a PR manager and new director *and* cover part of our journey across the country as well. Our journey was over.

Pedaling on Prayers

Paula

Day 360—Bainbridge Island, Washington

I chewed distractedly on a pencil as I stared out Robin's wide kitchen window. Should we stay on Bainbridge, or should we go? I could see Yvonne running outside with Hallie in the backyard—a beautiful wide green field surrounded by tall cedars and fir trees. Their laughter drifted over to me as they plunged through the grass, chasing each other. The girls seemed happy enough back home on Bainbridge. But every inch of me screamed to go.

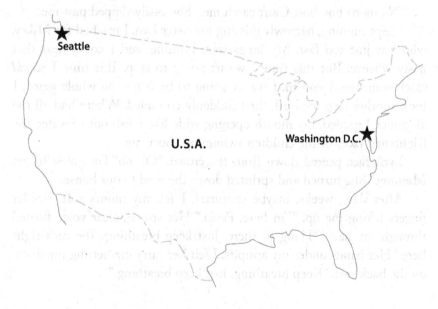

Seattle

U.S.A.

Washington D.C.

"Caught you!" Yvonne giggled, tugging on Hallie's shirt. Oh, to have run like that when I was a little girl!

—————

"Tag, you're it," my friend Janet shouted as she ran headlong into me, pressing her hand against my arm.

Friend sort of, I guess. On rainy days, when Janet was bored and her parents were still at work, she would slip next door to our house, bringing a favorite board game or doll, and ask if I was well enough to play. But at school it was different. When other kids were around, I was a ghost. She would walk right past me as if we had never met. It hurt every time. I tried hard to be Janet's friend. She was the only girl I knew who wasn't terrified when I hunched over, wheezing and coughing. But sometimes she was, well, kind of mean.

I looked around the cul-de-sac at the end of our street, trying to decide who to chase. Maybe I had a chance at catching six-year-old Tommy if my lungs could just hold out for the ten-second sprint. Tommy saw me headed toward him and quickly dodged behind a group of tall kids. I stopped, turned, ran for Sharon, who was flapping her fingers on her head, teasing.

"Na na na boo boo. Can't catch me." She easily slipped past me.

I kept running, narrowly missing my sister Lyn. I reached for Mikey, who was just too fast. My lungs were burning, and I could hear that nasty wheeze. But this time I wasn't going to stop. This time I *would* catch someone. I had to. I wasn't going to be *it* for the whole game. I took another step forward, then suddenly crumpled. Where had all the air gone? I gasped, my mouth opening wide like a fish out of water, the frightened faces of the children swimming above me.

Lyn's face peered down from the crowd. "Oh no! I'm going to get Mommy." She turned and sprinted down the road to our house.

After days, weeks, maybe centuries, I felt my mom's soft, slender fingers lifting me up. "I'm here, Paula." Her strong, clear voice floated through my haze. "Hang in there. Just keep breathing. The car's right here." Her hands under my armpits, I felt her carry me, setting me down on the back seat. "Keep breathing. Just keep breathing."

As my mom quickly backed our car away from the cul-de-sac, I stared out the rear window at the faces of the other children standing along the curb. Angry. Frightened. Irritated that I had spoiled the game. The band pressing on my chest was so tight, I was certain I was going to die before we got to the emergency room. For a moment I wished I *was* dead. I was still *it*. I was the one everyone ran away from. The one who couldn't catch up. The one who never made it to the end. *It.*

I focused my gaze back out the window. Hallie was now chasing Yvonne, giggling as they ran in circles across the meadow. I would never, ever be able to run like that! I gritted my teeth angrily. My whole life was filled with never-evers—with could nots and should nots! I couldn't bring a down sleeping bag on our bike trip—even though it would have been twice as light and much smaller (I was allergic to feathers). I shouldn't camp (ha!), pet cats, have carpets in my house, eat chocolate (right!), mow grass, dust my house (well, at least I agreed with *one thing* on my list), go outside in the spring when the trees were budding—or summer when the ragweed was in bloom. Or fall when the leaves were falling. Or winter when the air was cold. Heck, what was the point of *even being alive* if you had asthma?

But damn it! I *could* live, despite my asthma. Look—I'd made it around the world on a bicycle! Well, *three-quarters of the way*. Was that always going to be my story? The wheezing girl who couldn't make it to the end? I had to go! But—I paused, unsure. This was not just my journey. What about the rest of the family? Would they want to continue?

Sitting side by side on Hallie's guest bed, Anya and Yvonne looked up at us curiously, unsure why we had called this family meeting.

"Mommy and I have been talking about the bike trip across America. We've been wondering whether you want to stay here on Bainbridge," Lorenz said, looking at Yvonne, who was swinging her legs distractedly up and down under the bed.

"You mean stop biking?" Yvonne stopped swinging her legs and frowned.

"Well, yes." I twirled my hair nervously. "We need to know. Are you girls tired of cycling and camping every day? Would you rather stay here with your friends?"

Anya shook her head vehemently, her curly locks swinging back and forth. "But we have to go! It's your dream, Momma." She bit her lip, thinking. "I like biking and going new places every day. And meeting new people."

"Me too. That's how we live now!" Yvonne snuggled close to Anya. "I miss camping together. Anya's always busy with her friends here. I don't see her anymore."

Anya beamed at her little sister. How much had changed since we started! The two girls were inseparable now. As Anya put her arm around Yvonne protectively, I realized that we had all changed. From a family of four separate individuals pulling against each other, we had become a close-knit, well-oiled team, relying on everyone's unique strengths to make it around the world.

"All right then!" I reached out to Lorenz and squeezed his hand impulsively. His grin of relief said everything. It might be crazy, impractical to continue on, but then the whole plan had been audacious from the start. We'd already overcome so much together. Why stop now?

I stood up abruptly, making rapid lists in my head. "I'll have to call the board. Hopefully they'll be willing to continue the organization—at least as long as we're still pedaling." I chewed on my lip thoughtfully. "And we're still missing a director. Maybe it's time to talk to Robin."

I stepped toward the door and then paused, turning to Anya and Yvonne. "You girls are pretty incredible. You know that?"

The Connors' van sputtered to a halt in the wide asphalt parking lot at Fort Stevens State Park. We stood on the northernmost coastal point of Oregon—ten miles west of Astoria. To our right lay the wide mouth of the Columbia River. Almost exactly two hundred years ago, the Lewis and Clark expedition had stood at this very spot, realizing they had accomplished the impossible—they had arrived at the Pacific Ocean after more than a year of traveling by canoe, by horse, and on foot from St. Louis, Missouri.*

I stepped out of the van and breathed in the salt air, the cries of gulls filling the sky above us. Shouting and whooping, Anya and Tyson, Yvonne and Jordan piled out of the van behind us, running headlong, laughing, onto the long, flat, sandy beach.

"Shall we go?" Gary nodded to the beach in the direction of our disappearing children.

Lorenz and Gary strode out ahead, discussing engineering problems, while I walked quietly next to Julie, deep in thought. Julie strolled patiently beside me, waiting for me to speak first. I gazed out to the waves rushing to the shore, the dark, rusted bow of the famous shipwreck, the *Peter Iredale*, rising above the white crests. My head whirled with a confused jumble of thoughts and feelings. Fear, hope, despair, joy, gratitude, discouragement, doubt, faith—all tumbled around in my mind like clothes in a dryer, flipping over and over, rattling confusingly. Had Lewis and Clark struggled with similar bittersweet emotions as they gazed down on the Pacific Ocean—proud they had made it this far, and yet already worrying about the final return voyage back up the Columbia, over the deadly Bitterroot and Rocky Mountains, and down the Missouri River? We planned to follow in their footsteps, cycling along the Lewis and Clark bicentennial anniversary route laid out carefully on the Adventure Cycling maps in my handlebar bags. That is—until we ran out of money.

"Thanks so much for bringing us here," I said, fumbling awkwardly for the right words to say as I glanced over at Julie.

She smiled. "Of course! You need to finish this journey."

"We were so stuck on Bainbridge. It felt like we were moving in quicksand—sinking down farther and farther every day."

---

* On May 14, 1804, the Corps of Discovery, led by Captain Meriwether Lewis and his friend William Clark, set off from the banks of the Mississippi River, near St. Louis, in search of a route across America to the Pacific. One of the greatest expeditions in US history, the Corps paddled up the Missouri River, crossing the Continental Divide near Great Falls, Montana. Paddling down the Clearwater River in Idaho to the Columbia River, they glimpsed their first view of the Pacific Ocean over a year later on November 7, 1805. They wintered over on the Oregon coast near Astoria before returning along a similar route to arrive in St. Louis as national heroes on September 23, 1806.

"I know." She laughed, her voice warm and genuine. How did she always know when to do the right thing? I wished I had her certainty, her clarity.

"God put it in our hearts to help," she answered my unspoken question.

I envied Julie her unwavering faith, her complete trust in God. I loved the Connors for the exact reason that they were so different from us. While we could be labeled (as Yvonne dubbed us years later) the original hipsters, the Connors would fit in the category of fundamentalist Christians. They were central members in their church, held Bible study in their home weekly, and, most important, they had confidence in God's plans for them.

Me? I argued back—disagreed with God, debated about whether he really knew what he was doing, and questioned the fairness of his (or her) plans. For that matter, I doubted that God was male or even had human qualities and sometimes if he or she or it even existed at all. I was far too independent and headstrong to accept any particular church's interpretations. And yet, and yet—there was a part of me that understood Julie's faith. Maybe even shared it. There was no other possible explanation for why we were walking on this beach on the western edge of the North American continent right now.

We were cycling onward knowing, yes *knowing*, that we did not have the money in our bank account to do this. If we continued across the country, we would be pedaling on faith alone. I felt a wave of panic. No, we couldn't do this! We had to ask the Connors to drive us back to Bainbridge. They couldn't just leave us here! This was madness.

The adults had reached the wreck of the *Peter Iredale*, where the kids all stood, giggling and digging their bare toes in the wet sand, waiting for us. It was an unexpectedly lovely May afternoon. The sun shone brightly, and small clouds scudded above the long, green cliffs leading to the lighthouse in the distance. Lorenz took a few photos of everyone and then we stood awkwardly, no one wanting to be the first to say goodbye.

"I think we should all say a prayer for the Ebers before we leave," Gary said, beckoning us to form a circle. We all shuffled in the sand, reaching our hands out to grab each other's fingers. My fingers locked in

Julie's and Lorenz's hands, I bowed my head as Gary led the blessing. I believed in prayer—in theory. But seriously, it was crazy to think prayers would pay for our trip. For some strange reason, the little magnet I had hung on our fridge many years ago popped into my mind. "Leap and the net will appear," it said. I closed my eyes and saw, in front of me, a deep, bottomless abyss.

I took a breath. And then jumped.

At that exact moment, Lorenz and Tyson shouted out simultaneously, "Look—out there! Look! A whale!"

I opened my eyes to see not one but two majestic gray whales breeching off the shore in front of us.

Emails to bikeforbreath@hotmail.com

Wow!

I don't know any other way to start this note. Wow.
Asthma has been a part of my whole life and still
is. I am a forty-one-year-old male from Ontario, Canada. Biking has become a part of my life recently
too. Asthma still is a large part of my life, inhalers
nearby all the time, a few attacks during the year
no matter how hard I regulate my life. (Perfume in
church, yuk.)

Your family are doing a truly great thing, and I'll
be sending in a donation. If there is some way I could
help your group here in Ontario, I would be honoured.
If you need a place to put your tent or a meal(s), I
am more than happy to help.

WAY TO GO TO HELP THE FIGHT ON ASTHMA.

—George, Ontario, Canada

Greetings from Washington State!

I checked out Bike Bits today and caught up on your
adventure. I've already added it to My Favorites, and
we check it often. Although I don't gasp for breath,
I've got an exercise-induced asthma condition and use
an inhaler when I ride. I did a X-country ride this
spring and rode part of the Mississippi this fall.

I'm thinking the Lewis and Clark Trail might be my next trip, but I'm in total awe of your trip. I wish I was with you but will have to settle for watching by computer for a while.

—Fellow rider, Breeana, USA

Small Miracles

Paula

Day 368—Astoria, Oregon

My left index finger ratcheted down the gears as Anya and I leaned into our cleats and began the climb. Below us the green and brown islands of the Columbia River receded. We pushed higher up the hill. Drops of sweat rolled down my back. Down I pushed, left right, left right, my breath coming in and out hard as we climbed higher up the steep hill. At the top, we paused to take in a sweeping view of the silty green islands and the tiny buildings of Astoria below us. I felt my hair brushing my cheeks as it blew in the wind, smelled the sharp salt water in the air, heard the cry of gulls as they circled below.

How great it was to be back on the road! For the past three weeks, the cushioned beds, soft couches, and climate-controlled rooms had been seductively comfortable. But these luxuries had also shut us away from the world outside—the *real* world of pungent dirt, warm wind, wet grass, and sun-sparkled water. I spread my arms out, turning my face up to the sun in sheer joy. It was *wonderful* to be *feeling* again. Judging from the wide smiles on my family's faces, I was pretty sure they felt the same. Maybe it was not logical to keep going on this journey, but it felt so right.

The next two weeks whizzed by as we pedaled contentedly up the Columbia River along the border between Oregon and Washington—past breathtaking cascading waterfalls, through dark green forests, below steep snow-covered mountains. Cycling in our own country is so simple, I thought as I gazed down at the detailed Adventure Cycling map in my handlebar bag. The map plotted out a safe, carefully researched bike route along the former trail of Lewis and Clark, guiding us to all the important historical sites along the way. Nifty little icons indicated campsites, grocery stores, and even restrooms. Best of all the map—and the road signs—were in *English*! What I would have given for even half this information while we cycled around the world! Sure, the constant up-and-down hills along the Columbia River were tiring, but we could stop in a store and ask for directions; buy food we recognized with cooking instructions that we could read; and even plan out a camping or hotel destination for the day rather than cycling blind, hoping to find someplace to sleep before nightfall. This was biking at its best: great sights, easy planning, and no stress. Almost.

I would have been blissfully happy except for one major problem: at the rate we were going, we would definitely run out of money within six weeks, if not sooner. Lorenz and I had done everything we could think of to earn some more cash. I sent off another magazine article. We filed our taxes, hoping to get a refund. I even called Burley and asked them if they might consider making a large cash donation to World Bike for Breath to help cover the PR costs of promoting our journey for clean air and asthma. I figured that if the organization's costs were covered, the board might be more willing to help us out. But despite our efforts, our bank balance kept stubbornly decreasing.

I counted the money in my wallet carefully as we stood by the tandems in front of the Dayton IGA. The ride up and down gently rolling green hills from Walla Walla in eastern Washington had been easy enough, but lately it seemed we could work up an appetite just looking at the tandems. Anya and Yvonne were growing like weeds, and they just needed more food.

I stared, discouraged, into the wallet. Thirty dollars. How was I supposed to feed a family of four hungry cyclists for the next three days? That was barely two dollars and fifty cents per person per day. Still, that was the budget. Our bank account was hovering dangerously close to $2,000. Unless a check for one of my cycling articles showed up or we got our tax refund soon, we'd be out of money by Montana. Forget Canada. Or Washington, DC. We needed a miracle. And soon.

"Hey, guys, I'll be back in twenty minutes," I said, grabbing a shopping cart.

Anya barely nodded, her head already stuck in a book as she waited by the tandems.

Fiddling with the rear derailleur, Lorenz waved a wrench as I headed into the supermarket. "Get some chocolate, if you can," he called after me.

Half an hour later, I rumbled out of the supermarket, the shopping cart piled high with as many calories as thirty dollars could buy—bags of rice, pasta, granola, and trail mix topped with an enormous package of cheese, two dozen bananas, and several chocolate bars. To my surprise, Anya and Yvonne were chatting away animatedly to a dark-haired gentleman in a plaid shirt and cowboy boots, who was scribbling in a notebook.

"Paula, meet Jack. He's a reporter from the *Dayton Chronicle*." Lorenz waved me over. "Actually he owns it!"

"Hi!" I parked the shopping cart and reached out my hand. "Nice to meet you."

"Hello, ma'am. I've just been talking to your girls here. And your handy husband over there. What your family is doing is mighty impressive. Just about shocked the boots off me to be honest. Never heard of such a thing. Two little girls pedaling all around the world like this." Jack tucked the notebook back in his pocket and pulled on his chin in thought for a moment. "Listen. We folks here in Dayton would like to show you our appreciation for your project. And a bit of country hospitality." He reached into his checkered breast pocket and pulled out four green paper stubs. "We're having a rodeo here tonight, and I'd like to give your family four tickets. On the newspaper!" He winked at Anya and Yvonne. "You girls ever seen a rodeo before?"

They shook their heads, eyes wide.

"Well, there's a first time for everyone!"

I opened my mouth and then closed it. It was a fabulous gift. But—

"I know—" Jack broke in before I could protest. "The rodeo runs late. So hope you don't mind, but I took the liberty of checking with the Weinhard Hotel down the street here. It's the best in town. Lovely historic place built in 1890 or about then I think. They've done a fantastic job of renovating it. They happen to have two rooms available for tonight."

I smiled politely, swallowing hard. "That's ah—that's really nice of you. But—" I protested. A bed sounded great. Really great. But we'd just used up most of our budget for the next three days on the pile of food sitting in my shopping cart.

Jack put up his hand. "Don't you get worrying about this now. You're the town's guests of honor. And we want to pay for this. Put you up in style. It's not often we get such impressive world travelers in our little town out here." He grinned at the girls and handed them the rodeo tickets. "We aren't real slick city folk. But still and all, we know how to put on a good show sometimes."

❦

"Can you believe this? Our own room! In such a beautiful hotel." I sat on the canopied bed in our hotel room after the rodeo. "That was extremely generous of the *Dayton Chronicle*."

"Yeah, it's amazing. This room, the rodeo—" Lorenz pulled the ticket stubs out of his pocket, setting them on the antique dresser. "The girls were so cute—turning red when the announcer pointed us out as honored guests of Dayton! Jack certainly rolled out the red carpet for us!"

I smiled in agreement, images of the rodeo swirling through my head: Cowboys gripping the reins tightly as they flew up and down on the backs of wild bucking broncs. Cowgirls racing their horses around barrels, pigtails flying. The deep, booming voice of the announcer. The smells of hay and horses and manure mingling in the night air.

"Yeah, it seems that ever since we left Astoria, people have been so kind and helpful. Just think about it. There was that guy who owned the fishing lodge on the Columbia River—"

"Right, the one who invited us to stay on his private island."

Barely twenty miles east from Astoria, we had been invited to camp on the lawn of an avid fisherman, who cooked us a delicious dinner of fresh-caught fish that night. To our surprise, the owner invited us to visit his hunting lodge on a private island the next day. After cycling fifty miles farther up the river, we arrived at his log cabin the following night to find a delicious feast of venison meatloaf and moose jerky waiting for us.

"Or that family in Hood River." I laughed. "We must have looked a sight in our drenched clothes!" I pictured the lovely two-bedroom RV where a kind family had insisted we sleep and dry out after a day of cycling in pouring rain. Anya and Yvonne had been thrilled to hang out with the two daughters, Emily and Zoe, who were their age. And we had spent a wonderful evening laughing and telling stories as neighbor after neighbor poured in for an impromptu party and dinner at our host's house. How wonderful that these complete strangers and their friends had opened their hearts and homes to us!

I smiled at Lorenz as he sat down on the bed next to me. "You know, I keep looking for this big miracle that's going to pay for us to get across the US." I cuddled next to him as he put his arm around me. "But maybe I'm looking in the wrong direction. Perhaps it's these small, personal little gifts—the venison dinner, the impromptu party, our own room in this beautiful hotel—that are the real miracles."

Crossing Lolo

Paula

Day 395—Border of Washington and Idaho

"Hullo there!" a deep, cheerful voice called over from a cluster of tents in the Lewis and Clark Trail State Park. I paused, not expecting to see anyone else in the hiker-biker campsites set along the wide, slow-moving Touchet River near the border of eastern Washington.

"There's plenty of room! Come join us," the friendly voice continued.

I turned to the voice, surprised to see an almost six-foot-tall black woman, topped with wild curly black hair, dressed in dungaree capris and a bright yellow jacket.

"We're cycling the Lewis and Clark Trail," the woman explained. "How about you?"

"We are too!" Anya replied, pleased to find someone else following our route. "We've been stopping at all sorts of cool historic places since

we left Astoria. Did you see the Discovery Center in Oregon? They had this huge exhibit about all the cargo that Lewis and Clark brought on their journey—tents and blue beads for bargaining and even medicinal herbs!" Her eyes glistened with enthusiasm. "I've been collecting my own herbs and pressing them in a book just like the explorers did. I really like history—you know, doing things like people did from the past."

"Oooh—pressing plants is fun, isn't it? I'd love to see your book." The woman beamed, reaching out a broad, strong hand to Anya. "Hey, I'm Beth. And that's Moni over there." Beth pointed to a bustling gray-haired woman who was filling up water bottles under the faucet by the campsite. "And that's Paul." She waved to a thin bearded man wearing tights and Birkenstock sandals who was leaning over a camp stove. "We call ourselves the Try Try Again Gang."

Beth glanced over at a pile of crackers, beans, soup, and carrots stacked on the picnic table. "Hey, we're just starting dinner. Why don't you join us?"

⁓

"So why are you guys called the Try Try Again Gang?" Lorenz asked, sipping on a hot chocolate as we stood around a crackling fire after dinner, laughing and swapping stories.

"We each tried to bike across America before and didn't finish." Moni poked a stick around in the fire. "A couple of years ago, I started on the Northern Tier bike route. I crossed the Rockies and made it almost three thousand miles. But by the time I got to Indiana, I was worn out and went home."

"I didn't even get that far," Beth joined in. "When my youngest daughter was twelve—she was probably about your age actually"—Beth grinned at Yvonne, who had already taken a great liking to this warm, voluble woman—"we decided to bike across America from Seattle. We got off the plane and pedaled straight over Snoqualmie Pass. Two thousand something feet high. That was a big mistake. It took us three days to get over the pass. We were miserable. Two days later my daughter hurt her foot and couldn't walk. That was it. We went home."

"Well, I never even started." It was Paul's turn. "I wanted to bike across the States a couple of years ago. Bought a bunch of equipment. But I just wasn't able to pull it together."

"So here we are," Moni said. "This time"—she jutted her chin slightly and lifted her head upward, defiant—"this time is different. I just turned fifty, and I'm going all the way across."

Looking at her petite, determined figure, I didn't doubt it. I just hoped we would make it too. I really didn't want to be next year's Try Try Again Gang.

———

"Why can't we bike with Beth?" Yvonne pouted as we loaded up the tandems the next morning. "We always make friends and then have to go. It's not fair."

"Don't worry, we'll see you again!" Beth said to Yvonne, giving her a bear hug.

I doubted it. We occasionally ran into other cyclists, but once they pedaled off ahead of us, we never caught up to them again. Between my asthma and the kids, we moved significantly more slowly than everyone else.

"Look, I have this bag of chalk I carry with me so I can write notes on the road to everyone as I bike." Moni pulled out a collection of colored chalk. "I'll write notes on the pavement to you so you know where we are. What do you think?"

Yvonne still pouted slightly as the Try Try Again Gang pedaled off ahead of us. But she managed a small smile as Moni waved her bag of chalk and careened out of sight.

———

The sun beat down menacingly on us as we crossed a large bridge over the Clearwater River four days later. We had been pedaling through the poverty-stricken Nez Percé Indian reservation—a desolate land of shrub steppe and lonely high desert. I gazed over to the little dusty town ahead, relieved to turn off the silent, empty road and break the monotony of the unbroken parched sagebrush hills around us.

"Mom! Look!" Yvonne cried out, looking down to the wide river cutting its way through the arid basalt buttes lining its banks. "It's the Try Try Again Gang!" She pointed to a group of cyclists camped in the Kamiah town park by the river.

"It can't be. They must be miles ahead of us by now."

"*It is!* That's Beth's recumbent bicycle. No one else has a bike like that!"

There was no point in disagreeing with Yvonne's uncanny ability to find and remember people and places. I turned the tandem from the bridge and into the park.

"Hullo there!" a deep, cheerful voice called up from the tents. "Told you we'd meet again!"

<hr />

"Wow! Look at all those stars!" I gazed up at a broad twinkling sky as our little group stood around a crackling fire after dinner. Four other cyclists had pedaled in to join our campsite in Kamiah that evening. Including the Try Try Again Gang and our family, that made eleven cyclists in one spot. Definitely a first!

"Maybe Lewis and Clark made a fire right here, looking at the same stars two hundred years ago!" I whispered to Anya, imagining I heard the noises of the Corps of Discovery in camp—the sizzling of fresh-caught fish frying in a pan, horses neighing quietly as they munched on the grass by the river, the playful barks of Lewis's dog Seaman, and the canoes banging on the river shore.

"Do you really think they camped *here?*" Anya's eyes glowed with imagination.

"Well, somewhere near here for sure," I said, thinking of the latest entry we had read in the book about Lewis and Clark's encounter with the Nez Percé Indians. Not far from this campsite, the Corps of Discovery had stumbled down from the Bitterroot Mountains, half dead from their dreadful ordeal on the Lolo Trail. Battling fierce snow and unable to find game, they had practically frozen and starved to death trying to cross over the pass. If the Nez Percé Indians had not taken Lewis and Clark in and supplied them with food and horses, they probably would have died.

I certainly hoped our own journey over the Bitterroots would not be as disastrous. According to our bike maps, more than one hundred and fifty miles* of desolate highway lay between us and Missoula on the other side of 5,235-foot Lolo Pass. There were no towns, only a few hardy houses and *maybe*, if we were lucky, one camp store along our route for the next four or five days.

"So what's your bet? Will the camp store be open? Or not?" Beth asked the crowd of cyclists standing around the fire.

As we all placed our bets, I glanced over at the two panniers I had stocked up with food for the coming climb, worried. We had bought over thirty pounds of dried soups and hot cereal, pasta and cheese, chocolate and trail mix. It was a lot of extra weight to be carrying. But the way our family was consuming calories lately, I still didn't think we had enough. I bet on the store being open. I certainly hoped I was right.

For the next two days, our family climbed slowly up the steep Bitterroot Mountains, following the banks of the beautiful, rushing Lochsa River as it twisted and babbled among deep, silent forests of Douglas fir and lodgepole pine trees. On the second day, we ran into a chalk note from Moni. "Good place," it said, with an arrow pointing to the Lochsa Historical Ranger Station.

"Moni was right. It's a cool place," Yvonne said as we finished touring the wooden buildings housing displays of life as a forest ranger in the 1920s. "I hope we find more notes from Moni." She skipped back to the tandems cheerfully. "This is fun."

—◦—

Her wish was fulfilled. The next day we ran into the Try Try Again Gang sitting on a bench at the Lochsa country store. (I had bet right, thankfully. The store *was* open.) After climbing forty-three miles uphill on a couple of granola bars, a small bag of trail mix (mostly just peanuts at this point), and a meager lunch of cheese and crackers from our dwindling food supply, our family immediately raided the little store. A

---

* All of the world—with the exception of the US, Myanmar, and Liberia—calculates distance in kilometers, which is the measurement we used as we traveled around the world. However, since all distances in the US are in miles, during this portion of the journey, we reckoned our travel in miles.

few minutes later, Yvonne was sitting next to Beth, chatting away as she munched down her second bag of chips. Anya was raptly licking an ice cream cone on the bench next to them, while Lorenz was alternating bites of beef jerky with a Mars candy bar.

Moni's bike toppled over just as I was about to pop a second brownie into my mouth. Without warning, a huge gust of wind suddenly swept around the corner of the store and *bam*! Moni's heavily laden bicycle flipped over. As Moni lifted up her bicycle, it was clear something was dreadfully wrong. The handlebars tilted crookedly. She lifted the curved handles, tangled in a web of brake and derailleur cables, and gasped. The bars had snapped completely off from the bike stem!

Lorenz dashed to the bike, a wrench in hand. Soon a little crowd collected around the bike, everyone shouting out suggestions. Even the store owner stepped out to see what the commotion was about. He quickly disappeared back into the store, returning with a hand-powered electric drill and began to bore a hole in the metal handlebar stem.

"Try that," he said as he tightened two new screws to the stem.

Moni straddled her bike, looking rather doubtful. Stepping up on the pedals, she cycled down the hill to the campground behind the store. The repair didn't even last to her campsite.

The news about Moni's handlebars spread like wildfire up and down the cyclist sites along the Lochsa River. It seemed that the entire campground was filled that night with cyclists preparing for the final climb over Lolo Pass the next day. Everyone stopped by to offer help.

A young cyclist pedaling solo was the first to pop over. "I have duct tape if that will help."

"I think I have some string," another cyclist added hopefully.

Lorenz ambled over with his extensive tool kit and began pulling out bolts, wrenches, superglue, and his handy repair-all staple: zip ties. Moni looked discouraged. The twisted mess of wires and steel really did look hopeless.

"If you want, I can drive you into Missoula tomorrow," the driver of a sag wagon for his cycling wife offered. "I'm following my wife over the pass. I can just throw your bike in the car while we drive behind her. I'm sure there's a bike store in Missoula that can fix your bike."

Moni looked crestfallen. "I appreciate the offer of a lift," she replied, fiddling distractedly with the brakes on her handlebars. "But isn't there *anything* we can do to fix the bars? It's cheating to drive over the pass. I said I'd *bike* across America. Not drive."

She slumped down on the ground and put her head in her hands. Beth and Paul stood next to her, uncertain what to say. Suddenly Moni lifted her head, determined. "No, I'm going to bike over the pass some-how. I've already quit once. I won't quit again. This time I'm biking the *whole* way across the US."

As the sunlight slowly faded, Beth and Lorenz worked furiously on Moni's bicycle, attempting to glue the bars to the stem with JB weld. Beth, it turned out, had retired from the Air Force as a certified flight engineer. As I watched Beth debate with Lorenz about the mechanical challenges of stabilizing Moni's handlebars, I shook my head. She was full of surprises.

Finally, Lorenz and Beth stood up triumphantly. I had to stifle a laugh. Up and down the bike stem, they had attached a dubious row of zip ties and hose clamps. To top it off, a thick layer of silver duct tape twisted along the handlebars, giving the makeshift repair the look of a homemade rocket entered in a school science fair.

"Are you sure that will hold?" I asked. I truly believed in Lorenz's magical abilities to fix anything with duct tape and string, but still, there was a limit even to his Superman engineering skills.

"We'll see. The JB weld needs to cure." Lorenz wheeled the bicycle carefully to the firepit. "We'll need to set the bike by the campfire for a couple of hours to make sure it hardens."

That night we sat around the fire one more time with the Try Try Again Gang, drinking hot chocolate and roasting marshmallows over the fire. But somehow it was not the same as before. Lorenz attempted to make silly jokes about JB weld and duct tape, but they all fell flat. Moni just stared into the fire. Every few minutes she glanced nervously at her bike, as if checking to see if the JB weld had dried sufficiently. Was she doing the right thing to climb over a difficult mountain pass on a bike held together with duct tape and hose clamps?

—◆—

"Don't lean on the handlebars if you can help it," Lorenz cautioned Moni as she stood next to her bike in the chill early morning, determined to pedal over Lolo Pass with the rest of us. He rubbed his fingers over the bike stem, checking that the JB weld seam was hard. "The bars look solid, but a sudden jolt could break them." He paused, twisting his Swiss Army knife between his fingers, uncomfortable sending this petite fifty-year-old woman off on the bizarrely bandaged bike. "Just take it easy. Watch out for potholes. And try not to brake suddenly."

Moni nodded, grabbed the duct-taped bars gingerly, and carefully lifted her leg over the frame. Jutting her chin forward, she cinched her helmet, short gray wisps of hair poking out. "I'll be fine," she said, a resolute tone in her voice.

For the next thirteen miles, the seven of us pedaled slowly up the mountain, stopping occasionally to check on Moni, who followed cautiously behind us. We passed through thick forests of mountain hemlock and tall Douglas firs, an occasional break in the forest opening to vast glorious views over the snow-covered mountains. With each mile the air grew colder, and we pressed on. My breath pulled in and out in short, sharp gasps in the thinning air. These high climbs were always hard on my lungs, but after more than a year of cycling, my lungs had become stronger, more able to handle the higher altitudes and steep climbs.

Finally, a beautiful log visitors center appeared, a large sign proclaiming "Lolo Pass 5235 feet" carved in the wood above the door. We had reached the top! As we parked our tandems next to a pile of other heavily laden bicycles, I waved at Moni slowly cycling in behind us. Holding the handlebars carefully as she dismounted, she looked over at me with a grin as wide as a Cheshire cat's spreading from ear to ear.

—◆—

"Can we stay in the motel? Pleease." Anya stared longingly at the Lolo Hot Springs Lodge. She shivered in front of the long wooden building, the first sign of life since we had crossed Lolo Pass twelve miles ago. Above us the snow-covered Bitterroot Mountains loomed over the remote lodge, tucked in a small meadow hewn from the evergreen forest surrounding it.

The ride down the mountains from the pass had been bitterly cold, with stinging wind and snow flurries whipping in our faces. No wonder Lewis and Clark had practically frozen to death up here! It was June 8, for crying out loud. But summer seemed months away.

Behind the lodge, enticing wisps of steam rose from the natural thermal hot springs for which the resort was named. I'd have given anything to soak in those springs! My long underwear lay cold and clammy against my skin, and I felt chilled to the bone. The rest of our little group seemed equally exhausted and miserable. Paul and Moni were stamping their feet to stay warm. Yvonne was huddled under Lorenz's wide arms, trying to absorb his body heat.

"Bad news. Rooms are a hundred dollars per night," Beth announced as she walked back from the front desk of the hotel to our frozen, dispirited group.

I glanced at Lorenz, our leader for the day. Last time I looked at our bank account, we had barely $1,500 left. We really should push on. Or take a site in the campground next to the lodge. But I was *so* dead tired. I just didn't have another mile left in me. And I was too cold to camp. From the looks of it, Anya and Yvonne were just as cold and exhausted— maybe more so.

It had seemed such a brave and daring decision to bike across the US on faith. But I had to face reality. Hope wasn't going to give us a bed, keep us warm, or feed us. It was impractical to keep going like this. Maybe even dangerous. I suddenly shivered in my damp clothes. We needed somewhere warm and dry soon.

"I have a suggestion." Beth's practical, cheery voice interrupted my melancholy musings. "What if we all took one room and split the cost? We might be able to bring in a cot or two. And if not, I'm used to sleeping on the ground anyway. I don't care as long as I'm warm and can get a hot shower."

Anya and Yvonne gazed up at Beth with such a rapt look of relief, there was no way we were going to say no.

You would have thought we were celebrating reaching the top of Mount Everest from the wild party we had in the room that night. Wild, at least, by a cyclist's standards. We had no alcohol. And the dregs of food left in our panniers were, in a word, quite awful. But somehow we managed to pull together a strange and wonderful feast of curry rice with tuna, split pea soup with barley, Italian spaghetti with meat (Moni bought a large uncooked hamburger patty at the lodge restaurant), and fried apples with trail mix for dessert.

We had crossed Lolo Pass, Moni's handlebars were still attached to her bike, and we had hot showers; a warm, dry room; and even hot springs to soak in. What more could anyone possibly desire?*

---

* The following day we all cycled together to the Adventure Cycling headquarters in Missoula. The Try Try Again Gang then continued on the southern Lewis and Clark route, while we took the northern branch. Moni and Beth both successfully completed their trips across the US. Paul's father died as he crossed the Midwest, forcing him to cut his journey short.

Postcard to World Bike for Breath

> June 13, Missoula, MT
>
> Hi Robin
>
> Well now begins one of the more interesting parts of being Executive Director—the Eber family monthly packages. A lot of the stuff is weight we're trying to reduce from our panniers and hope you can store until we get back.
>
> In the attached bag are receipts from our ride, and receipts for $250 of donations we received at the slide show we gave at the Adventure Cycling headquarters in Missoula yesterday. Hope you're having a great summer. Paula

World Bike Bits

Bits and stories about World Bike for Breath. A Bulletin for sponsors. Volume 6

Pedaling with Lewis and Clark

"MOSQUITOES VERRY TROUBLESOM," WROTE CAPTAIN MERIWETHER Lewis in his journal as he camped with the Corps of Discovery along the banks of the Missouri River near present-day Fort Benton, Montana. Reading Lewis's comments by flashlight, while our family huddled in our tents near Lewis's former campsite, brought peals of laughter from my husband and our two daughters—twelve-year-old Yvonne and fourteen-year-old Anya. Our arms and legs covered in itchy red dots from the day's relentless mosquito attacks, we could easily commiserate with Lewis's comments. Our family was pedaling along the route that the famed Lewis and Clark expedition had taken from the Mississippi River to the Pacific Ocean and discovering—to our joy and distress—that two hundred years later, it was still possible to experience some of the Corps's own trials, tribulations, and triumphs.

Our family began our journey from the Pacific Ocean (retracing Lewis's homeward-bound route) fittingly on a misty cool morning—much like the many mornings that must have greeted the expedition during their rainy layover in the winter of 1805. Like Lewis and Clark, we carried our own journals; unlike them, we were armed with maps and a fabulous guidebook for families: *Lewis and Clark for Kids*. We first pedaled along the lush waterfall canyons of the Columbia River past snow-covered Mount Hood. Continuing on thirstily into the barren hot deserts of eastern Oregon, we felt renewed respect for the courage of both the Corps of Discovery and the many pioneers who followed later along the dusty Oregon Trail.

In Idaho we fell to sleep at night to the dancing babble of the Lochsa River, sprinkled on its banks with the white flowers of the camas or bitterroot plant. Anya's and Yvonne's imaginations soared with visions of Captain Lewis, quill and ink in hand, sketching these nourishing (though bitter) roots and flowers in his botanical journals. During the day, we visited the archaeological remains of ancient villages of the Nez Percé Indians. The terrible fate of this tribe, who had befriended and aided the starving Clark and his exploratory party as they stumbled out of the freezing Bitterroot Mountains (named aptly after the roots), was told in tragic road signs on the road to Montana, along their ill-starred and fatal escape route from the US Army seventy years after meeting the Corps.

Pedaling over the frigid Lolo Pass, our family headed north to Missoula, Montana, and into the Rockies. Here we entered some of the loveliest high mountain country of our entire world ride. Unspoiled quiet roads meandered through rolling green mountain valleys, circled by silent white peaks. Pronghorn antelope sprang alongside of us, bighorn sheep climbed along the ridges, whitetail deer nibbled at grass in the fields, and bald eagles soared overhead: a teeming unspoiled world of wildlife, as awe-inspiring and astounding to us as it must have been to Lewis and Clark. We heartily agreed that this country was, as Lewis put it, "beautifull in the extreme."

The freezing descent over the Continental Divide—at 5,610-foot Rogers Pass—to Great Falls, Montana, presaged yet another change in landscape: to the long empty expanse of the great plains. After a day in the fascinating Lewis and Clark Interpretive Center (displaying life-size dioramas of the Corps's eleven-day portage around the former falls) and an exciting private plane flight over the falls courtesy of Lorenz's pilot friends Gary and Bill, our family pedaled north above the vermillion and sand-etched cliffs of the great Missouri River. Feeling the need to experience life on the river as the Corps must have seen it, we rented a canoe for two days at Fort Benton. As we paddled along pristine silent waters dotted with pelicans, eagles, whooping cranes, and other wild birds, we dreamed of the time when the cliffs once also teemed with buffalo, deer, and the "great white bear." Sadly, the *pishkun* or Indian buffalo jump, just north at Havre, Montana, is now only an archaeological reminder of the days when the great plains had such an abundance of wildlife that Lewis remarked in his journals that he could hardly turn in any direction without seeing a buffalo, deer, or elk.

It is with regret that our family will bid goodbye to the Lewis and Clark Trail at the reconstructed Fort Mandan in Washburn, North Dakota, where we will continue east to Michigan. We can empathize with Lewis and Clark's many emotions as the Corps returned to Mandan on their homeward-bound journey in 1806. As our family slowly approaches the end of our journey too, we each share many mixed feelings: joy, sadness, excitement, longing, love. Overlaying it all, stand out the days and days of unforgettable memories. I understand, perhaps too fully, the poignant final words in Herbert's book, *Lewis and Clark for Kids*:

> *How often in later years did Clark stand on the banks of the Missouri River and look west? How many times did he close his eyes and imagine the vast plains, the tall grasses swaying in the wind, and the herds of buffalo that dotted the countryside. . . . What marvels he and Lewis had seen.*

Thank you for letting us share with you some of the marvels our family has seen this past year and a half.

Email to bikeforbreath@hotmail.com

GREAT NEWS!

To: Robin Simons, Executive Director

Monday, 6/21

Hi Robin,

I'm so delighted to hear that Burley has pledged $4,000 to cover the PR costs of World Bike for Breath! We also can't thank the board enough for voting to cut us a check for $3,000 to help cover our costs biking across America. This *is* great news!

We should have enough money now (with a refund from Uncle Sam coming too) to get across the U. S. Burley is covering Jonathan's and your expenses (it might not hurt to just call and remind them about their pledge) and office costs—phone, etc.—until Sept won't be much more than $600. So every donation that comes in from now on can go straight to asthma. That's a great point to be at.

Paula

Country Roads

Lorenz

Day 418—Malta, Montana

Five point seven miles per hour. My thighs were burning. I could hear
Yvonne panting behind me. I could feel the power of her legs pulsing
through the steel chain that linked us together. We were crawling at cat-
erpillar speed along Route 2 in eastern Montana. We could have walked
faster along this perfectly flat road. Yet, bicycling, my bike computer stubbornly refused to raise above 5.7 miles per hour. Mercifully, the odometer
on the computer turned over to the next mile, and I lifted my arm up into
the howling headwind. In slow motion, Paula and Anya passed us on the
left, fighting the twenty-five-mile-per-hour wind, and took the lead in
front of us. For the next mile, I nosed my front tire within inches of Paula's bike, eking out every square inch of wind shadow. Yvonne and I were
still struggling, but behind the others it was marginally easier to pedal.

We had been playing this routine, drafting each other and switching
off every mile for the last three days. All we had to show for it was that
we had barely covered a total of sixty miles and had collapsed exhausted,

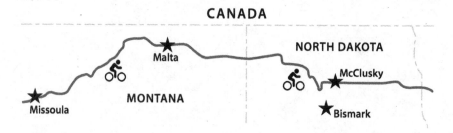

completely drained, into our sleeping bags every night. We talked about quitting or hiring a U-Haul truck to get us out of this wind. Get us out of this godforsaken place. Out of this desert.

At five the next morning, the alarm of my Casio watch beeped annoyingly into my ear. I had set the alarm early because it was the only way to beat the headwinds, which didn't really get going until about ten in the morning. I crawled out of our tent and stared bleary-eyed at the sun-parched landscape of dry, undulating hills draped in a thin layer of sagebrush. A patina of gray on an endless expanse of red-brown cracked earth. The wind was still calm. That much of my calculation had been correct, but standing there just in my shorts, I heard the dreaded high-pitched note of mosquito wings buzzing near my eardrums. When there wasn't any wind, there were mosquitoes. Some of the largest, most ferocious mosquitoes I had ever seen. Aren't mosquitoes supposed to come out in the evening? I wondered. It wasn't even six in the morning yet, and I could already feel the bloodthirsty critters settling all over my body, eager for their breakfast. Slapping wildly about me, I jumped back into the tent and put on long pants and a long-sleeved shirt. I noticed a small packet in my pants pocket, pulled it out, and turned it over appraisingly in my hand. It was a mosquito head net, one of four we had bought the day before in the dusty, eclectic country store in Dodson. The citizens of Dodson, Montana, were no fools. They knew the monster mosquitoes that the bottoms of their muddy creek beds were capable of incubating. They knew that leaving just an inch of exposed skin was plain tomfoolery. They knew. Everyone else learned the hard way.

I touched two nasty welts that were painfully blooming on my cheek from just standing thirty seconds uncovered outside the tent. Enough of that. I ripped open the head net package, pulled the mosquito net over my head, yanked the drawstrings tight, and headed out to make breakfast.

Forty minutes later, with the breakfast dishes quickly rinsed, I stuffed the still-warm camp stove into its stuff sack and shoved it into my pannier. The folds of my head net kept getting into my vision, and I somehow managed to get the fabric of the stove bag caught in the pannier zipper.

The girls stood, fully dressed in their head nets underneath their bike helmets, and watched me irritably as I wrestled with the zipper. They were slapping at mosquitoes, impatient to get on the tandems.

I set a brisk pace, hoping to outrun the mosquito swarms as long as possible. We shot down the road's skimpy shoulder on a downhill back to Highway 2. Gossamer mist floated just inches above the sagebrush. It was still cool, but the rising sun would soon burn off the morning mist. I could feel this day would be a scorcher. We were certain to roast under those head nets.

As we rounded a slight curve in the road, I saw what looked like a truck radiator hose lying on the white line, marking the shoulder. I had just enough time to swerve and avoid it when I suddenly saw the "hose" move, hiss, and rear up. The "hose" was a five-foot-long rattlesnake rising up from the pavement, where she had been soaking up the asphalt's heat.

"Snake!" yelled Yvonne behind me.

The rattlesnake rose to an alarming height, hissed once more, and struck. Whack! The snake hit us so hard, I could feel the vibration in my handlebars. Yvonne and I lurched to the left, swerving wildly across the road.

"Shit, shit, shit," I blurted, leaning into the brakes, trying to stop the careening bike. We skidded to a stop just before we hit the ditch on the other side of the road and jumped off the tandem, dropping it savagely onto the pavement. Patting ourselves down, we searched frantically for fang marks.

"Did she get you?"

"Don't think so." Yvonne sniffed as I patted down her legs.

"Nothing hurts?" I asked.

"No. What about you, Dad?"

I ran my hands over my legs. "I'm OK too, I think."

Just then Paula and Anya screeched to a halt next to us.

"Oh my God! That snake was huge! She hit your front pannier!" exclaimed Anya.

Dazed, I looked back and watched the big snake glide from the road and slither into the sagebrush.

"That was too close," said Paula.

"No shit," I said, inspecting the front pannier for fang marks, my hands still shaking. Why had we ever decided to bike through eastern Montana? This was hell on earth. Why were we biking against fierce headwinds, through swarms of mosquitoes, and into the fangs of rattlesnakes? This was nuts!

———

That afternoon, we were riding in the middle of nowhere, even though my map stubbornly declared that we should be near the town of Malta, Montana. Pedaling in the ninety-five-degree heat, I imagined that the tiny town of Malta had just evaporated like a swirling bead of water on a hotplate. The letters of *Malta* left on my map were just the filmy white residue that remained after the droplet of the town had completely vaporized.

With the wind blowing again, Yvonne and I had fallen behind and were riding in a stupor of discomfort up a steep embankment over a lonely railroad line. Out of the corner of my eye, I noticed a glimmer of gold in the gravel on the shoulder. I hit the brakes.

"Don't stop, Dad! We'll never get going again on this hill," moaned Yvonne.

"I saw something, over there by that bush."

"Dad, I'm not picking up another piece of trash for you," Yvonne replied, alluding to my newfound habit of collecting interesting roadside trash in the desert. I found it broke up the monotony. A quaint hobby of sorts.

"It looked like gold. Could you please get it?" I pleaded.

"No. Mom and Anya are already way ahead. We'll never catch them."

"Please?"

"OK, but I'm not getting one more bent-up license plate for you after this." She strode off in long determined strides.

I was still straddling the tandem, holding it upright, when Yvonne returned. She was excited. "Wow, Dad, look at this!"

"What is it?"

"I don't know. It's way cool though." Yvonne turned the thing over in her hands.

"It's a GPS receiver!" I ran my fingers over the screen and buttons.

"What's that?"

"GPS stands for global positioning system. It's a gizmo that communicates with satellites overhead and can tell you exactly where you are. Gives you coordinates you can find on a map. Sort of like an electronic 'You are here' sign."

"Really? Sounds expensive!" Yvonne was already pushing buttons at random.

"You bet, very expensive. They are about five hundred bucks new.* Look, the data plug in the back is actually gold plated. That's what I saw glinting in the sun."

"Wow! Dad, it still works! There's all kinds of stuff on the screen."

"It works?"

"There's no name on it. Can I have it?" asked Yvonne, hugging the GPS to her chest.

"Not so fast. Wasn't I the one who found it? We could sell it. We're super tight on cash," I said, wondering whether the check from Burley would show up before or after we ran out of money. We had, at best, $800 left in our bank account.

"No way! I want to figure this thing out. I'm super bored back here."

"Let's share it for now. Mom will probably want to send it home anyway. It weighs a few ounces, you know."

"Yeah, she's the 'Weight Witch.' She won't let us have anything fun, just because it's heavy," Yvonne said as she got back on the bike, still working the buttons on the GPS.

"Let's go and catch up to Mom and Anya! Finding a GPS! They'll have to admit that's pretty cool."

"Poor guy who lost it . . ."

---

* The Garmin 12 was one of the very first practical handheld consumer GPS units to come to market. We had considered getting one for the ride but had decided against it due to the extra weight and the very high cost. Handheld GPS units were very rare at the time, and finding one on a deserted road in Montana seemed incredible.

Email to bikeforbreath@hotmail.com

To: Garmin, Olathe, KS
cc: World Bike for Breath
GARMIN 12 GPS

I have been the proud owner of the Garmin 12 for six years. It is mounted in its bracket on top of my motorcycle gas tank. The Garmin 12 is my companion wherever I go. We have traveled north to Fairbanks, Alaska, cross-country to Washington, DC, south through Texas to San Diego.

On June 7, while traveling through Montana, Highway 2, at approximately 10:45 p.m., I demolished my Kawasaki Voyager XII motorcycle. I hit unmarked road construction and was unable to slow down quick enough to avoid crashing into the guardrail. When I picked myself up off the blacktop, somewhat battered, bloodied, and bruised, the motorcycle was still running. I limped over to the bike and shut it off. There was some moonlight. As I turned off the bike, I was positive my Garmin 12 GPS was still in its bracket mounted on the gas tank.

My belongings and motorcycle parts were scattered all over this two-lane highway. It was very black and dark, but I could see enough to start picking up pieces to clear a path should a vehicle come by. It was minutes, I think, and there were headlights off in the distance. I had no idea of direction. I was looking for my glasses along with those items scattered around.

I flagged down the approaching car some distance from my crash site. I think I scared these young people because I was a sight, bloodied face, blood in my eyes, tattered and bloodied dirty clothes. I was without my glasses, and I need them to see even in the dark. These young people had cell phones and called 911 by the time they had the window rolled down and were talking to me.

They had me go sit down on the guardrail that I had crashed into. They were still picking up pieces when the highway patrol arrived. I could hear sirens in the distance. The temperature was about forty degrees with an approximate elevation of two thousand feet. It was so cold my teeth were chattering and it was hard to talk. I had no concept of time. I tried to read my watch, but the crystal and face were missing. All I had on my wrist was a watch frame and a very sturdy band.

In Malta, Montana, I received emergency care in this small, friendly, competent, and warm community hospital. The physician was concerned about my condition, so he had me air evacuated to Billings, Montana, some two hundred miles away . . .

Michael Lewis

Take Me Home

Lorenz

Day 420—Endless Montana

"Dad, what does *home* mean?"

From the moment we found the GPS, Yvonne had wisely forfeited viewing hours of passing sagebrush and was instead figuring out her newfound toy on the back seat as we pedaled. While I still had trouble turning the GPS on, she was already querying billion-dollar satellites for information. Feeling a bit annoyed at children's superiority in all things electronic, I answered maybe a bit too gruffly. "What do you mean, what does *home* mean? That's where you live, of course."

"Well, if that's what it means, Dad, then the guy who owned this GPS lives seven hundred and eighty miles that way." Yvonne pointed straight down the road, toward the east.

A little stunned, I stopped in the middle of the latest hill that I was lacking the heart to summit anyway and asked, "How'd you know that?"

"Well, it's right here in this menu called 'Waypoints.' There is 'Home,' 'Mom,' 'Renate,' 'Hug22,' and all kinds of other people and places. Most

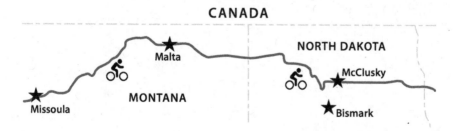

295

of them are about eight hundred miles away. 'Mom' is closer. Let's see, three hundred twenty miles to the southeast."

"He lives seven hundred and eighty miles east from here," I mused. "That has to be somewhere in Wisconsin or Michigan, someplace in the Midwest, anyway."

"Could be."

"And his mom lives three hundred and twenty miles from here. Let's see. That's got to be in North Dakota. Maybe Fargo? Or Bismarck?"

Email to bikeforbreath@hotmail.com

GARMIN 12 GPS (Part II)

I never once asked about my GPS. I know it was on my mind, but I never verbalized my thoughts. Once settled in Billings, I was far removed from the motorcycle. I was in the hospital eight days, then into a motel next to the hospital for the next four days. I did not ever feel that I would die. I did feel an overwhelming sense of loneliness and isolation.

I wanted to retrieve more of my belongings from the motorcycle. The clothes I was wearing were all cut off and were full of highway and my blood. Even my trusty and warm leather jacket looked very tattered and of not much use. They cut along the seams, but so far I have not repaired it. I left the hospital in "borrowed" menswear from the hospital laundry lost and found.

The motorcycle was in salvage some two hundred plus miles away, and it took eleven days to get it transported to Billings. I was somewhat anxious to see it, the Garmin, and some clothes. When I was able to get to the Billings salvage yard, there was *no* GPS. I was positive someone had stolen it because I was so sure I saw it in its holder on the tank.

BREATHTAKING

I stayed in Bismarck, North Dakota, some four hundred miles east of Billings, with members of my family another week . . .

Michael Lewis

To the Place I Belong

Lorenz

Day 423—Border of North Dakota

"Hey, thanks for the great directions," I said to the stranger we had just met in front of Lund's Landing Resort, where we had stayed the night.

The man handed me back my map of North Dakota and said, "No problem, my pleasure. Directions and whereabouts are my business."

"Well, you were the best guy to ask then. Are you a cartographer or something?"

"No, cartographers are a dying breed. I work for the prison system. I supervise house arrests."

"Huh ... What?" I was lost.

"You see, the prisons in North Dakota are well beyond capacity. So a few years back the state legislature started this new system for the less serious offenders. Instead of placing them in prisons with the hard-core criminals, who corrupt them further, the state puts them on house arrest."

"Great idea. But how do you keep them in?"

CANADA

NORTH DAKOTA

Malta

McClusky

MONTANA

Missoula

Bismark

"Well, that's where I come in," he added with a mock swagger. "The house arrest inmates receive this irremovable anklet that has a GPS transmitter in it and it sends the inmate's coordinates up to a satellite every few seconds. The GPS satellite network sends the data back down to me, and I can tell right here on my laptop where all my 'customers' are during all hours of the day."

"Awesome!" Yvonne broke in. "So if I give you coordinates of a person, you could find them?"

"Anywhere in the world! At the push of a button, kiddo," he said proudly.

"Dad, he can help us find the guy who lost the GPS!"

Within minutes our new friend was already powering up his laptop, and two minutes later the electronic prison guard had the answer.

"He lives smack in downtown Minneapolis. I can't give you the exact address with my laptop. It's not as accurate as the system back in the office. But it's within a half a mile or so."

"Hey, if we went to Minneapolis, we could bring the GPS back home, couldn't we?" Yvonne asked.

"Yes, maybe we could, but usually we avoid big cities. Also, what if he lives in a twenty-story high-rise with two hundred apartments? I'm not sure even the GPS will be accurate enough to get us to the right building, much less to the right apartment."

"We can do it, Dad. Let's bring the GPS home."

"You can do it, Dad!" The electronic prison guard smiled and slapped me on the back. He got into his car. Driving off, he yelled out the window, "Good luck bringing that GPS home! Make your daughter proud!"

After he left, I pulled out a rag and started wiping down the tandems, checking cables, chains, tires, and shifters. My morning safety inspection. The girls were busy dragging up the panniers from our cabin down by the lake. I was still thinking about bringing the GPS home when my rag snagged on something sharp. I ran my hand over it and discovered there was a half-inch crack in the rim of Paula's back wheel on both sides of where the spoke went in. I started checking other spokes. Cracks! More cracks! I checked her front wheel. Cracks! I checked my wheels. Worse!

Cracks everywhere! How could this be? Burley had just sent us these new wheels when we had arrived again on Bainbridge. Our trusty first set of wheels had lasted five times as long.

"Paula, this is bad," I said as she came up the stairs lugging two heavy panniers.

Ten minutes later I was on the phone with Marty Childs, vice president of Burley Design Cooperative, one of our biggest champions.

"Lorenz, do you think you can make it to Washburn? That's a hundred and twenty miles south of you," Marty asked.

"Maybe, Marty. These wheels are bad. They are literally splitting in half."

"If you can make it to Washburn, I can have new wheels at the post office there in three days."

"OK. We can try that," I said, feeling doubtful.

"When you get to Washburn, please send the cracked wheels back to Burley. The wheels need to go to the lab for analysis. We used a new manufacturer for the rims in this year's product line, and we think we need to start a recall. There appears to be a manufacturing flaw."

"Will do, Marty. Thanks for being a lifesaver again."

"Be careful. Take it easy on those cracked wheels."

I wrapped duct tape around the rim and tire at each cracked spoke hole. When I was done, the wheels were mostly duct tape. The bikes looked ridiculous. Like bicycle mummies escaping from the tomb of a deranged Egyptian pharaoh.

"Really, Dad? Really?" Anya said as she got on her bike.

"I'm all ears, if you have a better idea," I said, mounting my "Duct Tape Donkey" and pedaling off toward Washburn.

For the next two days, we handled the bikes with kid gloves. We avoided any unevenness in the road and lifted the bikes over every curb. Regardless, the cracks kept growing, and I was dreading every downhill for fear of a blowout and the potential of a nasty crash. We were constantly on edge, listening for the ripping sound when the twenty or so cracks in each wheel would grow long enough to touch each other and suddenly, catastrophically, split the rim in two, like a giant zipper. Thankfully the sound never came. In the evening of the second day, we dragged into Washburn, North Dakota, strips of duct tape flapping in the wind, rubbing with a grinding sound on the bike frames with each revolution of the tires. The Scotwood Motel was the first motel we came to, and I waited outside while Paula went inside to check us in.

"Your bikes look in bad shape, buddy," said a man who had just pulled up in a van behind me.

"You can say that again. These bike wheels are splitting in half. Good news is that I'm getting new wheels shipped to the post office tomorrow."

"Tell you what. If you need a place to stay and a garage to work on the bikes tomorrow, give me a call. I'm Mike, by the way," he said. He ripped a hardware store receipt in half and scribbled his number on the back of it.

———

As Marty had promised, four brand-new wheels by a different manufacturer arrived at the Washburn post office, general delivery. I replaced the front wheels on the lawn outside the post office immediately but could not get the cassette—the rear wheel gear cluster—off either my or Paula's bike. They seemed rusted on. I needed a shop with some better, larger tools.

"Mike, this is Lorenz, the guy with the crazy bikes from yesterday. Does your offer of a shop and a roof still stand?" I said into the phone, Mike's number on the hardware store receipt still in my hand.

"You bet it does. If you're quick, you can get a bowl of my wife's chili. She's made a ton. My son John's four kids are here for lunch. It's a mass feeding anyway."

We pushed our half-fixed tandems over to Mike's house, only two blocks from the post office, and were handed steaming bowls of chili as we walked through the door. It felt wonderful in a time of trouble to be taken in by complete strangers who treated us like family.

After lunch Mike gave me free rein over his tools and garage. To put the new rear wheels on the bicycles, I first had to take off the gear clusters on the old wheels and swap them onto the new ones that Burley had just sent. The problem was that the gears were rusted onto the axles of the old wheels. After beating on my old wheel with a hammer and chisel for an hour, the gear cluster finally came off and I could swap it onto my new wheel. Paula's gears, however, wouldn't budge. Mike and I tried for another two hours, heating Paula's gears and wheel with a torch and beating on it with a hammer and chisel. No luck. Frustrated, we went to bed without a plan.

The next day at six-thirty in the morning, Mike knocked on the door of the guest room, where Paula and I were sleeping. He told us that his son John, whom we had briefly met the night before, did not need to be at work until eleven and had offered to drive me forty miles to Bismarck, which had the closest bike store. I jumped into my clothes, grabbed Paula's wheel, and ran out to John, who was already waiting in his truck.

John and I got to the Bismarck bike store just as it opened. The bearded and ponytailed store owner put the mountain bike he was working on aside and gave Paula's wheel an appraising glance. He placed the wheel into a massive vice on the work bench and went to the wall to pull down a six-foot-long steel bar with a bicycle chain attached.

"I call this 'The Persuader.' My employees call it 'The Judge.' Regardless, something will give once I push on this pretty little puppy," he said, smiling proudly.

True to his word, the gear cassette came off, and ten minutes later I stood at his cash register with a brand-new rear wheel, cassette attached, paying my bill. In the glass vitrine under the cash register I noticed all the higher-priced items the store had to sell. High-end shifters, expensive pedals, *and* a GPS.

"Dang it!" I said out loud.

"What? You want me to put the cassette back on the exploding wheel?" asked the store owner, joking.

"No, not that. I just saw your GPS in the case, and it reminded me that I forgot to bring my GPS in the hurry this morning. There was someone I could have looked up in Bismarck—"

"An old flame?" he asked, winking.

"No, it's actually someone's mom. I don't even know her."

The Winds of Change

Paula

Day 432—McClusky, North Dakota

I wished I had never even thought of cycling across the US. Why hadn't we listened to the board of World Bike for Breath and just stayed home? Sure, the new tandem wheels we had put on in Bismarck two days ago seemed to be fine. But that had just been the last disaster after weeks of pain and suffering ever since we crossed Rogers Pass over the Rockies. Who would have guessed that eastern Montana and North Dakota could be pure misery? The wind was relentless. The mosquitoes were unbearable. I just wanted to end the pain. *Now.*

A week ago, the check from World Bike for Breath had finally gone through—which was great news. Sort of. Now we had enough money to get to Canada. But we were still short $1,500, and who knew when—or if—we'd get that tax refund from the IRS? If only we could put our bikes on the train—or maybe rent a U-Haul—and skip this awful section. If we cut off, say, five hundred miles, the trip would be two weeks shorter. We'd save ... about $1,000. Not enough. But close. Would it be cheating? I

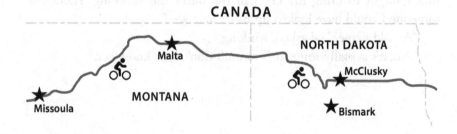

thought guiltily of Moni, who'd insisted on biking over Lolo Pass, pedaling *every single mile* across the country.

But we weren't Moni, were we? Who cared if we skipped a few hundred awful miles? We could catch a train to Minneapolis and make Lorenz and Yvonne happy. They were obsessed with Minneapolis. They'd been playing with this GPS they had found two weeks ago and insisted we needed to return it. Every now and then they would relate some new random destination on the GPS, for "Mom" or "Hug22." It was just the monotony and the agony addling their brains. Maybe we were all just suffering from a touch of heatstroke. We had been cycling under the burning-hot sun for weeks now. Today was no better. In fact, the sky looked rather creepy I thought as I lifted my head, bowed from the wind, to glance northward.

On the horizon I could see low black clouds, menacing and thick. At the bottom of the monstrous clouds, strange thin tendrils crept downward, pointing to the flat, dry North Dakota fields. The hair on the back of my arms tingled from the electricity in the air. It's just an afternoon thunderstorm! But I couldn't help glancing sideways at the increasingly ominous sky to the northwest. Something was wrong with this sky. Normal thunderclouds grew higher and higher in billowing white and black puffs. These clouds were thick and purple-green and close to the ground, with eerie wisps breaking off from the bottom.

"Those clouds don't look good," I shouted to Lorenz on the tandem ahead.

He pulled to the side of the road, and Anya and I drew up alongside him.

"What do you think that is?" I pointed to a thin, narrow tendril reaching toward the ground. I tried to sound nonchalant. Cool. Not worried. I didn't need to freak anyone out. Yet.

The sky rumbled, low and heavy. I fought an involuntary shudder as my skin suddenly crawled. We were pedaling along a straight, flat, empty road. Occasional low bushes or a cluster of oak trees indicated a farmhouse off on a side lane in the distance. But otherwise we were alone, unprotected on this silent, treeless road under a dangerous-looking sky.

"Not sure. It might be a good idea to find a gas station or town soon. Just in case whatever that is hits us," Lorenz replied, cleating back into his pedals. "No point in standing around debating." He pushed the tandem forward and sped off with Yvonne. Anya and I ducked our heads down resolutely against the increasing headwinds, pumping hard to keep up.

━━

It was not difficult to spot McClusky on the horizon. First the silver grain silos of the town's co-op grain elevator poked above the horizon, shimmering in the strange black sky. Then slowly the tops of leafy elm and ash trees appeared. And finally the low, flat, square houses of the small farm town came into view.

We locked our tandems in front of a gas station at the edge of town and hurried into the cool air-conditioned store.

"You on those bikes?" the stocky cashier asked as he rang up our pile on the counter: an ice-cold Coke, a lemonade, a Snapple, a sparkling water, and a stash of granola bars.

Yvonne and Anya nodded as they grabbed the lemonade and Snapple. "Where are you cycling to?" he continued good-naturedly.

"We're headed east toward Fargo."

"Well, you be careful. Lots of tornado warnings today," the cashier replied.

Yvonne blanched. My stomach did a little flip-flop. So those black tendrils creeping down from the sky *were* mini funnels. I'd seen photos and videos of tornado funnels reaching the ground and sucking up houses. I didn't want to know what they did to a family on bicycles.

"I wouldn't worry too much, honey," the cashier said, looking at Yvonne's white face. "The warnings are mostly for the towns farther north. But to be safe you might want to hang out in town for a few hours. The tornado warnings are supposed to end around four o'clock this afternoon."

What on earth were we going to do for three hours in this little sleepy town? The cashier must have seen the look on my face because he quickly added, "You might want to check out McClusky's swimming pool." He grinned at Anya and Yvonne. "I bet you'll like their waterslide." He put the cash in the register and whispered quietly to Lorenz, "If the tornado alarm sirens go off, they have a basement you can use as a shelter."

The sky to the north remained dark for most of the afternoon. Thankfully, no sirens shrieked warnings to interrupt Anya and Yvonne as they whizzed down the waterslide and jumped off the diving board, screaming and laughing along with most of the town's children, who crowded the pool, the decks, and the concession stand. If the pool had not finally closed at four o'clock, forcing us back out onto our tandems, I doubt we would have ever convinced the girls to leave. In fact, none of us were enthusiastic about battling our way against the nonstop headwinds again. But at least the eerie black tendrils on the horizon were gone. Or so we thought.

⌘

Anya and I had just finished staking down our tents in the Goodrich city park, sixteen miles east of McClusky, when a skinny young wild-haired cyclist whizzed in from the east. He sprang off his bike, full of vigor, and tossed it down next to the park's gazebo.

"Yo." He grinned at us. "I hear it's cool to camp here tonight." He pulled his dusty panniers off his scratched and worn touring bike, practically throwing them in the air. How did he have the energy? After another day of pedaling against the never-ending headwinds, I had barely been able to lift the panniers, let alone throw them halfway across the lawn.

"Don't you just love these little Midwest town parks?" he chatted on cheerfully. "So great they let you camp and use the bathrooms. Not like New England, where I'm from." He began setting up his tent, practically dancing and leaping around as he inserted the poles into the tent sleeves.

"So you're cycling from the east coast then?" Lorenz looked up from our camp stove. He and Yvonne were cooking up a delicious-smelling stir-fry from a package of chicken and a bag of fresh vegetables we had picked up at the Goodrich supermarket as we entered town.

"Yup. Started in Boston a month ago. It's been so awesome. Tail winds most of the way!"

I wondered how old he was. Probably not much past twenty, if that. "Everyone said I'd be biking against the wind. But it's been totally easy. I just biked eighty-five miles today. How about you guys?"

"Ah, we're coming from the west." Lorenz stirred a can of coconut milk and curry powder into the pot of chicken and vegetables. "It's been pretty much a month of killer headwinds." He interrupted the conversation for a moment—"Yvonne, can you turn the flame down? Thanks"—then he turned his attention back to our new campmate. "We're not making the same miles. We came from Turtle Lake today."

"Huh? That's only what? Barely twenty miles from here?" He threw his sleeping bag into his tent, munching on a PowerBar. I noticed he didn't have a rain fly. Probably figured the extra weight would slow him down.

"Twenty-five miles," I corrected him quickly. "We had to stop over in McClusky due to the tornado warnings."

"Oh, that's what those weird clouds were." Our apparent cycling superstar shrugged, unconcerned. "I wondered about those little funnel things but figured I was flying so fast on the bike, I could probably blow them away."

Thankfully he sprang into his tent at that moment, or I would have throttled his cocky little neck.

———

CRASH! Something loud and heavy woke me in the middle of the night.

I bolted upright in the tent, fumbling around in the pitch-dark for the headlamp. "Lorenz! What was that?"

BOOM! I jumped as something big smashed near the tent. Strange. We had deliberately pitched our tents in the middle of the grassy lawn in the Goodrich town park, away from any trees or buildings, just in case the black clouds in the sky decided to do something nasty. Like blow branches off trees—

Poking my head out of the tent door, I waved the flashlight over the grass. Or what should have been grass. It was covered with shredded leaves scurrying across the lawn. BANG! A large branch flew past the door, landing a few feet away.

"There's a huge storm out there! Stuff's flying around everywhere!" I shouted above the noise as Lorenz hurriedly pulled on a pair of shorts.

"Stay in the tent!" he ordered, crawling out the door. "I'm going to check out the gazebo. Maybe we can move the tents in there for protection." He disappeared in the dark, and I was alone in the tent. I held the headlamp in my hands, its light sliding eerily over the shiny blue surface of the sleeping bags. WHOOSH! Something flew past the tent, scraping the fly and bending the walls. I jumped instinctively. That was too close! What if a big branch landed right on top? Or a tree fell on our tent? Or Anya and Yvonne's?

I crawled to the door again, unzipped the mosquito netting, and flashed the light in the direction of their tent. Everything looked all right. Anya had staked the rainfly down tight, and their tent was holding up well in the wild wind, leaves and branches whizzing over the top.

"Anya! Yvonne!" I screamed at the top of my lungs. "Are you guys OK?" My voice disappeared with the wind, rushing, scurrying along with the dirt and debris swirling in the air past me. Nothing. No reply. I shouted again, "Anya! Yvonne!" They couldn't possibly be sleeping through this. Could they? Should I go look? Where was Lorenz? I hoped he was helping them.

I moved the flashlight over in the direction of the gazebo. For a second I thought I saw Lorenz's light. And then everything. *Everything.* Went dark. *Sssssssssss.* Raindrops began splashing, pouring, thudding down in front of me. No, not drops. Not even buckets of water. It was as if the tent, the whole town park, had been hit by a tidal wave. The walls of our tent bent inward as the deluge drove against the fabric, bending the poles.

The noise outside was deafening. Banging, crashing, swishing, roaring. I was certain that any minute now the tent would be lifted up into the air, like Dorothy and Toto, heading to Oz. The walls pushed down, laying almost flat over my face as I buried my head into the sleeping bag. Had Lorenz been able to help Yvonne and Anya into the gazebo?

For what seemed like forever, I clutched the floor of the tent, trying to hold it down. I screamed out to Lorenz and Anya and Yvonne, "Are you guys OK? Are you there? Anyone? *Anyone?*"

It was a waste of my breath. No one could hear anything over the thundering, roaring, and crashing of the storm around us. No, not storm.

I'd never seen a thunderstorm like this. Admit it. There had been tornado watches all day. I knew what it was.

~~

Silence. Complete and utter dead silence. I shone my light outside the tent. Everything was still. Not even a slight breeze to rustle the mess of shredded leaves, branches, and pieces of random debris on the ground. A soaking sock hung in a tree. An empty bag of Cheetos tilted on top of Anya and Yvonne's tent. Remnants of a soggy newspaper lay in front of our door. Just as abruptly as the storm had begun, it was over. The tornado must have passed around us. I had read that tornados move in weird erratic patterns, leaving one house untouched and destroying its next-door neighbor. I sent up a prayer of thanks that we had not been in its direct path.

My knees shaking, I crawled out of the tent. I could glimpse a light shining in front of the girls' tent and Lorenz bending in front of it.

"Are you girls all right?" I could hear him ask as he stuck his head inside their tent.

I knelt next to Lorenz in front of their door. Inside, Yvonne was sitting in Anya's lap, her sister's arms wrapped around her in a tight protective hug.

"Where were you?" Yvonne cried out, trembling.

"I was shouting to you ten feet away in the gazebo," Lorenz said. "Didn't you hear me?"

"We called and called and called, but no one answered." Anya squeezed Yvonne tightly. "Yvonne was scared. I told her I would protect her. That I wouldn't let her fly away."

"She was so brave." Yvonne looked up at Anya in admiration. "She just held on tight and kept telling me we'd be all right. She laughed and pretended there were giants fighting outside. She said she had a magic spell to protect me."

Anya loosened her grip slightly, looking at her sister protectively. "I would never ever let anyone hurt you, Boo. Never." She looked away, trying to hide her emotion. "You are more important to me than anyone in the world. You know that. You're my sis. Forever."

The next morning I poked my head out of the tent to a bright, clear, sunny day. Immediately something felt different. I looked over in the direction of our neighboring cyclist's tent. He was holding up a soaking-wet sleeping bag in front of a very sagging, bedraggled tent, looking extremely disgruntled.

"Helluva storm last night," I called over to him.

He just grunted. Then, limping with one shoe over to a nearby tree, he threw the bag over a broken branch. "Storm took my other shoe," he mumbled crankily.

I stared at the wet sleeping bag swaying in the wind. It couldn't be. Or? I pulled out the compass. Yes. Oh, yes! I knew what had changed.

I reached over to Lorenz and shook him awake, unable to contain my excitement. "Lorenz, look!" I opened the door and pointed to the bag blowing in the breeze. "It's a miracle! The wind! It's changed! It's from the west finally!"

He stared groggily at the bag, then grabbed the compass from my hand. "No shit!" he shouted with delight. "Oh, baby. We're outta here. *Yahoooo!*"

Lorenz leapt out of the tent, still in his underwear, and started his own version of a Native American wind dance. Our stunned cycling neighbor stared at him agog. Lorenz looked at him, then at me. I nodded and grinned. I almost felt a bit sorry for the kid. Almost. He had no idea what suffering he was about to face as he cycled west this morning. For a moment I thought I should warn him but then thought better of it. He'd figure it out soon enough.

Still, as I started to roll up our dry sleeping bags—protected from the rain by a tightly staked-down fly—I had to suppress a giggle. I could see our wild-haired cyclist pedaling west, wind blowing dirt in his eyes, his odometer stuck at five miles per hour, stopping to chat to an eastbound cyclist whizzing past. "Just about pedaled a hundred miles today," the eastbound cyclist would say with a grin. "How about you?"

Joy, pure joy, bubbled up unbidden as we sped off into a day without the wind beating us backward, without dust and bugs sticking to our sweaty skin and sun frying us to a crisp. For once, I was in harmony with the weather, flying down the road with the wind at my back. Laughing. Free. The tornado had not just cleared the air and changed the direction of the wind. As we pedaled away from the town park, the strong gusts propelling us forward, I could feel that something much more important had shifted.

The road ahead no longer intimidated me. We had survived a tornado, an earthquake, drug smugglers, Russian border guards, a broken foot, and a poisonous *molokau*. We had climbed over the Alps and the Rockies and numerous unnamed mountain chains in between. Slept under the stars and survived snowstorms, windstorms, and hundred-and-ten-degree days. We had refinanced our house to pay for this trip, camped five out of seven days a week to save money, and pedaled on nothing more than an empty bank account and faith. And we were still pedaling.

Suddenly I *knew*. Deep down I *knew*. We *would* make it around the world.

I felt the taut muscles of my legs thrusting down into my pedals, the blood pulsing through my veins as my heart beat strongly, powerfully, in my chest, and my lungs breathing in and out, in and out, in rhythm with the pedals.

It didn't matter that I had asthma, that I carried a bag full of inhalers in my panniers, or that I cycled up over mountaintops at the speed of a snail, struggling to catch my breath. I no longer felt ashamed that I was always picked last in gym class, that I ruined games of tag by rushing to the emergency room.

I took a deep, full breath of the cool morning air. No, my asthma did not define me any longer. I was *so* much more than this dreadful disease. In fact, maybe, just maybe, I was so much more *because* of this disease.

Minneapolis

Lorenz

Day 443—St. Cloud, Minnesota

After the tornado, everything seemed easy. With the wind behind us, the miles flew by. We whizzed into Minnesota, passing pretty little lakes and cute towns with strange giant statues. The town of Pelican Rapids boasted a fifteen foot tall concrete pelican that the locals called the "mother of all pelicans" while a nearby town displayed a twenty foot iron turtle affectionately called "Rusty." I guess our enthusiasm was contagious because everywhere we went, people invited us into their homes and fed us dinner, stretching our budget and cheering us on. Best of all, our $2,000 income tax refund came through! Finally, we had enough money to make it to DC!

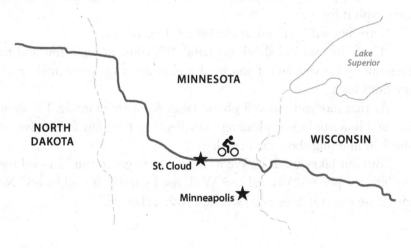

It wasn't just the wind and the towns that changed. Paula seemed different and more confident. I guess we all were. Somehow it was as if we all knew we had already made it—kind of like getting into college. Sure, we had to finish the final miles (our equivalent of final exams), but it was in the bag.

No one talked about *if* we would make it to DC anymore. Now we discussed *when*. Anya and Yvonne were already emailing their friends, making plans for their return home once we made it to the capital. With our new tandem wheels, I figured the equipment could make it to the end. And even if it didn't, given all the towns and bike shops around, I could easily get help. Compared to trying to repair bikes in Tonga, this was a piece of cake. It felt like nothing could stop us now!

On the last miles into St. Cloud, about seventy miles to the north of Minneapolis, both bikes started making terrible crunching noises in the bottom bracket, where the pedal crank goes through the frame. A quick inspection told me the bearings were completely shot. To make matters worse, it was Friday night. Fortunately, when we walked dejectedly into the Out and About bike store, Greg, the store owner, recognized us and said, "I know you! You're the family that's biking around the world! I saw you on the cover of *Bicycle Retailers* magazine!" He rummaged under the counter and proudly emerged with a copy of the magazine. "Will you autograph it for me?"

"Sure, but will you look at our bikes?" I bargained.

"Deal," he said and shook my hand. "I'll come in tomorrow and fix them all up for you, and if you need a place to camp, you can sleep on my front lawn."

At that moment our cell phone rang. An early-morning TV show out of Minneapolis was pleading with Paula to have our family live on the 5:30 morning show the next day.

"But our bikes are dead. We have no way to get to you," I heard her say into the phone. "A rental car? Well, yes, I guess that could work. No idea if we can still drive one," she said with a chuckle.

In minutes the situation was settled. We left our bikes in Greg's bike store and walked over to the rental car agency. We loaded our gear into the car and traveled in unaccustomed luxury to Minneapolis to stay in a motel for the night.

The talk show the next morning was very memorable and fun. Our TV hosts had set up couches and cameras on the rooftop of the TV station and interviewed us in the open air as the sun was rising. The girls had a blast, and after we said goodbye to our host, Yvonne had her day.

At 6:30 in the morning, GPS in hand, we drove toward First Avenue and began walking the Minneapolis neighborhood. Using the GPS to navigate toward "Home," we tried to zero out the coordinates on the screen. We knocked on a few wrong doors and were not too kindly received by bleary-eyed homeowners in bathrobes, but we persevered and ended up in an alley in front of a garage, where the GPS read "Home." We walked through the garden to the front door and rang the bell until we had to admit that the inhabitants were not just ignoring us but were not home. Disappointed, and doubting we had the correct house anyway, I quickly scribbled a note and stuffed it into the overflowing mailbox.

Email to bikeforbreath@hotmail.com

GARMIN 12 GPS (PART III)

It was day 20 since my accident when I got back to my home in Minneapolis. Along with my mail, there was a penciled note saying, "Hi there, I found a GPS receiver and the home coordinates led me to this house. If you lost your GPS, please call my cell phone." I immediately called. Got the answering machine. It took a day or so for Lorenz Eber from Bainbridge Island, Washington, to call me back.

He and his family are riding two tandem bikes. They are returning from bicycling around the world and are headed to Washington, DC. Coming through Montana going east, he spotted something out of the corner of his eye that was reflecting sunlight at the edge of the road as they were pedaling along an isolated spot on Highway 2. He asked his daughter to go over and see what it was. She picked up my GPS.

Lorenz replaced the AA batteries, and the Garmin worked. He learned its operation by trial and error but soon had it performing for him. Because of their tight schedule, they pedaled past Bismarck, North Dakota, but he noticed the coordinates of Bismarck are in the waypoint directory. While in Minneapolis this man took the time and effort to follow the "Home" coordinates on the Garmin 12. The Garmin led him to my backyard in Minneapolis.

I find this man and his family fabulous and resourceful. He could have said, picking up the Garmin, "Wow, what a find. Finders keepers, right?" What a wonderful person to go the extra mile and effort to trace and return a lost item. I was convinced it was gone forever.

Today I have my GPS. It is beat up with nicks and scars; after all, it survived the same crash I did. We look a little alike.

To Lorenz and his family, I find words escape me to describe my gratitude, appreciation, and thanks for his thoughtfulness and perseverance. I guess anyone who can go around the world on a tandem bicycle with his wife and two daughters is a tough act to follow. I encourage anyone reading this to look at the website (www.worldbikeforbreath.org) to see the journey, the faces, the cause of these marvelous people.

My most sincere thank you,

Michael Lewis

Route Update—Astoria, Oregon, to Saginaw, Michigan

Hi from the Ebers in Saginaw, Michigan.

When we last wrote we were in Havre, Montana, pedaling along Lewis and Clark's return route from Astoria, Oregon, to Fort Mandan in North Dakota. Little did we know that almost one thousand miles of flat, desolate, poverty-stricken, endless plains lay ahead of us. A month of what we can only term utter misery began. (I have just read this passage to my family, and they feel that I am missing certain important adjectives, such as "living hell," "blood-sucking, merciless, flesh-eating mosquitoes," "endless mind-numbing monotony," and "@@!!##!! dust-bearing, searing hot, insufferable headwinds.")

Then, two days from the border of Minnesota, the wind turned. For the first time in weeks, we suddenly found ourselves sailing effortlessly into pretty lake country. We were thrilled to discover trees and little towns with bakeries instead of ramshackle bars. As the population increased, so did our donations for asthma—and media interviews raising awareness for our cause. For the past four weeks, we have been averaging an interview with TV or newspaper reporters once a day!

We continued on through the deep woods of northern Wisconsin, where temperatures dropped to a pleasant seventy-eight degrees. And shade was abundant. We began to feel like human beings again rather than scorched, bitten, wind-beaten, mind-numbed zombies. Wisconsiners—thrilled and excited by our stories—took us in nightly, offering us long-forgotten luxuries like beds, showers, and home-cooked meals. Not wanting to be outdone by their lake neighbors, Michiganders have continued the incredible hospitality of the Wisconsiners, taking us in and listening to our stories until the wee hours of the morning.

We are on the home stretch now: three weeks and only 750 miles left. In a few days, we will cross the border to Ontario, Canada, cycling into our twenty-fourth and final country. After a quick visit to Niagara Falls, we'll head south through New York, Pennsylvania, and Maryland, ending in Washington, DC, where we have planned some exciting finale events. So mark your calendars for the following dates:

Saturday, August 28: Cycle into DC with the Ebers and join us for a great end-of-ride party.

Saturday, September 4: Join the Ebers in their finale ride to Seattle Children's Hospital followed by a great party for sponsors at REI.

Emails to bikeforbreath@hotmail.com

HI AND GIVING SUPPORT IN ONTARIO, CANADA.
Friday, August 13

I myself am a fourteen-year-old asthmatic, and I was just emailing you to give my support to what you are doing. I first heard of the idea in Port Burwell. We were just recently camping there and saw you and your family at the local restaurant, but I unfortunately did not get a chance to say hello and so therefore am doing it now. Keep up the good work, very proud!

—Callie, London, Ontario, Canada

PASSED YOU HEADING SOUTH IN NEW YORK.
Wednesday, August 18

What an inspiration! I passed you heading south on Route 219 about forty-four miles south of Niagara Falls. You must have stayed overnight in our town of Ellicottville, New York. We saw your bike at the grocery store. My wife and I are purchasing a tandem and starting to ride together. Seeing your family and reading about you gave us a challenge to ride for a cause. We will try to find any asthma rides and also participate. Thank you for your motivation, and good luck. You're almost there!

—Eric, Ellicottville, New York

RIDING INTO WASHINGTON, DC, WITH YOU.

Friday, August 20

Dear Eber family,

I just wanted to wish you an early congratulations. I envy the trip you're about to complete and admire the fundraising effort. Well done!

Last summer I rode across the country with two guys, Riley and Preston. Since we haven't been reunited since the end of our tour a year ago (I live in New Hampshire, and Riley and Preston are in Atlanta), we have planned to meet in DC to celebrate the end of your tour. We are all very excited to ride the last bit of your incredible tour. Anyways, best of luck in these last few days, and see you in DC!

—Bryson, New Hampshire

Last Dance

Paula

Day 478—C&O Canal

It was not a campsite really. Just a little hollowed-out nest of sand on the
banks of the sparkling Potomac River along the C&O Canal,* forty miles

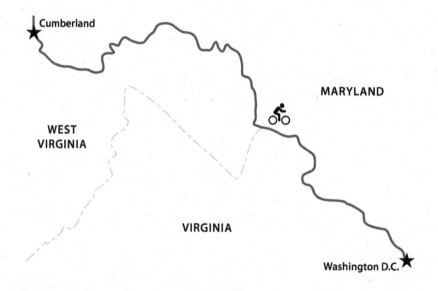

* The Chesapeake and Ohio (C&O) Canal was inspired by George Washington's vision of a canal
system that would allow boat traffic to move freely up and down the Potomac River. The project
began in earnest in 1828 and was finally completed in 1850, allowing boat traffic to move through a
series of locks from Cumberland, Maryland, to Washington, DC. Today, the 184.5-mile towpath is
a national historical park open to cyclists, hikers, and campers.

away from Washington, DC. A circle of charred stones suggested that others before us had camped in this beautiful spot.

Uphill in the woods, I selected a soft, flat corner under a large oak tree. As I had done for hundreds of nights before, I unrolled our patched and faded home, crossed the poles over the fabric, fastened the clips, and raised the Taj. Into the tent I crawled, breathing in the smell of earth, grass, and dried leaves, scents that had seeped into the fabric and become an indelible part of the tent over our sixteen-month journey—just as the tent and the scents had seeped into *my* soul, becoming an inseparable part of me.

For the very last time, I began our simple bedtime ritual, swallowing hard to suppress the tears welling in the corners of my eyes. Don't cry, I begged my heavy heart. This was it. The finale. Tomorrow, next week, next year I could be sad. But tonight I wanted to offer one perfect final performance in thanks for this unforgettable, impossible journey.

Lovingly, I repeated the steps in our nightly ballet. A simple, graceful dance. Meditation in motion. Close my lips around the round, hard plastic valve of my Therm-a-Rest. Blow deeply, inhale, blow again. Watch the green mattress slowly unfurl along the tent floor like a jelly roll in reverse. Press the toggle on my stuff sack. Slide it along the long, hard black cord. Clench a handful of soft, slinky fabric. With a quick flick of the wrist, fling the sleeping bag into the air. Shimmering and floating, the bag settles on the thin green mattress. Breathe. Count three beats and start the routine again. I don't believe we can find God in the big, dramatic rush of our lives. It's in the quiet, simple daily motions that he appears at our side.

I sat cross-legged on our humble sleeping bag bed, gazing out the tent door at the soft outline of the Blue Ridge Mountains rising above the banks of the river on the other side. I could hear the water splashing and gurgling as it leapt over the rocks in the shallow riverbed. The sun was sliding down the sky, casting a hazy glow over the clouds. Below, the river glistened a soft rose in reflection. The hot day was slowly seeping away, and for a moment there was perfect silence, as if the grass, the trees, and the animals were all, like me, quietly letting go of the day before settling into the evening. I held my breath, my lungs and heart bursting. With gratitude. With awe. With joy. And with sorrow. I ignored the numbing of my crossed ankles, wanting to sit there forever. Unwilling to let go of this one final moment before the curtain would come down on the performance and the dance would finally and irrevocably be over.

"Dinner's ready!" Lorenz called. The spell was broken. I unfolded my legs and crawled out of the tent, the delicious aroma of steak and corn wafting over the campsite. Kneeling next to a little campfire Lorenz had built in the stone circle, Yvonne pulled out blackened Pillsbury rolls wrapped in tinfoil from the embers, their moist, doughy scent making my stomach rumble. A feast. To celebrate our last night camping on the trail.

"*Efaristo, tishkir, grazie, danke, dankuvell,* thank you, *merci, tagesmukke, jinkyua, achoo, paldess, tannan, spasiba, bayla, she she, arigato, duo she, kapunka, ta mate, kiora, malo,* thanks," we all chanted our dinner blessing one last time—saying thank you in the language of every country we had visited during our journey.

As we sat on the ground around the campfire, licking corn on the cob and devouring crispy slices of steak, I looked around at my extraordinary family and world cycling team. Whispering to her big sister across from me sat little determined Yvonne. Her keen eyes and careful observation had helped us locate everything from hotels to temples to road signs along the way. The smallest of us all, she never stopped pedaling, continuing on despite drug smugglers in Russia, an earthquake in Taiwan, and even a broken foot. Next to her, Anya listened carefully, giggling and nodding as she bit off a piece of warm roll. My enigmatic daughter—cool-headed and independent, yet fiercely loving and protective of her little sister. She had been our diplomat and negotiator, saving our journey by suggesting we select a leader of the day. Finally, I looked over at my practical and humorous husband, who was lowering the flame on the camp stove. He had tirelessly assembled, disassembled, and repaired the tandems and maintained all our equipment across the globe. Ingeniously solving hundreds of logistical issues with duct tape, zip ties, and many jokes, he had miraculously succeeded in getting us here safe and sound.

And me? For better or worse, I had been the cause of all this. How strange that my asthma—my lifelong curse—could also be our blessing. Would we be here tonight if I had never been born with asthma? No. Of course not. I thought of all the extraordinary experiences that we would have missed. Sharing a meal of spaghetti with an Italian cycling club in the Alps. Visiting a pickled Lenin in Moscow. Sleeping with nomads in a Mongolian *ger*. Watching in awe as we pedaled closer and closer to the Great Wall of China. Startling an echidna waddling across the road in the bush of Australia. Being hosted as honored guests of the Dayton rodeo.

I would never stop hoping that, one day, I would not have to fight to breathe. But like a tree whose bark has grown around a foreign object embedded in its trunk, I had integrated my asthma, accepted it, and created a new shape—a burl, unique and oddly beautiful—from the wound.

I took a bite of the burned Pillsbury roll, strangely happy with the charred, sooty flavor. All too soon we would be home, eating perfectly cooked rolls, sleeping in soft beds. Back to the chaotic churn of swim lessons and carpools and course schedules.

But tonight we were still inseparable. I grabbed this moment hungrily—Anya and Yvonne laughing and cuddling together, Lorenz kneeling by the campfire, the scent and taste of burned rolls—holding on for one very last moment. We would bike together again. But it would never be *this*. Four of us bonded on an impossible journey. Of love. Of hope. Of faith. Of healing.

Email to bikeforbreath@hotmail.com

Dear Anya and Yvonne,
Hello. My name is Katrina. I read your article in *Teen*
magazine. As I read your article I was blown away.
I have been waiting for someone to do something like
Biking for Breath for the past five years. At the age
of seven, I was diagnosed with asthma. Over the last
five years, my asthma got worse and worse until last
year I was in the hospital for a week. Every day I pray
that someone would raise enough money so scientists
and doctors could find a cure. All I wanted to say was
thank you. You are my hero.

—Sincerely, Katrina

Final Route Update

On August 28, our family pedaled into Washington, DC, completing a full circle of the world by bicycle. We are happy, healthy, and proud. The final tally:

14,931 kilometers

9,332 miles

24 countries

4 continents

16 months

150+ media articles about asthma and clean air on 4 continents

$64,416 raised for clean air and asthma awareness

Air Pollution and Asthma

What Is Asthma?

Asthma is a disease of the respiratory system in which the lungs become overly reactive or sensitive to external substances such as dust, pollen, or air pollutants. When an asthmatic person's airways come into contact with these substances, the mucous membranes within the airways swell up and become inflamed. At the same time, the muscles around the airways tighten. As a result, it becomes more and more difficult for air to enter or leave the lungs, and the body becomes deprived of oxygen. During a severe asthmatic attack, victims may experience sensations of suffocating, and in extreme cases, if the patient is not treated, they can die. Currently there is no known cure for asthma. People with asthma, along with their loved ones, must learn to live with this disease for the rest of their lives.

Who Has Asthma?

Asthma strikes men, women, and children of all ages and cultural and economic backgrounds.

- In 2019, more than 460,000 people in the world died from asthma—more than 1,000 people every day.
- One in twelve people in the US have asthma, which affects over twenty-five million Americans.
- Asthma has been increasing since 1980 for all age, sex, and racial groups.
- People who have moderate to extreme asthma are at higher risk of developing serious complications from COVID-19.

Air Pollution and Asthma

What causes asthma? And why is it increasing? There are many theories. But one issue is clear: *study after study has documented that air pollution is related to asthma.* Here are some shocking facts, according to the Academy of Allergy and Asthma:

- Prenatal exposure to air pollution has been shown to increase the risk of wheezing and asthma development in children.

- Exposure to air pollution early in life contributes to the development of asthma throughout childhood and adolescence. Traffic-related air pollution in particular is associated with the development of asthma in schoolchildren.

- Air pollution, especially traffic-related pollution, can increase the chances of developing asthma in adults as well.

Clean Air So All of Us Can Breathe

Air pollution does not just cause asthma. According to the World Health Organization, *air pollution kills an estimated seven million people a year—* resulting in COPD, lung cancer, heart disease, strokes, and many other diseases as well as asthma. To learn more, go to www.bike4breath.com.

Acknowledgments

This story was the result of the dedicated efforts and contributions of hundreds of people and businesses across the globe. While our family undertook the fun part of cycling around the world, many others ran World Bike for Breath, donated funds, provided logistical and emotional support, and, ultimately, helped bring this book to fruition. While we would like to express our specific thanks to the amazing people and organizations below, we are also immensely grateful to the hundreds of other kind, generous people who helped in every way from offering roadside help or a free place to stay, to donating hours of their time, to interviewing us so that we could tell our story on TV, radio, and in the news. This book is your story too. Thank you for believing in our dream: to create a world where everyone can breathe. We extend our special thanks to the following:

- The hardworking board of World Bike for Breath—Dr. Maureen Koval, Tom Clune, Dr. Deborah Wheeler, Dr. Linda Warren, Chuck Veilloux, Katie Jones, and Tatiana Dudley. We especially thank the board's directors, Brett Thackray and Robin Simons, for their countless hours running a nonprofit organization while trying to track down the world-wandering Ebers. We apologize for making them store our many mementos picked up along the way and hope that our little random notes and postcards tucked into the packages provided at least a bit of entertainment in return.

- The tireless volunteer staff of World Bike for Breath: Mike Culver, who designed and maintained our website; Eileen Magnuson, who ran the office and spent countless hours logging donations; Tina and Gabriel Perez, who created the stunning logo, brochures, and marketing materials; Eric and Cheryl Fox, who received bimonthly packages of film and turned them into unforgettable photos and slides for the website and this book; and Matt Topham, our pro bono legal counsel. Thanks also to Jon Jones for his photographic expertise and assistance with the cover photo; and to Mindy Jones, Noni Baran, and Adrienne Williamson, who provided all-around fundraising, event, and cooking support. Finally, Jonathan Maus deserves recognition for essentially donating his PR help for free. We realize that trying to set up television and newspaper interviews with a cycling family that was never where they were scheduled to be (not to mention often pedaling far out of signal range) must have been hell. Hopefully our crazy antics provided food for some entertaining stories about one of your most unusual clients.

- Our corporate sponsors, who agreed with our philosophy that if we want to save our environment for future generations, we need to raise our children in the outdoors, teaching them to treasure the world around us. Thank you to Burley, REI, Patagonia, Arkel Overdesigns, Old Man Mountain, and T-Mobile. Your equipment is awesome, and we still bike with it everywhere. Any company whose bikes, tents, panniers, clothes, racks, and phones can survive two kids and fifteen thousand kilometers across four continents has truly had their equipment pass with flying colors!

- Our many generous local business sponsors: BI Cycle, The Traveler, Town and Country Markets, Starbucks, MSR, Cascade Designs, Virginia Mason, Wenzlau Architects, Crystal Photography, Eagle Harbor Chiropractic, Bell and Thomson DDS, Esvelt Engineering, and Dana's Showhouse. Thanks also to the city of Bainbridge Island, which generously gave Lorenz a year and a half leave from work to go on this adventure.

- Our faithful world sponsors, who sponsored us per kilometer and kept us committed to pedaling on those days when we really just wanted to go home, take a long hot shower, and crawl into a warm bed. While we cannot list you individually, you know who you are, and when this book comes out, there will be one wonderful big party for you!

- One world sponsor deserves extra special appreciation: Paula's mom, Barbara Sullivan. When Paula's mom heard about the proposed world cycling journey of her daughter, son-in-law, and grandchildren, she replied in her truly loving and magnanimous way, "Well, I don't like the idea of you taking my grandchildren around the world on bicycles, but I understand it is very important to you. So I'll do whatever I can to support you." And she did. She not only donated the largest individual sponsorship but also rescued us from cat- and flea-infested apartments in Moscow, boosted morale with a Christmastime visit in Hong Kong, provided a luxurious vacation in Thailand, and faithfully read all our mail and paid our bills while we cycled around the world.

Finally, there are all the amazing people who turned this story from a pile of journals and photos into a manuscript and book:

- Writing a book can be a lonely and never-ending project. Enter the amazing concept of coworking! We cannot thank the Bainbridge Island OfficeXpats run by Leslie Schneider and Jason Omens enough for the incredibly creative and supportive community they have created. Monday-morning check-ins for the past five years have kept Paula accountable to complete the chapter drafts she promised. Without these deadlines, she'd probably still be stuck in China (literally speaking)! We'd especially like to thank Xpats colleagues Karen Klein, Joanna Jenkins, and Paula Willems for volunteering to read the early drafts. Looking back on those drafts, we're not sure why they kept reading. But thankfully, something about the story kept them going and encouraged us to finish the book.

- We also co-opted two professional writing friends to read and comment on the more polished versions of the manuscript: Robin Simons, the author of fourteen books, and Kirstie Pelling, an award-winning British family travel blogger. Their gentle but truthful feedback taught us so much.

- Last but not least, we want to express our deep appreciation to our editors at Falcon, Mason Gadd and Kellie Hagan. When Mason made the offer to publish a book about an adventurous bicycling family of four, he had no idea what he was signing up for. The Ebers are, well, a rather independent-minded set of people; naturally, we had lots of debates about this manuscript before it finally made it to press. Mason handled the challenges with a calm and professionalism that was impressive. His enthusiastic support for getting this story in print, his personal attention to every aspect of the project, and his ever-open door make him a true treasure in the large and sometimes impersonal world of editors and publishing houses. We also want to thank Kellie, who like Mason, faced many unexpected challenges in editing and producing such an unusual book with a very complex layout. Kellie's amazing organization, efficiency, and painstaking attention to detail kept the project on track, resulting in a beautiful book interweaving narrative and archival materials in a seamless and aesthetically pleasing design. Working with Mason and Kellie and their hardworking professional team has made us truly thankful that we chose to publish our story with Falcon.